LOVE BIRDS

To Rebecca, my wife and best friend.
Thank you for believing.

LOVE BIRDS

How to live with the one you love

TREVOR SILVESTER

CORONET

First published in Great Britain in 2013 by Coronet
An imprint of Hodder & Stoughton
An Hachette UK company

1

A CIP catalogue record for this title is available from the British Library

ISBN 978 1 444 740875

Typeset in Plantin by Palimpsest Book Production Ltd,
Falkirk, Stirlingshire

Printed and bound by CPI Group (UK) Ltd,
Croydon, CR0 4YY

Hodder & Stoughton policy is to use papers that are natural, renewable and
recyclable products and made from wood grown in sustainable forests. The
logging and manufacturing processes are expected to conform to the
environmental regulations of the country of origin.

Hodder & Stoughton Ltd
338 Euston Road
London NW1 3BH

www.hodder.co.uk

Acknowledgements

Becoming an expert in anything usually involves failing at it repeatedly beforehand, and that's certainly true with my relationship history, so it feels appropriate to first thank all the women who've loved me and left me. I've been fascinated by relationships for a very long time, and I'm sure that's partly because I seemed to be so bad at sustaining them. So, along with my thanks goes an apology for my part in the many downfalls. (The rest of it was their fault.)

With the benefit of hindsight, I can see that the hard and painful lessons I learned became ways of helping others, who in turn taught me how to help still more, so I'm indebted to my clients who've shared with me the challenges of their relationships as well as being the source of the solutions we found that have made their way into this book.

I wholeheartedly agree with the notion that it's better to have loved and lost, but I've also found it's infinitely nicer to love and keep on loving, which is where my wife, Rebecca, comes in. It's not an exaggeration to say that she has been the springboard for everything I've achieved since I met her, and I've learned so much about how to make relationships work within the safety of her love. She's also been very patient in the face of her every foible being met with, 'That's going in the book!' – although they're not, because the book isn't big enough.

I don't know about other writers, but there comes a stage where I no longer trust my opinion about what I'm writing, so it's essential to have a team of people I can trust to tell me when it's drivel. And they do, if not sometimes with more relish than is entirely healthy. So my thanks go to Jan Gilbertson, Peter

Barker, Sue Knight and Ruth Ascroft, great friends to have help from.

I'd also like to thank my many friends within the Quest Institute. They start as my students while training to be cognitive hypno-therapists, and many end up as mates. They've been an audience for what is in this book for a very long time, so they'll probably be relieved to see it in print at last. Some of them even gener-ously shared stories from their own relationships, which you're going to read later.

Finally, my editors. Charlotte Hardman is the commissioning editor at Hodder who first approached me about the possibility of writing what you're now holding. She clearly has an eye for talent, and I'll be forever grateful for the opportunity. Mark Booth is at the top of the heap when it comes to publishing, and his encouragement and faith have been a lovely accompaniment to the writing of this book.

Contents

Introduction

We seem to be obsessed with relationships. Whether it's the endless stream of magazine articles detailing the latest celebrity gossip, the buzz in the office about so-and-so and their partner, or the long chats with friends about the state of your union, how we get on with others, and how others get on with others, seems to be an inexhaustible subject of interest.

I spend a good proportion of my working life helping people with their relationships, so I'm not surprised. Most people find relationships hard, and yet they're probably the single most important thing in life to get right. If you live in a supportive, loving state of intimacy you live longer, healthier, happier and more successful lives. No wonder we obsess about how to achieve such a state.

So why do we find it so difficult? After all, the human race has been a two-person relay from the beginning, so you'd think we'd have it sussed by now. In this book I'm going to explain why we find it hard, and how you can turn the things that cause relationships to be difficult into the very things that build the life together you've always wanted.

To do this, I want to share with you what I've observed in the many couples who've sat in front of me; many going through the kind of pain and distress that is unique to the threatened loss of love, because I've noticed the same thing again and again: *overwhelmingly, most people don't separate because they don't love each other; they do it because they can't live with each other.*

Opposites seem to attract . . . and then drive each other mad. It's taken me years to understand why this is so.

The introduction is (hopefully) the first part of the book that most of you will read, but it's the last part that I write, so as I contemplate what you're about to experience set down on these pages, I'm feeling a lot of hope: the hope that you'll find here something that will make you nod in recognition at yourself and the relationships you've had or are currently having, and learn some things that will enable you to create a fulfilling and rich life with someone you love. I absolutely believe that this is possible, and that the person you currently love is likely to be someone you can learn to live happily with.

There is, however, always a danger when you try to put people into boxes and describe them. We all know each of us is unique so can't be totally predictable, but we do have preferences in the way we see things that are identifiable in many situations – like whether you tend to be left- or right-wing in politics, or prefer the company of lots of people or something more intimate. So I'm going to talk about the tendencies I see most often causing the differences between people that we trot out as reasons for a break-up: 'They didn't understand me'; 'They were always winding me up'; 'They were too lazy/maniacal/anal/fluffy/undependable/boringly dependable . . .' The list may seem endless, but the differences that drive them aren't.

By reading this book, I intend to get you thinking about how you relate to people and to teach you how to do it better. While its focus is on intimate relationships, the benefits will be far broader – because if you can learn to relate clearly with your partner, then your friends, colleagues and bosses will be a doddle.

The differences between people that I'm going to be focusing on are the ones that fly largely beneath the radar. I'm expecting you to nod in recognition at them, and wonder how you never realised their importance in the daily impact on the way you live your life and run, or ruin, your relationships. I'm going to teach you to identify them in you and your partner, and how to turn how they cause you problems into what brings you closer.

Make no mistake, I intend for this book to change your emotional life for the better.

At the same time, while it's my fervent wish that reading this helps you to sustain and enrich a relationship you want to work, I know from working with my clients that reading this might also lead you to realise that your time together as a couple has run its course – that what ultimately separates you *should* separate you – and enable you to go through with it with the minimum of damage and hurt. I hope that's not the case, but it happens sometimes in my therapy room, so it's bound to happen here. That doesn't mean that you, or the relationship, is a failure.

Within our culture, we have an unspoken assumption that relationships are only successful if they last a lifetime. So many of us punish ourselves for 'failing' because the love we shared didn't fulfil the 'Til death us do part' promise. But does that need to be true? I've been in several relationships that were very successful, for a time, and what ultimately left the scars was the clinging on after the reason for being together – the initial attraction – had worn thin and we had insufficient understanding of each other's needs to find fulfilment in what was left. Instead we stumbled on, blaming each other for what was missing, and hurting each other in our own pain. If we had seen the endings as the conclusions of successful, but not lifelong, relationships, I think we'd have managed the partings with more grace. In fact, if we'd understood each other better, perhaps the break-ups wouldn't have had to happen at all.

But again, that won't always be the case: some relationships are meant to be a sprint, not a marathon. By this measure, I've been in three long-term relationships that were successful but not lifelong, and a few short-term, but still successful, ones. And if I'd seen them in those terms sooner, I wouldn't have struggled with their endings in the way I did. So I hope within this book you find a means of seeing exactly what you have with your partner; whether it's enough to be worth the journey and, if it's not, that the ending can be the beginning of something else that's good for both of you.

A contributing factor in how we feel about our relationships is typified in the way Hollywood focuses on two stages of relationships for its storylines: the burning, white-hot intensity of early love, and the burning, hurt-hot intensity of the ending. What wouldn't tend to sell tickets would be a film about the warm, middle stage of a relationship when passion is at least partially replaced by contented intimacy and shared hopes; when something is beginning to emerge between two people that is greater than just the sum of their *desire* it can be a lovely thing to be in, but not a very exciting thing to watch. And this emphasis on passion can persuade us that losing the rip-your-clothes-off-I've-got-to-have-you-now feeling is a sign that something is wrong, when it is more often just the natural consequence of the maturing of your union. In fact, instead of embracing this change, we more often look elsewhere for the re-ignition of the early fire. And, as for endings, it almost feels compulsory to turn love into hate and separation into drama. It doesn't have to be this way.

A dear friend of mine, Gil Boyne, was a great therapist for over fifty years and he came to believe that we all suffer from a universal neurosis: that we don't believe we're lovable or deserving of being loved. I don't believe there is any one thing we all suffer from, but I tend to see his point in most of my clients. If you feel unworthy, it's going to lead to a host of issues in your relationship, from jealousy to clinginess, attempts to dominate and diminish your partner, pushing away anyone who starts to get close, or holding onto someone you no longer love because you fear there'll never be anyone else. A good relationship is the best opportunity to heal these issues, and a bad one the best to make them fester. This book isn't therapy for that, but being half of a great couple can be, so I hope that by using the knowledge contained here it will help, not just with your relationship to your significant other, but also with your relationship to yourself. By having a language to describe the interactions between you and your partner you're more clearly able to see what problems are about you, what are about your partner, and why most don't really matter. Understanding yourself is a big step towards loving yourself.

I've wanted to write this book for a very long time, and I spent a good portion of it searching for a way of describing relationship differences, which would be both appealing to you and make the point. Overwhelmingly, my focus in this book is to provide the tools to help you meet someone you're attracted to and make it work from the beginning (once you've done the up-coming quizzes and read about which Lovebird you are, you can go to Part Three for some general advice on finding your suitable Lovebird type) or, if you're already in a relationship, to create a deeper level of intimacy and understanding. And while there is nothing more serious than making our relationships work, there is nothing more likely to stop you reading than to write about them seriously, I hope what you find entertains as it educates.

Inspiration for how to write the book came from an unlikely place. One day, I was out walking with my dogs, Betty and Fred. They were still puppies, so progress was very slow as everything they discovered became their favourite thing. This gave me time to think about a couple I was working with, on the point of separation, who'd come to see me as a last-ditch attempt to salvage their relationship. Theirs was a classic example: two people who wanted to stay together, who believed they were doing their best to love their partner, but who were both feeling unloved and misunderstood. And I knew why: they were different.

I know that sounds simple and obvious. We know that people are different to us – and yet we so often treat them as if their needs and wants are the same as ours. So it was in this case: the husband was doing for his wife what he would like done to him to show his love, and she was busy doing for him what she so wished he would do for her. That's got to be right, hasn't it? We're supposed to, 'Do unto others as you would have them do to you,' aren't we?

In a word: no.

When you stop to think about it, you will probably find that you know or feel yourself to be loved because of certain things your partner does. Similarly, your partner knows he or she is loved by certain things you do. Guess what? If your relationship is failing, they're probably different things: what you're doing for your partner is what makes you feel loved (and means nothing to them), and vice versa. My couple were love-starved in the middle of each partner's attempts to feed the other.

I had been searching for a good metaphor to explain this. My first attempt at a title for this book had the strapline: 'How to live with the alien you fell in love with', but this was a bit too much along the lines of *Men are from Mars, Women are from Venus* – and I disagreed with the premise that the problems with relationships are the differences between men and women, as gay couples who come to see me have the same problems as straight couples, so it's not simply a question of gender. But despite the strapline not being right, it made the point – there *are* differences between us that often make it seem like we're living with another species entirely, and this book is about the psychological preferences we each have that can lead to a number of differences between us and those we love, and how those differences don't need to cause the conflict and distress they so often do.

So it might have been this train of thought that brought my attention to a couple of birds sitting in a bush. One was a robin, and the other was a dove. The robin was singing its heart out, while the dove was doing nothing very much at all. When you listen to a robin, you should always focus on the silence between the songs, because more often than not, you'll hear a reply from another robin. They're not singing; they're having a conversation. The dove seemed completely unmoved by the beauty of the song, however, and it suddenly occurred to me that *here* was my metaphor. The differences between types of birds are blindingly obvious, presumably to them as much as us as they stick rigidly to their own in their choice of mates: robins sing to robins, doves cosy up to doves, peacocks hang out together and owls, well, owls do secret owl things.

But imagine if they didn't. Imagine if a robin tried to relate to any other type of bird the way they do with other robins. Imagine a wren shacking up with a thrush. An emu with a blackbird? They'd soon be in the same state as people often are, feeling unheard, misunderstood, ignored and unloved, and there would be bird divorce lawyers with a branch in every tree. (Vultures, probably.)

So I'm going to use the metaphor of different birds to help represent the differences I perceive in individuals that I think cause most of the difficulties so many of us experience in our love lives. I will use eight different types of birds to describe eight different types of people.

My method isn't meant to be taken too seriously, however – think of each type as having a bit of overlap with the next one, to accommodate the infinite variety that is a person's character-istics. (If you're a bird watcher, you may grind your teeth at the liberties I've taken in describing the characteristics of particular types. Sorry, I only intend them as a means of easy reference, not a depiction of the bird itself. Please don't set Bill Oddie on me.)

What this book is going to show you is how to recognise your partner's love song, because the chances are you're going to be a robin living with a kingfisher, or an owl trying to catch the eye of a dove. Opposites don't need to drive us mad; you just have to learn to sing more than just your own song. And I'm going to teach you.

Finally, here's a little joke that later you'll see covers a lot of what I'm talking about (it's important that you focus on the nature of the misinterpretation, not the gender of the participants):

Wife's diary:

> *Richard was acting weird tonight. We had made plans to meet at a nice restaurant for dinner. I had been shopping with my friends so I thought he was upset at the fact that I was a bit late, but he made no comment on it. He didn't say a single thing about the new dress I was wearing. Conversation wasn't flowing, so I suggested that we go somewhere quiet so we could talk. He agreed, but he didn't say much. He didn't take hold of my hand when we walked back to the car; he kept his hands in his pockets and looked down the whole way.*

I asked him what was wrong. He said, 'Nothing.' I asked him if it was my fault that he was upset. He said he wasn't upset, that it had nothing to do with me, and not to worry about it. On the way home, I told him that I loved him. He smiled slightly, and kept driving.

I can't explain his behaviour. I don't know why he didn't say, 'I love you, too.' When we got home, I felt as if I had lost him completely, as if he wanted nothing to do with me any more. He just sat there quietly, and watched TV. He continued to seem distant and absent. Finally, with silence all around us, I decided to go to bed. About fifteen minutes later, he came to bed. But I still felt that he was distracted, and his thoughts were somewhere else. He didn't hug me or say goodnight. He fell asleep; I cried. I don't know what to do. I'm almost sure that his thoughts are with someone else. My life is a disaster.

Husband's diary:

A four putt – who takes four putts to sink a ball? My life is a disaster.

PART ONE

Differences that make a difference

We've been raised in an age where the movies drip-feed us the ideal of the perfect love: that just around the corner is 'The One', who will tip orange juice over us in Notting Hill, or emerge dripping from a pond, and sweep us off to a better life. Most of us at some time or another have had the experience of falling madly and deeply in love, a place where for a time – sometimes a long time – we believe we have found what all the fuss is about. Then the gloss begins to dull. Did he always have that annoying way of cleaning his teeth? Did she moan about my mates at the beginning?

It isn't long before you're saying to your friends, or at least yourself, 'I don't know what I saw in him in the first place' or 'It took a while for her true colours to show through' and for you to be saying to your partner, 'I just need a little space' (without you in it) and, 'Maybe we just need some time apart' (like the rest of our life).

It's been estimated by evolutionary psychologists that for most of the time that our species has been on the planet, couples would only stay together for about six years – roughly the length of time it takes to raise a child to a point where the mother and child could survive independently. It lends a certain sense to the seven-year itch. Within those six years, very little space would have been available for 'quality time', as the couple would have been too busy hunting for food, avoiding predators, keeping their children safe and finding shelter. Back in those days, the average life expectancy was about twenty-five years (so there was less scope for getting into trouble or forgetting anniversaries): you got together, you had kids, you fought to raise them for a few years and then either split or succumbed to the perils of the world. I suspect our ancient ancestors spin in their graves at the very mention of the words 'quality time'.

Most of us now have the luxury today of living in a bubble of security that gives us the room to have expectations of happiness with the perfect partner who will 'fulfil us' – expectations that wouldn't have occurred to even our great-grandparents.

What we're left with is a mismatch. We're not evolved for monogamy – that's just a cultural thing – and our genes don't select a partner according to how likely they are to fulfil us. Unconsciously, things are a lot simpler than that. The question our unconscious asks first is: who will provide good genes for my child, and will they make a good father/mother?

This takes us a long way from what we think we're looking for when we look around for a prospective mate. For example, what do you think first attracts you to someone? Their eyes? Their smile? Their car? Nope. Their smell. That's pretty ironic considering the billions we spend every year dousing ourselves with something to attract mates, but it's no less true. Professor Robert Winston was the subject of a televised experiment where he and six women had their blood tested for six genes that are markers for their immune systems. The women then slept in a T-shirt for two nights that were then placed in separate jars. Professor Winston was invited to sniff each jar and rate them for attractiveness. An interesting thing happened: unerringly, he rated them in direct relation to the dissimilarity between his genetic markers and those of the women. In other words, he was most attracted to his opposite. This makes perfect evolutionary sense: if your child has the broadest possible immune system, it's more likely to survive what life throws at her or him.

I mention this only to highlight just how unconscious our mate selection system is. As the philosopher Blaise Pascal said, 'The heart has its reason, whereof reason knows nothing.'

When Cupid – i.e. your unconscious – points its bow at someone, it releases a cascade of chemicals in your body, the best known of which is oxytocin, the so-called 'love chemical'.

This hormone is involved in bonding and building relationships. It's released in large quantities in the brains of new-born babies and their parents, as well as in the brains of two people falling in love. It's been shown to activate an ancient area of our brain below our thinking systems, even below our emotional areas. It's also the part of the brain that becomes active when we take something like cocaine – love affects us like an addiction, it's the highest of natural highs, and it shares similar characteristics to obsessive compulsive disorder (OCD). We can't stop thinking about that person, we lose appetite, our sleep gets disturbed and we act in ways that are geared towards getting a reciprocal response to the love we feel. And if we don't get that response, often we do more of what isn't working with that person, like stalking, bombarding them with texts or poking them on Facebook (you know, the things that tend to endear you). In a way, it's not your fault, as oxytocin makes you a bit obsessive – hang out with the mother of a new-born to see how single-mindedly focused she is on her offspring if you don't believe me.

In a situation of requited love, it's estimated that we're actually a bit nuts for about eighteen months, but at least we're nuts about each other, that's only annoying to . . . everyone else. Then things calm down a bit, and the tint on the rose-tinted spectacles starts to lighten. Things we may have found endearing now start to grate. Changes we hoped for in our partner don't materialise despite our best coaching, and our eyebrows may begin to twitch in sympathy with those raised by our friends when first confronted by our choice of partner.

This is where the work begins. We're waking up out of our love trance.

Scientist Helen Fisher suggests that we move through three phases of attraction: lust, romantic love and long-term attachment. The first two tend to get all the headlines, but it's the latter by which we tend to judge our success in relationships as we get older. Why? Maybe because it's so hard to do. Without the mainlining thrill of oxytocin keeping us in a love-fog that obscures from view what we're really getting into, we can be left with the after-party moment of waking up beside someone eighteen months into the relationship (at the latest), and asking ourselves, 'Did I really?'

I mentioned in the introduction that most couples I see, and all I help, aren't struggling with each other because they don't love each other; just that they don't understand each other or feel valued. I think the selection of differences goes beyond immune systems, and embraces aspects of personality, too. This book isn't so much for people who are like each other – generally I find people who are tend to rub along quite happily together (there's a saying that people like people who are like them), although there are some tips for those people, too. No, this book is for those of you who look at your partner and shake your head at what they do or don't do that upsets, annoys or bothers you.

But, here's the thing: **everyone has reasons for doing what they're doing; they're just not your reasons.**

One of the great flaws in us humans is that we know we think, but we don't think about *how* we think, and we assume that how we do it is how everyone else does it. Newsflash! That's not so. There are differences in the way you and your partner interpret and interact with the world that have a major impact on how you get on. The trouble is, we keep making the mistake of thinking that our partners think like we do, and see the world the same way. This means that when the person you love does something you don't like, or doesn't do something you *would* like, you tend to behave as if it's a deliberate thing to annoy or disappoint you. Over time the dripping tap of these disappointments can build into a tsunami of frustration and rage that sweeps the love out of sight and leaves you surrounded by the debris of failure. And solicitors' fees.

The good news is that it doesn't have to. If you were attracted to someone in the first place then you have chemistry on your side, and I'd put some trust in that. All things being equal, the oxytocin might diminish in quantity, but its work will have been done in terms of bonding you to your partner. What weakens those bonds subsequently, in my opinion, is the conflict you feel between the love you have, and the negative emotions that arise from living with someone you don't understand, or who you feel doesn't understand you. If my friend Gil Boyne is right and we do carry within us a doubt about our self-worth, then it's not surprising that our partner's 'not getting us' carries so much weight on the love scales. 'My wife/husband/partner doesn't understand me' is a deserved cliché; we smile when we hear it in a bar, but it's a cliché because it drives so many people into the arms of someone who they hope will understand – and hence value (love) – them better. And they'll probably be disappointed again.

In my opinion (and you can take it as read that from here on in everything you read is just my opinion, so I don't have to keep writing that), being understood – and understanding your partner – is purely a question of communication, and I'm about to teach you the language in which to communicate. Living with someone you love, successfully, isn't easy, but it is possible. And creating a sense of mutual understanding of the weirdness of each other, and hopefully an appreciation of it, can be something that leads to a greater sense of worth in yourself, too.

How this book is arranged

In a moment I'm going to ask you – and your partner, if you have one, and if they're sharing this book with you – to complete a quiz. It comes in two parts: the first part is to put you into one of two nests (you see how I've begun with the bird analogies already?). In the language of the book, the answers you give to the quiz will place you either in the *ground-bird* nest, or the *sky-bird* nest.

A thing I want to stress from the beginning is that there is no type that is better or worse than the other in any way: there are no 'good' birds and 'bad' birds, there are just consequences; so do your best to give an answer as honestly as you can, rather than one you think will put you in the best light. I'll explain about the differences between sky-birds and ground-birds after you've answered the following questions.

Quiz 1

When you've completed the quiz, circle the 'G' or the 'S' letter in the grid below that corresponds with each answer.

1. Which is most true of you?:
(a) I like most things to be done a certain way
(b) As long as things get done it doesn't matter much

2. Is it worse to:
(a) have your head in the clouds?
(b) be in a 'rut'?

3. Do you tend to be more annoyed when:
(a) people do something the wrong way?
(b) people insist there's a right way?

4. Are you more interested in:
(a) what is actual?
(b) what is possible?

5. In doing ordinary things are you more likely to:
(a) do it the usual way?
(b) do it your own way?

6. I am better at working with:
(a) the big picture?
(b) the detail?

7. Are you more attracted to:
(a) sensible people?
(b) imaginative people?

8. Do you:
(a) prefer to look for patterns and go with your gut instinct?
(b) prefer to systematically work through problems?

9. When asked a question would your friends say you:
(a) tend to be brief?
(b) tend to go into detail?

10. Would you say you are best at:
(a) strategy and ideas?
(b) organisation and planning?

11. Is it better to:
(a) deal with what comes up as it comes up?
(b) prepare for any eventuality?

12. Are you more:
(a) methodical?
(b) creative?

13. What's worse:
(a) to be unprepared?
(b) to be over-prepared?

	1	2	3	4	5	6	7	8	9	10	11	12	13
(a)	G	G	G	G	G	S	G	S	S	S	S	G	G
(b)	S	S	S	S	S	G	S	G	G	G	G	S	S

Now add up the total number of S and G responses and insert each number in the box below. If you have more of the letter S circled, you are predominantly sky-bird; if you have more of the letter G circled, you are more of a ground-bird! (What this means is explained below.)

Scores

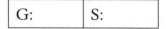

G:	S:

One of the best-known ways of describing differences in the way people think is the Myers-Briggs Personality Inventory. It's been used on over thirty million people, and aspects of it became integrated into an area of neuro-linguistic programming (NLP) called metaprograms. NLP was originally developed by Richard Bandler and John Grinder as a means of describing an individual's way of seeing the world (and the different ways individuals do so), and using the knowledge that came from it to help people gain control of their own behaviours. Metaprograms are just a set of descriptions of particular differences – such as the differences you've just answered questions to identify.

Ground-birds and sky-birds

As I mentioned, 'G' stands for ground-birds and 'S' for sky-birds: the names I'm giving to what, in Myers-Briggs and NLP, they term as *sensors* and *intuitors*.

Ground-birds

These people are the sensors: those more likely to trust information that is concrete rather than speculative. They're much more comfortable with what exists now, rather than what might happen in the future, and value what they can touch – they're big on living in the 'real world'. If you ask them for information they'll probably deluge you with it; they love to get down in the detail of things. Ground-birds like things a certain way: their way. They have rules for most things, use the word 'should' a lot – as in 'you should do it this way', 'you should have been home on time . . .' etc, and treat transgressions of their rules as the act of a mad person or someone deliberately trying to put a crimp in their day, i.e. they can overreact to a breach of their rule book. (Only yesterday, for example, my wife watched me feed the dogs and told me that I was doing it wrong: meat should go in the bowl before the biscuits. I'd got to fifty-two years old without realising there was a 'best' way of feeding a dog.)

In their careers, ground-birds will be excellent at organising things and making sure something runs smoothly. They need to be careful because if they get overworked their tendency is to work even harder rather than delegate – think Monica in *Friends*. In a management role, they can be prone to micro-managing, and if they rise far enough to take on a strategic role they might struggle. As parents, they can be a little controlling but everything is done for a good reason. Usually theirs. (And I didn't really mean usually.)

If there's someone in the house who knows where everything is, it'll be the ground-bird. I was looking for examples of the different types in well-known characters from film and TV, and two genres came to mind, mainly because I'm a fan. In *Star Trek*, Scotty is a great example. He knows everything about the Enterprise, can navigate the wiring diagram for it with his eyes closed, and knows exactly how much power he can give the captain to play with. Similarly, if we think of great detectives, then Poirot or Miss Marple come to mind: painstakingly connecting together little clues until the finger points in only one direction, both only trusting hard evidence, and having no time for fanciful theories. They only announce their conclusion when they're absolutely sure.

Sky-birds

The intuitors, the sky-birds, on the other hand, trust information that is more conceptual or abstract. They go with their hunches, are turned on by possibilities and tend to spend more time in the future than in the reality of the present. They like looking for connections between things and seek the bigger picture – partly because it keeps them away from dealing with detail, which bores them senseless. Because they avoid detail, they can be quite poor at keeping tabs on bill paying and the like, and will read something enough only to get the gist of it, which might mean they miss reading the one thing to which they really needed to pay attention. (If they're helping you build a flat pack wardrobe, for example, you'll barely see them look at the instructions, as they'll just expect to be able to figure it out. And there will always be some screws left over at the end.) They can repeat the same errors because they don't create systematised responses to things; they just go with what comes up. If you ask them for information, you're likely to get quite a short, 'in a nutshell', kind of response. They're poor at following rules. While they might be attracted to the idea of them, and accept the need for them, they lack the attention to detail that makes following them systematically possible. Whoever said 'rules are for the guidance of the wise and the blind obedience of fools' was a sky-bird. The person who hit him over the head for saying it was a ground-bird.

At work, they can be guilty of slacking if given something that is menial or boring. And because that is what starting at the bottom usually entails, they can seem like late bloomers, but it's actually only that it takes a while to reach a level where their strengths – usually creativity and vision, which are what people who head companies are usually paid to provide – come into play. Once they find their aptitude matching their role, then they can really seem to transform in front of your eyes. Sky-birds can be great to work for if you value your freedom because they are happy to give you a direction and then leave you to do the job your way. The downside of this is that through this macro-managing, things can go wrong because they don't keep track of the small stuff – if they have a subordinate who doesn't thrive without closer supervision, then problems can occur. As parents, they can be a little too *laissez-faire*, letting the kids roll along without paying enough attention to whether they're rolling in the right direction. Think Joey in *Friends*.

If I continue with the *Star Trek* theme, Captain Kirk is a sky-bird. He wants to boldly go and explore new galaxies, and he hasn't a clue about what poor Mr Scott has to do to get him there. But if the universe needs saving by seeing how to make a nuclear weapon out of three matchsticks, a shoe lace and a pair of pants, he's your man; sky-birds are great at innovation and putting things together in new ways. When it comes to detectives, then Sherlock Holmes is a prime example: making connections between such seemingly unconnected bits of information that his conclusion almost seems magical – and yet on other occasions, being oblivious to the mundane things that are under his nose.

Ground-bird and sky-bird differences

When it comes to detail, the difference between these two types could be summed up in the following conversation:

Ground-bird: 'Weren't you on holiday the same time I was? Did you have a good time?'

Sky-bird: 'Yes, I did. It was great. How about you?'

Ground-bird: 'Well, we always have a holiday at this time because it doesn't get too expensive, and this time we went to Florida. We booked with BA and took a package that let us explore a little, so the first day we . . .'

Both people have answered in the style of their type, and both will feel their response is appropriate to the question. However, because the way *we* do things is clearly the right way (or we'd do it differently), it's very easy to label negatively people who respond in a way you wouldn't. In this case, the ground-bird might feel that the sky-bird was a bit aloof and evasive by answering as succinctly as they did, while the sky-bird, after the first couple of minutes of the blow-by-blow recollection of Florida, might feel themselves losing the will to live and think the ground-bird a boring windbag. Neither is necessarily true – they're just different. If you listen to politicians you can often tell which nest they flew from, too. Martin Luther King's 'I have a dream' speech is pure sky-bird, big-picture oration, while someone like ex-Prime Minister Gordon Brown was more comfortable talking about the nuts and bolts of economic reality. Interestingly, a King is more exciting and inspiring to listen to, but they'd need a Brown-type figure somewhere working out how exactly to get to the promised land.

My first wife was a ground-bird and I'm a sky-bird (I probably made that obvious from my descriptions of the types). In the evening, we'd sit reading our books before bedtime, and at a certain point she would turn to me and say, 'How's your book?' I'd say, 'It's great, thanks.' Then, with a sinking heart, I'd say, 'How about yours?', knowing it would then lead to a twenty-minute update of her latest bodice-ripper. If I had known at the time about ground- and sky-birds (or sensors and intuitors), I might have listened with more patience.

Because ground-birds have quite fixed ideas about how things should be, it can often seem as if their partner is a project, someone to be viewed as a work in progress, a soul to be saved. And the sky-bird is likely to continually frustrate them in their efforts. In my mind, that's a good thing for any sky-bird living with a ground-bird because, as one of them, I have a theory that if we became who our ground-bird partner is trying to change us into, they'd lose interest and no longer respect us. (In a way, frustrating them is in their best interests; I just hope my wife doesn't read this bit.)

Don't think of these two types as me trying to fix people to one telegraph pole or another; think of the idea as two poles linked by a wire with people somewhere in between the poles. Some will be sitting on the pole, most on the line closer to one pole than the other, and some will be right in the middle.

To make my point, I've tended to exaggerate my descriptions, so it sounds as if everyone is strongly one way or another. When it comes to the quiz, the higher your score, the more likely it is that my exaggerations will describe you accurately. The closer you come to sitting in the middle of the wire, the more I'd advise you to read the bird types at both ends, and how they combine with your partner's type. I'll explain more a little later.

Now we'll find out a little more about you to help us identify your Lovebird type.

Quiz 2

For each of the following statements, please place a number 1–4 next to every phrase. Use the following system to indicate your preferences:

4 = Closest to describing you
3 = Close to describing you
2 = Less close to describing you
1 = Least close to describing you

To come to a decision:
1. ___ I habitually talk to myself in my head (T)
   ___ I need to talk things through with other people (So)
   ___ I go with my gut feeling (F)
   ___ I like to see everything clearly in front of me (Si)

At parties:
2. ___ I hate having to stand around, I like to be comfortable (F)
   ___ I hate it when the music is so loud it's hard to talk (So)
   ___ Half the fun is having the chance to dress up (Si)
   ___ I get bored making small talk (T)

To find my way:
3. ___ I prefer to look at a map myself (Si)
   ___ Things seem clearest when someone describes them to me (So)
   ___ I really need to have been there before (F)
   ___ I need the route to make sense in my head (T)

When listening to an argument I go with:
4. ___ What feels right (F)
   ___ Which way sounds the best (Si)
   ___ What looks best to me (So)
   ___ What makes most sense (T)

What I tend to enjoy most about holidays is:
5. ___ The sights (Si)
    ___ Visiting places interesting to me (T)
    ___ The chance to relax (F)
    ___ The opportunity to talk to different people (So)

What attracts me is:
6. ___ The way someone looks (Si)
    ___ The way they make me feel (F)
    ___ A good listener (So)
    ___ Someone who is interesting (T)

What turns me off is:
7. ___ A horrible voice (So)
    ___ A bore (T)
    ___ Someone who is scruffy (Si)
    ___ A cold personality (F)

I learn best:
8. ___ From hands-on experience (F)
    ___ From watching someone or something (Si)
    ___ By getting the chance to discuss things (So)
    ___ By making sense of the subject (T)

I find it hardest to:
9. ___ Listen to music I hate (So)
    ___ Sit somewhere really uncomfortable (F)
    ___ Have to do something that doesn't make sense (T)
    ___ Wear something that doesn't suit me (Si)

STEP ONE:
Copy your answers from the test to the lines below.

1. T ____   2. F ____   3. Si ____
   So ____   So ____   So ____
   F ____   Si ____   F ____
   Si ____   T ____   T ____

4. F ____   5. Si ____   6. Si ____
   Si ____   T ____   F ____
   So ____   F ____   So ____
   T ____   So ____   T ____

7. So ____   8. F ____   9. So ____
   T ____   Si ____   F ____
   Si ____   So ____   T ____
   F ____   T ____   Si ____

Totals

Enter the number you put for each question in the grid below.

	Si	F	So	T
1.				
2.				
3.				
4.				
5.				
6.				
7.				
8.				
9.				
TOTAL				

STEP TWO:

Now compare the total scores with each other and write Si, F, So and T below in their corresponding descending order: e.g. if you have your highest total for F, then that will be the letter you put in 1st place.

1st _____ 2nd _____ 3rd _____ 4th _____

What was that about?

Another idea from NLP is that people tend to have a preference for which sense they pay most attention to, dividing people into the categories of visuals (seeing), auditories (hearing), kinaesthetics (feeling) and a fourth category of people who pay most attention to their own thoughts: to what is going on inside their head as a result of what is going on outside. These are usually described as auditory digitals. (Catchy, huh? In this book I'm calling them thinkers.)

So, the quiz you've just taken will have identified you as a *sight* bird, a *song* bird, a *feeling* bird or a *thinking* bird. Again, none is better than any other. I do find that sight and feeling birds are most common, followed by thinking birds, with song birds being the rarest – some estimates I've seen put them as low as 10 per cent of the population.

You'll see from the list below that I've created the eight types of bird and grouped them as either ground- or sky-birds: i.e. birds that tend to spend most time hopping around the garden, or sitting high in a branch (my apologies again to anyone with even a passing interest in birds, I know that several I've chosen can be seen doing both; it's strictly a metaphor).

	Ground-birds	Sky-birds
Si – Sight bird	Peacock	Swift
So – Song bird	Robin	Nightingale
F – Feeling bird	Swan	Dove
T – Thinking bird	Kingfisher	Owl

By matching the two quiz results you've taken, you'll be able to see which Lovebird you are. If you came out with little difference between ground- and sky-bird in quiz 1, then it might help you to read more than one of the types – i.e. if you came out a song bird in the second quiz and evenly balanced as a ground- or sky-bird in the first quiz, then I think you'll find it useful to read about both the Robin and the Nightingale in Part Two, and how both types get along with your partner's type in Part Four. And if you don't have a partner at the moment, I suggest you go to Part Three. From your reading, you should be able to extract a mixture of things that apply to you, and discard others that don't.

Similarly, if your top type in quiz 2 is close to your second type – let's say you're a ground-bird and got 30 for thinking bird and 28 for sight bird, then you might like to read about both Kingfisher *and* Peacock, and how each one relates to your partner's type in Part Four. If you came close in both quizzes, and so did your partner, you've got a lot of reading to do, but it'll give you lots to talk about.

I suggest you read your own(and your partner's) Lovebird profiles in Part Two, answer the questions I ask at its end, and then find your combination in Part Four. Within each combination in this chapter there are two headings: 'Cuckoos in the nest' highlights the potential challenges and drawbacks they might face, while 'Feathers for the nest' gives some ideas about do's and don'ts that will help a couple work more harmoniously together. In Part Five, I give you some things to do over the next couple of months to really focus both of you on understanding yourself and each other like never before, and making that understanding the basis and birth of a more enriching relationship.

PART TWO

Lovebird profiles

With your Lovebird type identified, or at least narrowed down, I want to go into more detail now about each one.

As I've already said, I'm going to be generalising about the characteristics of each type – and occasionally going for cheap laughs – so don't be surprised if I've made you sound worse (or better) than you actually are. If the book makes you nod in recognition about some of the situations you've been in then it's doing its job, by getting you to think about the differences between you and other people in a new way.

Sight birds: Peacocks and Swifts

When I think of sight birds I'm often reminded of the cartoon character Roadrunner, who always seems just a little ahead of everyone else and is absolutely uncatchable once he's in motion. Sight birds usually buzz with energy and if there's something they want to share with you, they seem to feel as though their mouth is going to close for business any moment, so they need to get as many words out as they can. Often, fast-paced and slapstick, slip-on-a-banana-skin-type humour is what makes their sides split.

As you'd expect, sight birds' interests and hobbies also usually reflect their love of the visual. Whether they paint or enjoy collecting art, have an interest in design – whether soft furnishings or cars – or love to hike to enjoy the wonders of nature, somewhere within their passion will lurk the need to see what they find as beautiful. In fact, sometimes it takes gifted sight birds to teach us to see the world in new ways – like Salvador Dali or Vincent van Gogh.

Extrovert sight birds are likely to dress to impress and will often be pretty flamboyant. They'll be the person in the bright pink or yellow car. They'll be the person who wears shades in all weathers – sometimes it's just because they think they look cool, but some sight birds actually are very sensitive to light and do need them (so try not to laugh when they walk into a wall indoors). Being around an extrovert sight bird can be quite exhausting, as they'll never want to settle in one place: a pub crawl will always seem more fun to them, as what's going on over there will seem better than what's going on over here, and

they'll often seem to be juggling three things at once as ideas
occur to them. I've occasionally wondered if a study would show
that sight birds get more speeding tickets than other types because
they always seem in such a hurry, not just on journeys, but to
get to the next thing, whatever that is, even if it's just the next
course of a meal. Savouring the moment isn't something that
comes naturally to them.

Introvert sight birds are a bit easier; they may be going at a
million miles an hour in their head, but on the surface there's a
bit more calm about them, which often translates into intensity.
To be the centre of their attention can be like looking up at a
microscope from a glass slide, and what they can achieve in this
state of mind is immense because they're able to work at such
an amazing rate. Comedian Eddie Izzard strikes me as a sight
bird, not just for his stylish cross-dressing, but for the epic mean-
derings of his stand-up and the speed of his thinking. I'd put
him alongside Lady Gaga – who else would think of wearing a
suit made of meat? – and Kylie.

Sight birds will be, in a word, stylish – even if it's not your
style. Understated but perfectly presented – the look that says
'Oh, this? It's just something I threw on,' but probably took a
few hours of careful thought. If fashion is a focus for them, that's
the kind of thing sight birds will spend their free time thinking
about: outfits they have, what goes with what, what items they
need to complete their perpetually incomplete wardrobe. And
even if it's not, how things look in their world will always be
somewhere in their mind.

When you visit the house of a sight bird, you tend to have
one of two experiences. One will be where the house is decorated in an original and often truly stunning way. The colours
may clash, the mix of styles eclectic, and you'll get a sense of
someone in pursuit of an idea. You may hate it, but you won't
be able to deny its originality. Or you may walk into a show
home. I know people who have literally decorated a room in
their house precisely from a magazine article or style catalogue.
Clearly there's nothing wrong with this: to a sight bird, it's the

highest form of praise to buy a dress someone else looked great in.

When it comes to careers, there are few limitations. Sight birds learn quickly in the main, as more information comes through our eyes than all our other senses combined, so they tend to be adept at picking things up quickly. The career paths they're most likely to choose include architecture, interior design, painting and decorating, cooking – they'll love making a plate look great or decorating a cup cake – but most things in business would be open to them. What they'd hate to do is work in a confined place with nothing to look at – a call centre would be their idea of hell.

If I'm painting sight birds as people without limitations, I'm over-egging the pudding: for a start they're easily distracted, particularly if they're extroverts. Whatever they're in the middle of, no matter how deeply they're focusing, there will always be something that can catch their attention, whether it's an item on the telly, a passing pert bottom or a piece of fluff on their jacket. Which reminds me: they can inadvertently come across as flirtatious. If they see something amiss with your outfit, like your tie's askew or you have a stray hair on your jumper, they're likely to groom you – not a perfect stranger, hopefully – but casual acquaintance upwards. Also, they'll always return eye contact because they'll think you're trying to communicate something – and therefore they will be prone to holding your gaze for too long. They are also the world's worst for staring at something (or someone) they like the look of. It's probably another reason why they wear sunglasses a lot.

Sight birds can be in such a hurry that they either leave you behind or wear you out. Sometimes people vote to take a break from their sight bird friends, not because they've gone off them, just because they need to refuel. But it'll only be temporary, because sight birds are good to be with. They'll take you to new places, be the first to introduce you to new experiences and generally give your life an injection of va-va-voom. They'll know how you're feeling from just a look, and be the first to send you flowers, or come round to console or congratulate; they're great at keeping in touch – especially the extroverts. In fact, that's another thing that can be a bit wearing. If you don't keep in touch sight birds can take that very personally, and the first ten minutes of a catch-up call is likely to be spent with them telling you what a bad friend you are. (Hands up if that makes you more or less likely to want to ring them next time? I thought so. What they're doing to motivate you to keep in touch can actually have the opposite effect.) Sight birds just need to learn to chill a little, because they would realise they have the world at their feet if they'd only slow themselves enough to look down.

Peacocks

'I don't mind making jokes, I just don't want to look like one.'
Marilyn Monroe

Peacock types are people who connect to the world strongly through their visual sense: how things look really matters to them. They're also ground-birds – they have rules that need following and like to know the detail of things. Combined, these preferences make for some interesting characteristics.

The look of things
You've only got to look at a peacock to know that looks are a big deal – I bet you've never seen a scruffy one. It's much the same with Peacock people. Looks matter, both their own and, if you're thinking of being in a relationship with them, yours too. I once heard one say to their partner, rather cuttingly, 'I don't know what look you were aiming for . . . but you missed.'

This fixation with the importance of appearance doesn't necessarily imply that they're always going to be dolled up, but it does mean that they'll hate to be caught in their grots and hate to leave the house without looking 'right'. I have a Peacock friend who used to wake up in the morning before her boyfriend and brush her hair and freshen her make-up before languidly rearranging herself on the pillow in readiness for his first sight of her. I'm sure that behaviour didn't last, but first impressions for a Peacock count – and last longer than you might imagine. You know the way you tend to ease up as a relationship progresses? When you both get more comfortable with each other, stop being on your best behaviour and feel okay sitting together on the sofa in your old jammies? Well, if you're with a Peacock, leave out the last one, at least for a while. You starting to slob out could be taken as a sign of your lessening romantic interest, so wait until they begin to relax a little in their clothes choices before you do – although I bet their lounge pants will still be ironed immaculately.

An interesting thing with Peacocks is that although not all of them are going to be fashion plates, they'll all have strong ideas about their appearance in some way or other. Some put particular emphasis on something like their hair, or nails, or six pack, while others will focus on a single colour, or label or style. As I mentioned earlier, extroverts will tend to be more eye-catching, while introverts will aim more at the 'subtly chic' side of the street.

If you get into a relationship with a Peacock, be ready for them to demand a say in the way you look, because it reflects on them (in their world). 'I can't have you going out looking like that!', 'Do you really think those shoes suit you?' and 'If you were taller that would look good on you', are just samples of the things I've heard in clothes shops over the years.

Peacocks will tend to love things that stimulate them visually, so the interior décor of their house will usually be interesting and quite striking, sometimes with daring combinations that you'll love or hate, or something that seems to have come straight from a shop display. Because sometimes it will have done. As you might expect, their hobbies will often be in alignment with their love of the visual, but can take many forms, from art to bird watching – it really depends on what they find beautiful or visually stimulating. While they might be embarrassed at turning up to an event in the same outfit as someone else, they'll be less embarrassed at seeing someone else copying their style; in a way they kind of expect it.

If you move in together, be ready to lose a lot of your stuff. If it doesn't match the theme your Peacock has in mind, the only time you'll see it again is if you happen to pass the window of your local charity shop at the right moment. But the upside is that you'll live in what looks like a show home. And you'd better keep it that way.

Gifts

Buying presents for Peacocks can be tricky. Clothes you'll almost certainly get wrong unless you know them really well, and something for the home – beyond a pot plant – is a no-no, unless you happen to know they collect something or are replacing something you broke. I know an Owl and Peacock couple who spent six months with nothing on their walls because they couldn't agree over paintings. The Peacock wanted something pretty that would complement the décor, while the Owl wanted something thought-provoking, or meaningful to them as a couple.

I remember being in a museum looking at the picture van Gogh painted shortly before he shot himself. It depicts the field where it happened, and is full of dark swirling portents of doom: at least, it is if you're an Owl. My Peacock leaned across to me and I felt a quickening of my pulse – at last, she was getting it. She whispered, 'Isn't it bloody ugly!' I knew we were doomed.

Pace

One thing that often makes Peacocks easy to spot is their pace. They'll often talk really quickly – think of racing commentators during the final furlong or Robin Williams in full flight. They can be pretty exhausting in that regard, but it's simply that they tend to process quite quickly and attempt to communicate at the same speed. If you're someone who likes to think before you speak, you're probably not a Peacock – but I expect you can think of a time when you were steamrollered by one; overwhelmed by the sheer speed of delivery. A relationship with a Peacock is definitely life in the fast lane, from the minute they throw back the curtains, to the minute you slip a sedative into their cocoa.

Part of the reason for this pace is because Peacocks pay most attention to the things that they're seeing around them, and that tends to be a lot of things. This can mean that you can lose them mid-sentence to something that passes by the window, a magazine cover they suddenly spot on the coffee table, or a fly buzzing round the living room; the more extrovert they are, the more difficult they are to keep on point.

Time

Everyone's heard the saying, 'Absence makes the heart grow fonder.' That will make Peacocks snort with derision. 'Absence means you don't care' is a more likely belief of theirs. For some reason, for Peacocks, the amount of time you spend on something is an indicator of how strongly you value it. If, for example, work starts eating into your relationship time, it's likely you're going to start getting accused of 'caring about work more than me'. Whilst working in the police force, I was building up my therapy practice and putting in long hours working as an instructor at Hendon Police College during the day and then seeing clients four evenings a week, plus Saturdays. I think it was the thing that finally pushed my relationship with the Peacock over the edge. Even though I felt I was working towards our future, she couldn't overcome what we weren't having in our present: quality time. It's vital if you're living with a Peacock that concentration is given to spending time in and on the relationship.

Peacocks will prize sharing experiences – trips to the theatre or the cinema, a day at the seaside; anything where the two of you get a chancc to spend time together and talk about what you're both seeing. Making a Peacock watch a magical sunset on their own is almost an act of cruelty. If they are feeling you're not investing enough together-time, they'll start talking of 'drifting apart', 'not seeing eye to eye any more', 'life being dull', or 'losing the spark'. They're using the words that describe the internal picture they are making of the relationship. If you start hearing that kind of talk, you'd better start putting some hours in at home.

Peacocks really will 'believe it when they see it', and not unless. A couple coming for relationship therapy were going through some serious problems. The guy was feeling really hassled by his girlfriend's demands to spend more time with her. He was having a very busy time with his work and felt he had to honour a number of commitments to his family and friends. She accused him of not caring. He would phone her several times a day and tell her he loved her, and make sure he always got to spend what time he could with her – time which was increasingly filled with her recriminations. Eventually, he was so desperate that he broke down and cried in front of her. He was amazed that this actually made her feel better because at last 'she could see he cared'! Therapy was easy; I just got him to carry an onion with him at all times. Seriously, once he realised how important face-to-face time was to her he adjusted his schedule, and when that wasn't possible he made sure they had something special to do together booked for her to look forward to once the busy period was over.

Rules

Peacocks belong to the class of birds I call ground-birds because one of the key things with this type is that they like things the way they like them. They have rules, and they need to be followed.

I had a girlfriend once who was a big time ground-bird. I'll call her Susan to spare any embarrassment (or libel action). As I said before, I'm a sky-bird, so I realise now we were always destined for a bumpy ride. I remember the first time she saw me wash up. As a sky-bird, I tend not to have rules for things. With me, everything to be washed goes into the bowl, and everything comes out, without any pattern or sequence. Susan was horrified. She said to me, 'Don't you know how to wash up? You start with glasses, then cutlery, then plates, then pans.' Implicit but not spoken was, 'Anything else is a sin.' Explicit, and unwisely spoken, was my reply: 'People are dying in droughts in Africa, so what does it matter?' Instant row. It set the pattern for the two and a half years of our relationship. You might think that dishwashers would solve that particular problem . . . but I bet her husband has had to learn how to stack it the 'right' way.

For me, the relationship was like living in a strange, dark room, around which this Peacock had strewn her rules at random for me to trip over. And for *her,* it must be realised, it must have seemed like a familiar bright room, around which I was kicking her rules just to annoy her. I remember another time, when we were in a department store. We had bought some chocolate and were walking out. I opened the chocolate and offered her some. She looked aghast: 'You don't eat chocolate in a clothes shop!' she exclaimed. 'But we're not shopping for clothes – we're walking out,' I replied, somewhat puzzled. It didn't matter; it was a rule. If I'd known then what I'm writing about now I would have been much quicker to have picked up on the importance of such things to her, rather than dismissing them as silly. They matter, so honour them.

Detail

Peacocks can like information seemingly for the sake of it. Susan started studying for a qualification in canine psychology. Before she got started, she went out and bought pretty well every book on the market, just in case they would be useful. When she got into gardening the same thing happened. Most of the books she never even opened, but having the information to hand, in case it is ever useful, is classic Peacock behaviour.

Ask a Peacock for information and you can forget the *Reader's Digest* abridged version, as the Peacock will give you everything they know. If they ask you a simple question like, 'How was your day?' and you reply with, 'It was okay,' this can seem like a slap to them. They want to know what happened, and they'll expect you to sit through the same level of detail. And it doesn't matter if the detail is trivial to you. In Peacock world, there is no such thing.

The plus side to this attention to detail is that your life is likely to be well organised – for some, almost militarily so. Bills will get paid on time and you'll never be without your passport at the airport. The downside is that sometimes Peacocks' focus is so in the detail that they can miss the big picture. They can get so immersed in the running of the day-to-day that they forget why they are doing it, so sometimes you might feel like you're more a member of a team than a partner in a relationship. It's something you may have to talk about from time to time.

In the bedroom

There's no getting away from the fact that in the Peacock universe, looks count. No problem if you look like Sandra Bullock; big problem if you feel you only look like the bullock part. As appearance is a big thing for Peacocks, sex is usually better for them with the lights on. So if you're with a Peacock who suddenly prefers it in the dark, the bad news is it's probably not you he or she is getting down with in their head. Partners of Peacocks can feel under pressure from the demands of their partners to keep in shape – the way you looked on the day they met you is the comparison you're going to be judged by. It's not very fair, but then what is?

For male Peacocks, sexy clothing is likely to be a big winner – less so for many females, unless we're talking role play, as this is often a big turn-on for both sexes. I'm not talking dirty stories; I mean getting into different fantasy situations and acting them out: stranger in a bar, naughty nurse, school teacher and detention, the Tupperware saleslady (but enough about me) – the sky's the limit. Dressing the part can really escalate the effect, as can the building of expectation by planning it for the evening after next, when the 'game' is on from the minute you come home.

Some Peacocks will enjoy voyeurism – men particularly will enjoy being out with someone, watching them, knowing what they're wearing, and perhaps being rewarded every now and then with a glimpse.

For the man, doggy-style is likely to be a favourite position because there's lots to see; for women, being on top has the same advantage. If you're making love face to face then often the Peacock will stare intently at you, gauging your enjoyment from your 'sex face'. Practise it in a mirror first . . . (no, not really!). Oral sex may not be a favourite thing for either of them to do because there's not much to see – but they will probably like it done to them; again, especially the man, because the image is such a strong one.

Pornography will probably be something that turns Peacocks of both sexes on, especially if it mimics their fantasy situations. I know some people don't like it – that's fine, but do try your best to be accepting if it floats your partner's boat.

So, to titillate your Peacock partner, take the time to look good for them. Flirt with them. Ask them which bits of you they like the most and dress to make the most of them. Find out their fantasies and engage them in playing them out. Become aware of the position they tend to favour and see if it matches my prediction – even if it doesn't, become more proactive in suggesting the one they like. Make love like you're on camera – be aware of how good you look in certain positions and avoid the less flattering ones. And give them feedback on how good they look to you, because they'll be assuming that if you're not saying they look good, you don't think they do.

Swifts

'Margaret liked this smile; it was the first thing she had admired in this new friend of her father's; and the opposition of character, shown in all these details of appearance she had just been noticing, seemed to explain the attraction they evidently felt towards each other.'
Elizabeth Gaskell, *North and South*

If you've ever been entranced by the sight of swifts racing around the skies, narrowly avoiding buildings and each other in their hunt for insects, you won't be surprised to hear that people who belong to this bird family are strongly responsive to what they see. They are also what I call a sky-bird: one that spends more time looking down at the big picture than on the ground amongst the detail.

The look of things
Swifts miss nothing – especially when it comes to what they see. For them, not only is seeing believing, it's also approving. If they don't like the look of something, or someone, then you're probably on to a loser. On an online dating site, they'll probably scan

photos at an amazing rate and reject or accept in a heartbeat. Love at first sight is probably their ideal. As with Peacocks, that means that they'll be assessing you on a first date with a beady eye – if they've seen you already, then the first test has been passed. If it's been from a photograph then it had better have been a recent one – and not one that's been Photoshopped to death. In fact, I'd advise that you look as close to the picture they've seen as possible, so you live up to their expectations. And if it's a completely blind date then it's a lottery, but you'll soon get wind of any lack of interest, because it'll be almost instant. This makes it sound as if they're superficial, but that's just a non-sight bird judgment: the heart wants what the heart wants, and for Swifts, the heart wants what it likes the look of.

If you've passed the initial eye-candy test, your turnout is next on the list for scrutiny. Your dress taste is your own, so dress in a way that is right for you – it's who you want them to fall for, not the version of you that you think they'll like: that rarely works for long. Instead, just make sure you've made an effort, because that's the most common criteria I hear Swifts and Peacocks complaining about – that they didn't feel their partner cared because they had 'let themselves go' in relation to their appearance, dress-wise or physique-wise. Whatever you choose to wear for a date, make it look like you've taken time with your appearance. Your Swift will appreciate you taking care over how you look, and showing appreciation for how they do, too.

Swifts look for meaning in things they see, so they'll often communicate how they feel through a visual medium: a beautifully laid table, flowers, a thoughtfully wrapped something if you're in their good books – or a particularly withering look or a sign pointing towards your latest failing if you're not. Sight birds have a look for everything, and they expect you to know each one, from the raised eyebrow which says, 'Stop drinking, you've had enough' to the little smile that suggests you're the funniest person alive. Make sure you can tell the difference between the two.

★   ★   ★

Their houses are likely to have a certain style about them with deliberate combinations of colour, for example, but are also likely to tell a story. Not only will furnishings be chosen for what they contribute to the house, they'll also be there because they're a reminder of a good memory, or a connection to an interest. When you're first shown around a Swift's house, prepare to be regaled with a story about something in every room; you'll almost see them dying for you to ask something about the painting over the fireplace, and finally bursting out with it anyway if you don't put them out of their misery. To a Swift, everything relates to something else, so they can become very sentimental about prized possessions and be heartbroken if one gets stolen or broken. This can be in marked contrast to the Peacock, who are less driven by emotional connections to things and are more likely to regularly recycle their ornaments to complement a change in décor. Swifts are ones who'll pass on heirlooms, Peacocks won't keep anything that long.

Gifts

The way sight birds feel or know themselves to be loved is by the amount of time you spend with them, the presents you buy, or a special look you share. Buying presents is the tough one. Not only does it need to go with whatever it needs to, but it also needs to answer the question 'Why?' By that, I mean a gift that has some meaningful connection will be loved, whereas something considered 'thoughtless' won't. I remember one Swift client who negatively compared an expensive brooch her partner had bought her with a 'delightful' but cheap dolphin ring her friend had got her that was considered 'thoughtful' because it reminded her of a holiday they'd gone on as teenagers. So, if you're in the market for a present, put some thought into your joint history, their present interests, or past gift successes, and then match your ideas to their current taste. You might want to start early.

Pace

With swifts being birds that have to expend most of their energy on what they're hunting – those flies can travel *fast* – at times, it's going to seem like Swifts are following suit. They'll often be energetic; more specifically, they'll be really energised by things that take their interest, and you're probably going to need to work to keep up with their speed. They're often fidgety and may find it difficult to settle to watch a film because there will be two or three other things that need their attention; consequently your pause button is likely to take a bashing. Swifts are even worse than Peacocks when it comes to sticking to what needs doing. They're really not shirking – you'd never mistake them for lazy – they're just like the birds they're named after: they rarely land, and the minute they've caught a fly they're off chasing the next one.

If you're not a morning person, Swifts might take some getting used to because when their eyes open on waking up they're usually ready for business; there's no snooze button installed in a Swift, it's more 'Wakeywakey, rise and shine!' You'll grow to love it. (Then again, maybe you won't. You could always get them a paper round, because there is little you can do to slow them down. Either you need to keep out of their way while you come to, or you need to give them a reason to be busy early.)

Time

Do you dream of having a job where you can spend all day with your partner and then come home and spend even more time together? No? Well, be careful, because for some Swifts this will sound like heaven. Swifts feel that the amount of time you spend with each other is an indicator of how much love there is between you; widen the time gap, and the love may start to trickle away through it.

We all have times when other things take our attention away from the relationship, like work pressures. If that happens to a Swift, they are likely to work themselves to a frazzle to keep all the plates in the air, rather than compromise their quality time with you. And guess what? If the situation is reversed, they'll expect the same from you. Spending more time at work than you spend with them is, in their eyes, the same as saying you prefer work to them. How many people plough their energy into promotion only to find the locks changed one day when they return home? That won't always be because they were living with a Swift, but it'll be one of the reasons a Swift would do it. Pay attention to them by being with them (at least until hologram technology catches up with your need).

Swifts will love being taken out for experiences the two of you share and which you can talk about afterwards. They'll often be deeply into the theatre, or film, or dance: something that is performed in a visual medium. They might also be into art – as an appreciator or as an artist – so feeding that passion will go a long way towards breeding intimacy. The husband of one Swift I know scored massive partner points by surprising her with a weekend watercolour workshop they both attended. It was a double pointer, in fact: sharing something that was her passion, and way better than packing her off with some paintbrushes while he stayed at home and watched the rugby. (If your budget doesn't go that far, a paint-by-numbers kit might go further than you think. Again, think two brushes.)

Details

This is the major difference between Swifts and Peacocks. Peacocks like detail; Swifts avoid it like kids avoid vegetables. A Swift's strength is in seeing the big picture, in putting things together, in spotting patterns. It means they can be great ideas people, but not so hot at finishing things – especially if finishing involves tedium. I warn you now: Swifts have low boredom thresholds. Generally speaking, Swifts will need reasons for doing things: 'Why?' is their favourite question. It means they won't follow your rules unless they make sense to them: not because they mean to breach them, but just because they won't notice that now is the time for that rule to swing into action.

As a sky-bird myself, I've lost count (although Rebecca, my wife, will have it written down somewhere) of the times I've come unstuck by not following instructions because they didn't explain themselves fully. Once I decided to put up coving in the living room. For a change, I had all the right tools. The first instruction was to draw a line under the coving all the way around the room. I couldn't see the point of that, so went straight to the next part. It was only at the end of a dreadful afternoon of trying to get the bloody things to stick that I arrived back at the place where I started, to find I was now about an inch higher than when I began . . .

'Ahhh, *that* is why you need the line,' I said, in a tone of wonder at the revelation.

'Why didn't you just – – – –' began Bex's response.

(Fill in the blanks yourself.)

In the bedroom
I'm afraid we're back to appearance again. Swifts are likely to have a strong preference for what turns them on visually. This can be a bit of a pressure, because if your weight changes from how you looked when you started out they'll notice and probably comment. They'll also let you know what they like to see you in, and it can be a real treat for you to indulge that, from a tuxedo on a night out to the Marge Simpson outfit in the bedroom. They are also likely to love to be visually teased. Often pornography can be a turn on – it's nothing perverted (unless it's something perverted); it's just the way their brain is wired.

Lights on. Swifts are going to want to see you, and mirrors might be a real stimulant so they can see both of you. Don't be disconcerted if they like to look at your face during sex as they're getting pleasure from your pleasure – so let's hope you're not a poker player. Also, role play can be enjoyable for them, so if they come home dressed as Maverick from *Top Gun*, or Lara Croft, be ready to bring out the inner actor. Remember, it's all about what they see, both in terms of what's in front of them and the pictures they're making of it in their head. With a bit of thought, you'll have them aroused in no time – it's one of the upsides of the pace to which they respond to things – as they'll often come to the boil very quickly in response to something they see, so 'quickies' will definitely be on the agenda. Again, it's a compliment to you, not a sign that they're 'sex mad'.

Men are likely to enjoy sex from behind because it's beautifully visual for them: woman will enjoy a well-positioned mirror for that one, or being on top. Men are likely to enjoy oral sex being done to them, but might not get as much from giving it because there's not much of a vista. For women, the same thing probably goes.

So, for Swifts, making love is a bit of a cinematic event. Act like you're being filmed, and they're holding the camera, and you're likely to be rewarded. Look your best, and pay attention to the compliments they give you – they're a guidance mechanism about what to wear and do more of.

Song birds: Robins and Nightingales

Robins and Nightingales are probably the least common of all the Lovebird types, although I have no idea why. But who wants to be common? For them, sounds make the world. I know several song birds who pick a tune in their head to start their morning with to avoid being infected by something on the radio on the way to work, which they'd then be stuck humming for the rest of the day. They'll often be good mimics and unconsciously adopt the accent or phrasing of those around them.

In terms of careers, many will find their niche in sales – either battering their customers into submission with the volume of their sales pitch, or by becoming brilliantly subtle persuaders who can listen to a client and connect their need to the product with an invisible web of influential language. I've known others use their sensitivity to sound to become piano tuners, music engineers, teachers and, obviously, performers.

For others, it's through their hobbies that they get to express their auditory gifts, from getting up and speaking as toastmasters, to playing in a band, dj-ing on hospital radio or taking part in amateur dramatics. I spent a wonderful evening once listening to a client of mine who had suffered from performance anxiety giving a reading of her poetry to a group of friends in a cricket club. The sheer sense of liberation she exuded was equivalent to watching a caged bird fly from an open door, because a fear of public speaking is probably the worst kind of torture for an extrovert song bird. At a karaoke night they will long to be up belting out 'I Will Survive' but have legs that refuse to get them onstage. I suspect their hairbrush microphone gets a lot of action in the bedroom. Jane Horrocks in the film *Little Voice* perfectly captured a song bird trapped by her own shyness.

Extrovert song birds without this impediment will love to engage in activities where groups get to hang out and talk, sometimes with it seeming as if the activity itself comes second to the getting together. They'll be the loudest one in the room, the one you listen for as you enter a crowded pub, and always with a thousand stories and a million jokes. Nowhere is home more than centre stage.

Introverted song birds will be more controlled in how they engage with others. They'll be online gamers, be members of interest clubs like chess, pigeon racing or knitting circles, where talk – especially about their passion – will be part of the experience, but where the spotlight is on the activity itself. You sometimes see introvert song birds suddenly come out of their shell when they have a child because they have someone it's okay to talk about without the attention being on themselves. (The danger with them, however, is that you think you're going round to their house for dinner and end up sitting watching a two-hour home video – with commentary – about their little angel's school play.)

In some ways, I feel a bit sorry for song birds. In a modern world, noise surrounds us, from the chatter of people on trains, to road works, background music seemingly everywhere – even on the telephone when you're put on hold. On many occasions this can really feel like pollution: on public transport, many of the people with huge headphones stuck to the sides of their head will be song birds protecting themselves. I wonder sometimes if they're listening to music or just a soothing voice saying 'Sssshhhhh, it'll be okay.' There'll be occasions when they just want to sit in a quiet room, probably darkened, not even to think, just to enjoy silence, especially if the noise they've experienced that day has been beyond their control. That's something most other bird types won't recognise: the sheer pleasure of certain auditory experiences, like perfect quiet, the opening bars of a favourite song, or just the cadence of a word, like 'opalescent', or 'campanula'. So while it can seem as if song birds just love the sound of their own voices, it's not so (usually): they simply love the sounds of the words themselves. If you listen to the way Stephen Fry forms a sentence, there's a certain pursuit of the poetry within it – the rhythm, the timing, the timbre – that makes it a pleasure to listen to (I know some of you will disagree), whereas other presenters might be an instant turn-off for song birds, whether because of their accent or just because of the way they misuse words. In the political arena, Barack Obama is a master of perfectly weighted delivery; George Bush less so. Margaret Thatcher was tutored in public speaking when she became leader of the Conservative Party because a high-pitched voice is heard to lack authority and assurance. If you listen to her as Prime Minister, her voice is much deeper than when she cancelled free school milk as Minister of Education a few years before (and made me redundant at the age of nine, by the way, seeing as I was the milk monitor who delivered it to class). Song birds will be exquisitely tuned to those kinds of auditory subtleties, and affected by them.

Song birds can be great fun because they'll often have a huge reservoir of stories, comedy sketches, quotes and jokes that can be wheeled out to suit any occasion, or just be plain witty. Victoria Wood's wonderful use of language – who can forget the 'Let's Do It' song? – is one example, and, of course, Ronnie Barker's 'Fork Handles' sketch could only have been written by a song bird.

They can be very sensitive to your voice tone and squeeze out of you exactly what *is* wrong when all you said was, 'I'm fine' in response to their question, 'How are you?' They'll be happy to sit for hours talking over your worries and travails, or let you waffle on about your new love interest, especially if they're down the introvert-end of the spectrum. If they're extrovert, you'll probably have to listen to quite a bit about their life in the process, too. Extroverts care for you just as much; it's just that conversations are more of a collaboration for them. In fact, if there is a downside to the company of a song bird, it is that they can run away with themselves and forget to tune in to others. At the end of time spent with them, their friends could walk away knowing absolutely everything that's going on in their life, but the song bird has learned nothing new about their friends. Striking a balance is very important.

Also, because many song birds need to hear their thoughts on the outside of their heads – it's their way of ordering their thoughts – they're quite reliant on the company of others, even if it's only one other. My youngest son is a song bird and pretty much got through his 'A' levels only because my wife sat down with him and listened to him talk about his revision every night. In school, song birds tend to get labelled as disruptive because, in order to learn, they need to talk about what they're learning. I have even found that not being able to read questions aloud during an exam can reduce song birds' marks because somehow reading something in their heads isn't as clear to them.

Now, I got stuck here with the *Star Trek* character theme I've been using. I couldn't think of one as a song bird, but if I switch to *Star Wars* it's easy. C-3PO, the gold protocol droid: always talking and needing someone to talk at. In the world of detectives, Starsky, from *Starsky and Hutch*. (I was going to say Hutch as well, but I've heard him sing.)

Robins

'One advantage of talking to yourself is that you know at least somebody's listening.'

Franklin P. Jones

In many gardens, if the beauty of a bird's song captures your attention, there's a good chance it will be a robin singing. For their human equivalent, sound is going to be equally important. They are likely to be people who cling to their sound systems – complete with gold-plated leads – in preference to an iPod dock because of the superiority of the sound. They will swoon at a sexy accent – think Sean Connery or anyone Italian – and wince at one less-kind to the ear.

Robins like to know the detail of things and have rules for how things should be. Breaking one of their rules is the same for them as scraping your fingers down a blackboard, and their pain will quickly become yours.

The word's the thing
A key idea in this book is that we all have a preference for which sense we pay most attention to. In the case of Robins, it's sound,

words and music. They are likely to be people who spend a lot of time speaking on the phone – they'd much rather hear your voice than text, and like nothing more than a heart-to-heart, whether with someone near and dear or, if all else fails, with whoever happens to sit next to them on the train. It'll sound like they happen to meet interesting people more than you do, but that's just because they'll tend to engage with anyone who comes within hailing distance.

As music is an important part of their day-to-day experience, with a bit of time Robins can, very often, map the story of their life to a sequence of songs that helped them, consoled them or inspired them – so don't be surprised if you see them reduced to tears by the soundtrack to a deodorant commercial. I'm a believer that a few may even use lyrics as part of their everyday repertoire. And why not? As I said to my wife Bex the other day, everybody hurts, down in the tube station at midnight, but we can work it out because all you need is love.

Wordplay can be enjoyable to them, so they'll enjoy clever puns or the comedy of people like the American Steven Wright, and Briton Milton Jones (who once said, 'It's difficult to say what my wife does . . . she sells sea shells by the sea shore').

Don't expect to win any arguments over who said what to whom and when, with a Robin. They have a disconcerting ability to recall conversations more or less verbatim, which is great if they overhear people chatting about where they hid the treasure, but not so good if you have to listen to the playback of a row they just had with their mother on the phone.

Getting their thoughts straight

As I have mentioned, there will be some Robins who seem to need to speak what they're thinking in order to know what they're thinking. If you ask them an apparently simple question they seem to go on forever answering it – but if you interrupt them or attempt to end their sentences, they will just go back to the beginning. Also, they may ask your advice but then actually not let you speak; they just use you as someone to speak at so they're not caught talking to themselves (because we all know what *that* means). They can be difficult, because people often write them off as chatterboxes or people who like the sound of their own voices, but in reality it's just another difference in the way we communicate, with ourselves as well as with others.

Not all Robins are like this to the degree I've just described, but most will need company or contact with others to be happy, will talk more than most, and never go shopping without a friend – however uninterested you may be in dresses, handbags, fishing rods or terabyte hard drives.

Silence can be a real challenge for the more extroverted of them; a Buddhist retreat is the stuff of their nightmares unless they're choosing the silence themselves. If it's foisted on them, they'll struggle. They'll interrupt a film by whispering a question about it to you, and will keep hold of the remote so they can pause it every thirty seconds to tell you something they just remembered about their day. Paradoxically, if they're deeply immersed in something they're listening to, they are likely to hate the sound of the rustle of sweet papers or a fly buzzing around near them.

It's the way you say it

Whoever came up with the little gem about, 'Sticks and stones may break my bones . . .' never met a Robin. Words can wound them terribly, and so can thoughtless tones. There is no such thing as a meaningless word to them, so use them carefully and don't ever say anything you don't mean, because not only will it hurt them, they'll remember it – and remind you of it – for ever.

Robins will let you know they love you very simply: they'll tell you. Of course, they might also buy you music, and if they do, be ready for it to turn into a quiz. They'll want to know which track you liked best and why, and which lyrics meant the most to you (top tip: think of what would mean most to them if you particularly want to please them). If it's something old, there's a chance it's significant to you as a couple so be on your toes: you'll get a lot of partnership points for remembering that track three of the CD was what your first dance was to at your wedding, and no points at all for mixing it up with your first kiss with someone else behind the bike sheds at a school disco.

Because words are Robins' 'thing', make sure you tell them you love them frequently. And remember that they will have a recording of a time you said it *when they believed it* stored in their heart, so don't say 'I love you' as a throwaway ending to a phone call: hold them in your heart for a moment and then say it. If the tone you use doesn't match the recording, it's worse than not saying it at all.

Do your best to pay attention to them when they're talking, because they often link the act of listening to them with being liked. If you ignore them or only pay passing attention it's the same as saying 'you're not important to me', so focus, or get them to wait until you can – 'I'm really interested in what you have to say. Can you wait until after I've finished this because I really want to listen.'

Robins are great at arguing. Not only can they draw on everything you've ever said to be used against you, but they can marshal their words quickly and swamp you with them: even if they're not perfectly thought out, the volume is likely to overwhelm your resistance. Because they're big on detail, you have little hope of having something they could use pass them by – it's seemingly alphabetised in a library somewhere in their head.

The devil is in the detail

Robins are people who naturally seek the detail of anything that catches or requires their attention; they can actually take comfort from it. If you are a Robin and your boss asks you how a meeting went, they're probably in for chapter and verse, right down to the type of biscuits, whereas they'd get a 'It went alright, thanks', from a Nightingale (more of that, later). *Reader's Digest* is the devil's publication as far as Robins are concerned. Why cut short a good story?

What that means is that when you get together, Robins will want to tell you about their day, in some detail. They will also want to hear about yours. If you cut it short they might take it the wrong way and think you don't want to involve them, or have something to hide. Include the details! If you do, when your workmates meet your partner for the first time it might seem like they've known each other for a long time because your partner knows so much about them. It's another example of the sound library in their head. Everything you say is catalogued and stored in case it comes in useful. The downside is that Robins will involve you in the minutiae of their working life too, and expect you to keep up with it as well.

Ground-birds like to collect information. More detail is always better for them: a thick brochure means a better product, a longer film probably better than a short one. So if you want to drop them a text don't think you'll get away with 'I'm fine, how r u?'(And, of course, the reply is going to cost them big time unless they've got unlimited texts as part of their phone contract.)

Rules

As a ground-bird, a Robin likes rules. Scratch that, they live by them – and expect others to do so, also. The way it tends to work in relationships is that they have rules, they're eminently sensible, don't argue with them if you know what's good for you, so just follow them. I've found that works pretty well.

My wonderful wife is a ground-bird. Did you know there is only one way to hang washing properly, make a bed, or take the top off an egg? Honestly? It drives me nuts but, in her words, she's 'only trying to help'. Apparently, I've proved much harder to train than her first husband. (And I'll probably be harder than her third too if she doesn't . . .) It's a challenge. If you're not also a ground-bird, it's going to be the hardest part of your relationship to manage. Surrender, it's your only hope.

In the bedroom

For a sexual partner who is sensitive to sound, guess what's required of you? That's right, you'd better make some noise! The sounds of your pleasure will arouse them greatly, and also guide them as to what to do more or less of: when to use the feather, and when to use the whole chicken. Don't underestimate the importance of this point. I've known men who've walked away from good relationships simply because the woman orgasms silently. The sound of an orgasm is likely to be a large part of the point of sex for Robins.

Robins might like the light off – the better to focus on the sounds – and will favour positions where they can whisper in your ear. Talk is likely to feature in lovemaking, whether it's talking dirty, role play, or simply hearing how good you and they look and feel. And one of the sexiest words available to you? Their name. Whispered at the right moment, it can produce deep feelings of love, intimacy and recognition. They might also enjoy phone sex, but pick your moments.

Music can be a great accompaniment to lovemaking, and nothing beats it for getting Robins in the mood. Making a playlist specially for the occasion, and based on songs you know they like, will garner you big points.

Plus, the good thing is they stack over time: if you make love to a song, it's likely to be added to their mental collection, so listening to it in the future will trigger that association. Good news if you're snuggling up at home (but tricky if your Robin partner is dancing with someone else . . .).

Nightingales

'Your name is a golden bell hung in my heart. I would break my body to pieces to call you once by your name.'

Butterfly, in *The Last Unicorn*

As you might expect from people named after one of our most famous song birds, Nightingales are all about sound. They are the people who sit in the middle of the cinema because you get the maximum benefit of surround sound that way. Music is likely to be important to them. Often they are great chatter-boxes and can remember verbatim whole conversations (or arguments) they had years ago, yet not be able to follow a map unless the directions are read to them. And, as a bird that likes to look down from up high, they're not really into the details of life.

The word's the thing
We all pay attention to every sense we have, it's just that most of us have a preference for one over the others. Nightingales tend to be very tuned into the sounds in their world. Words will often

be a source of pleasure – they'll enjoy clever puns, ambiguities and reframes.

Many can be moved to tears by a lyric or a moving piece of music. I know one bride who picked a piece of music that had a deep significance for her to walk into the registry office to. By the time she reached the groom, she was crying louder than the music. (Nobody was in a hurry for *that* veil to be lifted.)

Sound can also bring Nightingales pain: they'll often have strong opinions on accents and find it really difficult to listen to voices that aren't easy on the ear. If you have a voice that curdles milk, you're unlikely to make it to a second date with a Nightingale – or beyond the phone call to arrange the first one. People who are loud can make them wince, and unless the context is right, noisy backgrounds will irritate – but then so will being in an empty restaurant where you feel like you have to whisper so as not to involve the waiters in your conversation. For Nightingales, sound will create the right ambience, but it has to be the right kind of sound, in just the right amount, for the place you're in. Tricky.

Getting their thoughts straight

Some Nightingales seem to need to hear their thoughts on the outside, as if they're unaware of them otherwise. Have you ever known anyone who, when you ask them a question that requires a ten-word reply, speaks uninterruptedly for five minutes? You could walk into the kitchen and make tea while they rambled on and come back just in time to catch the bit you were interested in. People who say, 'Can I ask you something?' and then proceed to talk about a problem without you having any real input, but then say, 'Thanks, that really helped,' are likely to be Nightingales or Robins. As I said with Robins, this can be irritating, but it is just their way of working things out. They are not empty chatterboxes or people who love the sound of their own voices – it is just that they don't know what they think unless they hear it outside their own heads. If you interrupt their flow they often need to start again, and if you ask them something, they may repeat it before answering. It may appear strange to you, but it's perfectly natural to them.

This is not true of all Nightingales, however: some appear to think inside their heads perfectly well. But, in either case, they may not like silence much unless it's of their choosing (sometimes they can be overwhelmed by noise pollution), and will nearly always prefer to be surrounded by some sort of sound, meaning that the radio or TV will always be on in the background 'for company'. They can be a bit irritating to go to the cinema with because staying silent is a torture for them: you can count on them breaking on several occasions and whispering plot points to you, or asking you if you let the cat out before you left the house. This is more a thing to learn to cope with because, unless you have a gag handy, the words just have to come out of them or they'll be too distracted by them to be able to watch the film.

It's the way you say it

When Nightingales are in love, they will know how you feel about them by you telling them. As a result, they will often be the ones who ask, 'Do you love me?' To you the answer is obvious – didn't you just give him your special hug/take her to the pictures/have dinner? But they need to hear it in your voice, so if you're working late, for heaven's sake ring them!

Nightingales can also be very sensitive to voice tone, so an exasperated, 'Have you seen my . . .' type of question can be the beginning of a row, as they will often associate the tone with some accusation about them.

Using 'I love you' as a casual way to end a conversation may not work for the same reason. 'You're just saying that – you don't really mean it' is their way of telling you that you got the tone wrong. Nightingales seem to have a tape recording in their head of when you said it and (as far as they are concerned) meant it, and will compare your latest offering with 'the real thing', so you'd better get it right.

They will also like to hear about your day, but not too much because they'll love to tell you *all* about theirs. Often the minutiae of the detail into which they go will take minutes to communicate, particularly if it's a conversation with their boss, or their friend, or a complete stranger who tried to sell them a ferret. Quality time together for a Nightingale means *talking*. Going to the pictures will only be worthwhile if they can go back over it afterwards over pizza, including laughing again at the lines you were listening to with them. Expect them to repeat them to you for several days to come, because often humour for them is the retelling of old sketches. Do you know someone who can recount word for word every Monty Python sketch verbatim? Very likely they're a Nightingale. (Just don't, whatever you do, get stuck with a pair of them in a bar.)

If they are into music, Nightingales will often strongly associate particular songs to particular events, so if you can't remember that Abba was playing in the background the first time you made love, be prepared for a pout when 'Dancing Queen' comes on the CD player and you don't know why you're being looked at expectantly.

Don't try to beat them in a dispute over who said what. You'll lose, and they will feel affronted. Nightingales have an uncanny knack of being able to re-run every stupid thing you've said over the last five years. They will also take you to task for not remembering every promise you ever made, however drunk you were at the time. They are great at arguments, not just because they're often very eloquent people, but because of their memory for past conversations and their ability as a sky-bird to see how things connect together. A typical argument might go something like this:

Partner: 'But I thought we'd agreed to go to Greece this year for a holiday.'

Nightingale: 'No, I only said it was on the list.'

Partner: 'But I've learned Greek and everything.'

Nightingale: 'Yes, but what about six years ago when we had to cancel the trip to Egypt because of you?'

Partner: 'But I was in hospital with a life-threatening illness!'

Nightingale: 'Yes, well, I got stung by that insect when you
      made us go to Spain.'

Partner: 'I didn't make you – I just said it was a place I
      fancied.'

Nightingale: 'Actually, I remember distinctly you making a fuss
      about it and I said yes because I love you. My leg swelled
      up for weeks. It still itches in hot weather . . . like they have
      in Greece . . . and I so want to go to Clacton this year. It's
      only fair!'

It's often only afterwards that you look back and realise that, even
though you were in the right, the Nightingale has somehow
managed to move the argument onto something that restored the
moral high ground to them.

If you live with a Nightingale, you may also sometimes
mistake your phone bill for your mortgage. Leave them alone
for longer than a minute (ninety seconds, top whack) and
they'll be 'catching up' with a friend, their parents, or the guy
with the ferret.

Words make their world go round. Say nice things to them,
about them, and make sure you sound like you mean it!

The devil is in the detail
In this book, I distinguish between two types of birds, ground-
birds and sky-birds. Nightingales are sky-birds – they prefer to
be up high rather than on the ground. They don't much like
details as they find them boring. This might seem to contradict
the fact that Nightingales will happily talk for ages about something, but that's different, because that's *their* detail. Detail coming
at them from others will be a thing they'll look to avoid.

Nightingales look for possibilities in situations and are more
concerned with patterns and the relationships between things.
Their imaginations are going to be very important to them and

you need to be ready to join in discussions about ideas that might seem fanciful to you. They are happiest when they're being creative and gain tremendous energy by following something that has captured their interest, so much so that their life can be a succession of what my dad used to call 'five-minute wonders' – things you immerse yourself in completely for a short period of time before moving onto something else. Nightingales' houses are likely to be littered with the evidence of these fads: musical instruments, the latest piece of fitness equipment, an easel, a horse. Don't expect them to settle on one passion, but if they do, they can achieve amazing things.

Nor will Nightingales tend to have rules about things, often appearing to make things up as they go along. This can lead to them repeating the same mistake again and again because they're so focused on something else that the mistake only registers as a minor irritant, not something to focus on enough to make a rule about. Instead of rules, they have their gut instinct. Often their decisions will be based on what may appear to non-sky-birds to be vague goals, but these goals are enough for them to be guided. They'll trust that the specifics will emerge later – and hope someone else provides them. In other words, they're great at pointing in the right direction, but don't expect them to be able to explain how to get there.

In the bedroom
Song-bird types are quite straightforward – only screamers need apply. If you're one of those people who barely raise a moan while your Nightingale partner is raising the neighbourhood, then it's time to start wondering if you want to keep your partner. There is an up side – Nightingales can be incredibly sensitive to the sounds you're making as guides to what they're doing – how much, how well and when they should do it harder. Without sound to calibrate to, they can get a little lost, and I've known Nightingale men who got out of relationships because the woman orgasmed too quietly. The sound of orgasm is likely to be their biggest turn-on, and guide.

Talking dirty can be another big arouser: some Nightingales will use words they reserve strictly for the bedroom; some will want you to use them. If your partner wants to hear you call them a 'naughty girl', or 'big boy', what's the harm? Just make sure you say it in the right tone.

Phone sex can be fun. If you're happy to turn your Nightingale lover on by talking dirty down the phone, just make sure it's them who answers before you start (or dinner round their mother's could be a bit awkward next time).

When having sex, they'll often like positions where you can be speaking in each other's ears. Using their name in these moments will often be more special than you'd imagine.

Nightingales are also likely to have favourite mood music, so an iPod in the bedroom is a good move. They often have a good sense of rhythm, so be aware of this in your manoeuvring – think more Barry White than the 'Hokey Cokey'.

Feeling birds: Swans and Doves

'Feeling' birds have a special place in my heart. In the nineties, at Hendon Police College, I was in charge of a unit helping the students who were failing the new constables' exams. I would estimate that at least 60 per cent of them were either Swans or Doves. Many felt they were failing because they were stupid – they'd always had trouble learning things. I came to realise that 'things' meant academic learning as, in fact, many of them were brilliant mechanics, nurses, chefs and crafts people who picked things up perfectly well in a practical setting, but struggled more if they had to learn from something on a page. Essentially, if they could *feel* what they were doing – were closely physically involved with it – they could work happily with it. I discovered that most of these feeling birds left school at the earliest opportunity and found their way – if they were lucky – into a profession where on-the-job training was available; where they could learn by observation or trial and error. The unlucky ones tended to end up under-achieving in a job they were comfortable doing but which didn't stretch them, and not feeling confident enough in their abilities to do better. I've since found this to be only too common an experience for feeling birds. Teachers find feeling birds slow, but this is mainly because the education system doesn't support their style of learning. Feeling birds tend to pick up practical things – from dance moves to how to strip an engine – very quickly. Writing about how to do that is harder for them, and the jobs they are in will usually be ones that don't involve too much paperwork.

When it comes to hobbies and interests, you tend to get two distinct flavours of feeling birds. As they are so connected to physical sensation, it won't surprise you to hear that many are adrenaline junkies, loving the excitement of sky diving, fast cars or climbing. The other type tend to be more into the savouring of gentler sensations, so may well be into cookery, wine tasting, making clothes or soft furnishings. It needn't be one or the other: you may well find someone who races motor cycles by day and throws on a pinny in the evening. The unifying element here is that it is the pursuit of a sensation, whether it's physical, like playing a sport, or enjoying the tastes and smells of, say, good cuisine, which will be driving feeling birds' passion.

Whether feeling birds tend towards extroversion or introversion will make for interesting differences, too. Introverts lose energy from being around people (at least that's how I define it), so they will be more into solo sports and interests, like running or collecting things, rather than team games – although there can be notable exceptions.

Meditation and yoga are likely to be attractive to introverted feeling birds – yoga classes give the illusion of sociability without actually having to spend too much time with people. Many feeling birds take up a physical skill as a hobby, whether it's building miniature steam engines, doing massage or calligraphy. Throw a net over a tent of people at a craft fair and you'll snag a lot of feeling birds selling the products of their hobbies.

Extrovert feeling birds, on the other hand, get energy from being around people. Boy, do they. They're the friends who invite you out for a quick drink and you turn up at your door three days later with only a hazy recollection of what happened, and usually wearing a traffic cone. These people can be overflowing with life. I'm always reminded of the bearded gay man in *Four Weddings and a Funeral* – Simon Callow's character (Gareth). You know it when they enter a room, and when they leave (both can be a happy event, depending on your mood). Their hobbies are going to include team sports, playing in a band and helping out on committees.

If you've ever sat next to someone who has ants in their pants, it's likely to be a feeling bird. They get fidgety sooner than most, don't find sitting still easy, and will often keep popping up to 'do' something, say, in the middle of a TV programme. They'll be the thirty-year-old child in the car asking, 'Are we there yet?' when you're only popping down the road to the shops. Things that are likely to distract, disturb or annoy them are scratchy labels in clothes, badly padded chairs, scabs that have reached the itchy stage, shoes that start to pinch, and smells that are coming from a undiscovered source – they'll spend an evening sniffing that last one down.

There are many positives to a feeling bird's character. They tend to be hard working – if they're doing something they enjoy. They have excellent social intelligence so they're often the peacekeepers of the family, and put a lot of energy into making sure everyone is all right. Their homes will be homely with an ambience about them in which visitors will relax happily, and even if their style wouldn't make *House & Garden* magazine, it will fit their personalities perfectly – comfortable, warm and friendly. They're usually very tactile, using touch as part of their punctuation as well as a communicator of their feelings. They'll usually shake hands with a stranger but be ready to hug by the time it comes to the goodbye at the end of an evening, and they have a gift for making you feel special because, for most people, touch is a very powerful communicator of positive emotions.

To be with a feeling bird friend is to be wrapped in their emotions – something that can, of course, also be a negative. Feeling birds live very much in the moment, so whatever they're experiencing emotionally is the way the world is, and how it might always be, and therefore being with them can be a roller-coaster. 'Level' isn't where they stop that often: it's usually just a waypoint between 'up' and 'down'. This can make them a lot of fun to be around when they're on the up, but harder work when they're not. They'll also tend to carry their feeling from one situation into another; they're not great at compartmentalising their life. This can mean that a bad day at the office will mean a glum evening at home, and a row before you leave the house will usually lead to a day staring out the office window or snapping at colleagues.

In a relationship, for a feeling bird, to love is to care for. People lucky enough to live with a feeling bird will tend to find their needs taken care of whenever they're expressed, and often even before that.

If I return to my theme of *Star Trek* characters, Bones would definitely be the feeling bird of the crew: gentle, humane and unhurried; while Columbo fits the detective category: seemingly slow to get things, but building up a head of steam until he's unstoppable.

Swans

'To those few who know me my religion is well known. I believe in bodies, arms entangling and untangling. I believe, and I know it to be so, that there are so many curves and hollows in a single body that none of us, none of us, can come to know them all within a lifetime. But I'll go on trying.'

Rod McKuen, *Alone*

Doves and Swans are all about feelings, which is why, to many of us who aren't part of their gang, another name for them is 'high maintenance'! That's not to say they're not worth it (at least if I want to stay married it's not – my wife is a Swan), it's just that they seem involved in a perpetual search for perfection in every possible sensory experience: the perfect cup of coffee, the perfect bed, the perfect pair of trainers . . . the list extends as far as ways of feeling does.

Swans tend to be as sensitive to the emotional states of others as they are of their own, and are often attracted towards caring professions. In fact, they need to be careful to avoid burn-out because of how strongly they take on the feelings of other people.

If they aren't very good at visualising, they may have found school tough, and have a feeling that they're not very clever. This simply isn't so: it's just that the educational system doesn't suit their type because they pick things up best from personal experience and physical involvement in the thing to be learned; something that tends to stop in schools once you're made to leave the sandpit and get on with 'real' learning. What you'll find is that Swans will pick up practical things really well and, if they're lucky, will have found a way to earn their living from it; from engineering and nursing, to catering and mechanics. They may not be able to read a map, but they can ice a three-tier wedding cake in the dark.

Words are not usually a Swan thing, either. In new situations, they might struggle to find the right words to express themselves, and often their pace of speech is quite slow, but translating from feelings to words takes time and there's no rushing them.

Because words don't excite Swans, they're not likely to seduce them: actions are what are going to count. They like to hug and will be quite 'touchy' in face to face communications (even on Skype, they've been known to give the monitor a cuddle . . .).

Keep in touch

If you tie a Swan's hands behind them, you'll deprive them of a great percentage of their capacity to communicate. Often their hands will be kept busy drawing shapes while they talk, and they may not be able to remember their pin number without tracing the keypad in the air.

When they're talking to you, Swans are likely to touch or stroke you quite a bit – if you're getting on together. If you're not, well, who do you think invented the cold shoulder? Swans probably can't think of a harsher punishment than withdrawing their little huggie-wuggies (you can tell I'm not a Swan, can't you?).

Some Swans – and I have to say most of them would be men – use sex as an expression of love. Sometimes their partners mistake this for thinking that either they have one-track minds, or that sex solves everything. It doesn't mean either of these things as, if they love you, they can't think of anything better than expressing intimately how much they care. (If you prefer a cup of tea and a chance to chat things over, you can see that confusion is going to arise. Not to mention broken crockery.)

For both genders, sex can be a barometer of the strength of the relationship, both because a good feeling needs to exist for it to occur, and because it's likely to be a major way Swans communicate their commitment. Female Swans, particularly, will withdraw sex if they're unhappy with their partner. Male Swans will try to, but probably just end up doing it with a bit of a pout.

Swans are slow burners. They'll prefer to wake up slowly with as many taps on the snooze button as they can get away with, and then at least one more. If you bring them tea in bed you'll get big points – if you dress them, the sky's the limit. Don't engage them first thing with the news headlines or with a debate on the Hadron Collider's search for the God particle, because their response won't be pretty. In fact, arrows from the sleep fairies hit Swans and Doves more strongly than others, including in the middle of what they're doing, whether it's watching TV, eating their dinner, or, if you're not putting enough into it, making love. When the arrows hit, it's over for them for a while, no matter how much they're enjoying something.

Similarly, Swans need a run-up when faced with a need to change pace, whether that's in a meeting, or when the in-laws pay a surprise visit when they're having a cuddle with their partner on the sofa. Pacing is everything with these people.

Swans live in the moment and often aren't that great at imagining something they've never experienced. For example, the first time my wife and I went on a Segway (you know, one of those futuristic-looking, two-wheeled things that you stand on to travel around) course in our local forest I was bouncing with excitement for hours beforehand, while Bex was pretty underwhelmed, scoring herself at about seven on a scale of excitement. Within seconds of bombing around the course, however, she was whooping with exhilaration and came past me grinning like the Cheshire Cat . . . straight into a tree. (Did I mention not good with directions?)

In a relationship with a Swan, you have to stack up good experiences close together. You may be able to delay your gratification from January until the spectacular cruise the two of you have booked for Christmas, but your Swan won't, however much they protest otherwise at the time of booking. They might get really excited by the new car you've bought together instead of going on holiday, but within a few months they'll be wistfully looking at brochures. By all means have big projects planned for the future, but make sure you have things closer to look forward to as well, and beware of pawning your future to pay for something nice today.

Self or Others?

One of the main themes of this book is that there are many layers of difference between one person and another, and many of these differences revolve around preferences. So it is with Swans. Some have a preference for paying attention to their feelings, and some put most focus on the feelings of others. It's a continuum so bear in mind that many will be a mixture of both, but you'll know it when you meet one who is strongly at one end of this continuum or another.

'Self-referenced' Swans (i.e. those that place a larger importance on themselves than others, generally) can be mistaken for being selfish. They're not, they just tend to focus most on things affecting their own feelings or relate what is happening to others through what has happened to them. This can lead to conversations like, 'Ooh, I've got a really bad headache.' 'Have you, you poor thing, that's like me the other day, my head was really pounding . . .' I say they're not selfish because what they pay attention to can include your feelings, so they can be wonderfully empathetic (they'll come back to your headache in a minute), but their own comfort tends to dominate their lives. Here's what another husband of a Swan has to say on the subject: 'At any time of year, a trip out with my wife usually involves about three clothing options, because weather can be really changeable, can't it? Meals out can be great, but for her "great" is a much harder target to hit than it is for me. If it looks like it's supposed to, is as hot or as cold as it should be, and is a decent size I'm about done. Mary has a much longer list of criteria, from salty enough to too much, to too flavoured to not flavoured enough. It must be exhausting for her.'

For Swans generally, but 'selfs' in particular, acts of service float their boat. Anything you do that increases their sensory pleasure, which might just be a peppermint tea at the right moment, or decreases their discomfort, like a peppermint foot rub at night, will elevate you mightily in their eyes.

One of the things I've always been impressed by with Swans is their relationship with their bodies. While it makes them incredibly aware of every creak and knock, they are also able to enjoy the sensations their body can give them beyond the range of most other mortals. I can barely tell if I'm being massaged, whereas it will transport a Swan to another dimension.

'Others-referenced' Swans place their sensory awareness on the world around them. They can pick up a bad vibe from across a room and will work effortlessly but relentlessly to clear up a bad atmosphere. They hate conflict and people being hurt. 'Others' Swans will go to extraordinary efforts to support their friends through bad times, often at the expense of their own wellbeing. Being less aware of their physical self than self referenced parts, they must be careful not to burn-out through their efforts to support others.

At the same time, they can be a bit explosive, but their fuse is long. Because of their dislike of bad atmospheres, they'll endure things that upset or annoy them for a long time, but when the straw does that thing with the camel, step back, because when they let go it's short-lived but blinding. So, when they say, 'No, it's fine', just take a moment to listen to the tone and look at the body language. Is it really?

Swans are the kings and queens of touch. Many will actually

train in massage such is the good feeling they get from giving pleasure to others. They can seem flirty because they employ touch in their communications sooner, and to a greater extent, than any other bird type and I imagine they get used to dealing with people who mistake friendship for flirtation.

The interesting thing is that, probably because they communicate how they feel so much through touches and strokes, you might find them getting jealous if you appear over-familiar with someone else. While they know how they feel when they're touching others, they might project how you make them feel when you touch them, or what it communicates to them about your feelings, onto the person you're touching.

It's in the detail

Swans are very much ground-birds when compared to their Dove cousins as they are more comfortable with hard facts than big concepts and 'airy-fairy' dreams. They feel themselves to be grounded in reality, i.e. theirs, and expect their partner to share it. If you're a sky-bird who's just shared a big idea with them, expect to be confronted with questions like, 'How exactly is that going to work?' and 'What about X? You haven't thought of that, have you?' They can feel a bit of a cold shower to your creative processes.

They will almost certainly have a list of rules they live by, from how to properly air your undercrackers to which direction the cans should face in the cupboard. Swans can be a little (I mean a lot, but Bex is going to read this) bossy in their policing of these rules, because they make obvious sense (to her) and only an idiot (me) would fail to follow them, and only a moron (err . . . still me) would *repeatedly* fail to follow them. High maintenance.

Swans will expend no little time and effort in saving your soul. My advice? Do your best to be saved, because those rules were made for following. While the downside is that Swans can be a little inflexible, the upside is that your life is likely to be beautifully organised and squared away.

In the bedroom

If you know how to massage, you're halfway there. While quickies will be okay occasionally – and when they are, they'll be red-hot quickies – Swans are more likely to want to take their time. Scented candles, subtle lighting, massage oils, yoghurt without pips . . . Swans will like as many different senses engaged as possible, and the more the mood is set, the more involved they'll be.

Returning to the 'self' versus 'others' continuum, some will get most from you worshipping them, while others will love to pleasure you. As before, most Swans will be a mix of both, but some will be at the ends of this line, and it'll be important that their preference matches yours. With two 'selfs', you end up with two people making love to themselves; two 'others', and it's a wrestling match. Most will love any position where they can feel you: oral sex is likely to be a favourite; as will the wearing of nice textures like silk and velour (okay, so that's just me), or they may be into things like rubber and even, in one case I can remember, being wrapped in cling film. (At least she was always fresh.)

Doves

'Her lips on his could tell him better than all her stumbling words.'
Margaret Mitchell, *Gone with the Wind*

Doves and Swans are the sense-monsters of the universe. They can be incredibly sensitive to the physical conditions around them, to their level of comfort, to their own emotional feelings and, in many cases, the feelings of those around them. They usually pick up practical skills very quickly, but they can be slow to understand verbal instructions and can forget something they are told within minutes.

They will often speak quite slowly and deliberately. The extreme is the type of person who makes you want to end their sentences for them. Doves need to take their time and you need to give them the space to warm up. For many of them, words don't come naturally to them – they're all about feelings and those are often hard to verbalise, aren't they? Instead, they tend to express themselves through their actions and they'll often show they care by what they do for you to make your life nicer. Sweet words will bounce off them – they're cheap; it's what you *do* that you'll be judged by.

If they are a strong Dove with a low ability to visualise, they will get lost going somewhere new, and probably had a rough time at school because the education system doesn't support them at all well. As adults, they may sometimes have an inferiority complex around their intelligence because of their negative experiences at school. I cannot count the number of clients I have had who describe themselves as 'slow' or 'thick', yet who can strip an engine blindfolded, or cook a meal fit for angels.

Keep in touch
In any relationship, it's about how you make the other person feel. Often, this will be linked with touch. Many Doves are very 'touchy' people and respond to hugs and strokes and any kind of physical expression of affection. As you might expect, that is also how they communicate their feelings, too. They will often find it difficult to speak to someone without some physical touch being involved, so you'll know you're in their bad books when they don't – these are people for whom the phrase 'to be frozen out' was invented.

Some Doves (men in particular, but not exclusively) use sex as an expression of love, and because of this can be accused of thinking that sex solves everything. They can be genuinely hurt and upset when their attempt at calming you or cheering you up after a hard day at the office is met with the rebuff, 'For God's sake, stop pawing me, I'm not in the mood!' 'Strange,' they think, 'if I'd had a bad day I would have loved you to have pawed me.' Exit disgruntled partners stage left and right.

If the frequency of sex decreases, it can mean for them that the relationship is going through a rough patch. Even though any number of other factors may be present – like pressure of work, moving house, your team hitting a losing streak – the Dove will often connect a downturn in lovemaking with the general state of the relationship.

Dove women (again, particularly, but not exclusively) will tend to withhold sex if they are feeling unloved because it doesn't 'feel' right. It just underlines how mood is the key in any situation where you want to communicate with a Dove.

Most Doves are not too hot first thing. Waking up can appear almost physically painful to them, as does staying up past their bedtime. Some appear incapable of speech for quite a while after waking and will communicate by pointing and grunting. If you are one of those bright morning creatures living with a Dove, then learn to button it or risk a bread knife in the back one fine, chirpy morning. Similarly, it doesn't matter how interesting a film is on the TV, if the sleep fairies arrive nothing will keep your Dove with you, and you'll know nothing about it until half an hour later when they ask you to catch them up with the plot. Especially annoying if they fall asleep again mid-explanation!

Doves tend to live in the 'now': the things that are going on right now are the most important things, which means that the relationship is only as good as it is today. It's no good having good times stacked up in the future – Doves need regular sensory experiences to enjoy, and their memories can be short. It really won't matter if you agree that you won't go on holiday this year so you can refit the kitchen – once the excitement of the new cooker has diminished, they're going to start talking about how they need a break. Don't trust them to stick to a long-term plan: they are led by their feelings *now*. This makes them sound hard work, doesn't it? I can't offer an argument. They can be. They are also absolutely worth it.

Self or Others?

Doves tend to be either internally or externally focused. For internal, 'self-referenced' Doves, how *they* feel is of primary importance. Don't mistake this for selfishness. They can be wonderfully giving, but if they are uncomfortable it tends to dominate everything else. This is very much the Princess (or Prince) and the Pea story.

'Self' Doves have an incredible connection with their bodies. They will complain about being too hot or too cold within minutes of each other, but can get pleasure out of a simple act such as lying down, that is denied other mortals; or buy a car purely for its air conditioning or comfy seat. If you are into foreplay and like to wake the neighbours, marry one.

'Others-referenced' Doves focus more on the 'vibe' going on around them. They can be extremely sensitive to the feelings of people around them, and hate a bad atmosphere. They will often go to great lengths to 'keep things running smoothly', even at the expense of their own feelings. They'll hide behind a determined smile until they reach boiling point, at which time it's best to stand back, because when they erupt it can be as spectacular as it is unexpected, and can leave their partner feebly struggling with phrases like, 'But I thought you said . . .' and, 'Why didn't you mention . . . ?'

'Others' Doves are often the life-and-soul-of-the-party types; they get high off good atmospheres. They can be incredibly warm and empathetic, and notice you're feeling low almost before you do. They can also be vulnerable to negative atmospheres, or be brought down badly by the misfortunes of their friends because they tend to 'live' other people's feelings.

They are the Doves who will most value cuddling, hugs and strokes, because it literally 'gets them in touch' with your feelings. A lack of physical contact will leave them feeling lonely and they'll often have a pet to provide a source of affection. They can appear flirty because of their high level of tactile behaviour while they are talking to someone, and I've had to help many relationships where partners have found their Dove partner's need to touch while conversing with others irritating or threatening.

Perversely, sometimes 'others' Doves can be jealous of your doing the same thing, possibly because they know what feeling they are communicating when they do it, but they only know *your* touch for what it is when you touch *them*, so it feels as if you are touching someone else the same way.

Finally, this may sound unkind, but some Doves and Swans dress terribly. (You did hear me say *some*, didn't you?) They will dress for comfort rather than appearance, and sometimes that leads to . . . ahem . . . unconventional colour combinations or style choices, like Crocs and socks. Bad at the best of times;

but to a dinner party? To balance that out – and to prevent my wife from killing me – some also have a weird sixth sense. I've seen Rebecca know a dress looks great on her without even checking in a mirror, and combine colours in her head and 'feel' that they'll work. And they do.

It's in the detail

In nature, doves are sky-birds. You often see them climbing steeply in the air as if to enjoy the wind in their face as they zoom back closer to earth.

People who are Doves share this distinction: they are going to avoid getting involved in details wherever possible. They tend to have low boredom thresholds for tasks like doing the accounts, or organising the minutiae of a family event. They're at their best providing ideas and directing the action.

Creativity is likely to be an important feature, and Doves will often involve themselves in learning new sports or hobbies that involve physical sensation, from a pottery class or mountain climbing to learning the piano. They'll accumulate hobbies, but might not stick to them for long periods because novelty is attractive, and their interest span can be short. Have a root through their cupboards and you'll probably find a host of hobby materials that create a trail through time of the things they've fallen in love with and then moved on from. (There might even be an old flame in the attic.)

If you're someone who likes rules and systems, then Doves will probably frustrate you quite a bit because most of the time they won't even notice them and will do things their way – even if your way is better. From the outside, it looks like things just don't matter to them; certainly things don't tend to bother them, so many are untidy and more than a little disorganised, but happy about it. You might choose to try to reform your Dove partner – after all, there are many ways to waste your energy – but don't make the success of your project a factor in your relationship. We all have to give a little in our life with those we love, and this will almost certainly be one of your allowances.

In the bedroom

Break out the baby oil. Doves are usually all about sensuality and therefore demand involvement and lots of touching. Often they prefer the lights out so they can focus on the sensation more. More into the slow-build-up-with-massage-and-play than the wham-bam approach, they really appreciate you worshipping their bodies and making them feel good. Doves fall somewhere along a continuum of 'do to me' and 'do to others' – where some will spend hours pleasuring you, while for others it's more what you can do for them that really gets them going. They are creatures who live in the moment, so their mood is crucial. Spontaneous hot sex can emerge from any peak moment of positive emotion, whereas if they've had a bad day it can take time to get them out of the doldrums and into the mood. Patience is definitely a virtue.

Male Doves often express love through the desire for sex; females often need to feel loved before they'll have sex. This can be a real bone of contention where a couple is mismatched in this area – if he wants to get down and dirty after a row, you can bet he's a Dove or a Swan. If she wants to hold hands and eat chocolate first, the same holds true.

Smells and taste are often very important, so make sure you've had a bath, and think about experimenting with yoghurt or Nutella. Doves are likely to love oral sex – whether giving or receiving will depend where they sit on that continuum I mentioned above. Any position is good – male Doves will often enjoy being underneath so they still have their hands free to play, while female Doves will really enjoy the feeling of a body moving over them.

Textures can add to the experience as well: silk will probably be more of a turn on than winceyette, but make sure there aren't any crumbs – so any fancy tricks you know with biscuits are going to be wasted.

Thinking birds: Kingfishers and Owls

Out of all the Lovebird types, thinking birds are the toughest for me to predict. It's my opinion that they're made more than born, in that their way of relating to the world tends to be a response to their childhood.

As a therapist, I most often see thinking birds who are the result of negative experiences that they've had, which has led them to disappear inside their heads and talk to themselves about what they don't like seeing, hearing or feeling – it felt safer for them to *think* about their feelings rather than just go ahead and have them. But that's not all of them. Some might have developed this way because they were an only child or had limited opportunities to interact with others, or who were extremely shy and found living in their own world easier than having to join in the real one, or who were just naturally introspective people who enjoy thinking their thoughts.

Whatever the reason, a person starts life as a seeing, hearing or feeling bird and then changes into a thinking bird as they go inside and spend more time with their thoughts, so there can be wide variations in how they behave. It's why it's important to look at the quiz you took at the beginning of the book and, if you came out as a thinking bird in either first or second place, it's a good idea to read the profiles of both your first and second Lovebird types, and how they interact with the Lovebird type of your partner (or prospective partner – for more on this, please see Part Three).

That said, there are several things that distinguish thinking

birds from other types. Probably the strongest thing is that everything has to have a meaning. They hate things not making sense
or being senseless; so, for example, having a stupid boss will be
very hard work for them. But, generally, getting them to do
anything that doesn't seem a good idea to them is like pulling
teeth.

Their need for structure and sense tends to make them very
good planners and problem-solvers and you'll find them working
a lot in IT, HR and strategy roles such as marketing and advert-
ising. A lot also prefer to be self-employed – to avoid stupid
bosses? – and I also found a disproportionate number of them
in the police (perhaps because they don't like mysteries. I'm
joking, but only sort of).

They can suffer from insomnia, because if something is buzzing
round in their head they won't be able to let it go until they've
solved it – like a challenge at work, or where to go on holiday,
or a crossword clue from that morning. Anything and everything
can interfere with sleep.

Another key characteristic of thinking birds is their love of
control – mainly of themselves. Emotions tend to be an issue:
there is a common fear that any feeling or emotion will lead to
it running out of control, so they can appear reserved, aloof and
even a bit robotic in situations where a more emotional response
might be thought the norm. That's probably another reason why
they fit so well in the police. Concluding our round-up of *Star
Trek* characters, Mr Spock is a fine example of a thinking bird,
as is House from the TV hospital series of the same name. In
real life, Bill Gates is (as was Steve Jobs) a fully paid up member
of the thinking-bird club. The billionaires' branch.

Thinking birds are great shoppers, but that does depend on
your definition. They will loathe 'window shopping'; it has to
have a point or it's painful. As a thinking bird myself, there is
nothing I detest more than wandering around the shops without
a target. My clever wife learned long ago to say something like,
'I'm looking for a cream blouse' to give me a target to lock onto
(a challenge in the butchers, I'll grant you, but it keeps me

occupied).What makes thinking birds great shoppers in my book is that they'll have researched what they want before they go into a shop, be able to scan quickly for whether it's there, and move on quickly if it's not. No browsing for alternatives: it fits the bill or it doesn't. In a way, thinking birds have a list of criteria in their head for whatever they're looking for: a car, a pair of jeans or a partner and, as they examine possibilities of each, they tick off the features in their head. If they get to the bottom of the list they'll buy. If they don't, they'll walk away. That might explain some dating experiences you've had with thinking birds where you didn't make it to the main course. Don't take it personally – it was probably a very long or difficult list to tick. Really, it wasn't you.

I mentioned earlier how there will be variations on a theme with thinking birds. If a sight bird was second on their list from quiz 2, then what they *see* will be the major focus of what they need to make sense of, or what will feature on their checklists. For example, in their home, for a thinking/sight bird things like paintings might be very important to them, but it won't be the colours or style that will be the major reason for giving it wall space, it will be the personal meaning it has for them – the holiday where they saw it, a favourite animal, a painter they have a particular fascination for (and who they're likely to be very knowledgeable about). I had an interesting moment the other night with a friend of this persuasion. We'd finished washing up and I was putting away the wine glasses. I have a white wine glass that is the last of a set from about eight years ago. It's my favourite, and I always choose it in preference to the other matching ones we have. As I put it on its shelf, my friend said, very disapprovingly, 'Why on earth are you putting it with those? It's taller. I'd put it with the red wine glasses.' (All said in a tone that suggested that what she meant was so should I.) I replied, 'Are you crazy? It's not a red wine glass, why would it go there?' I'm a thinking/song bird combination, so the look of things doesn't mean much to me, but in typical thinking-bird style, things being in the 'right' category do. For my thinking/sight bird friend, the way they *looked* was a much more important criteria.

I find the thinking/feeling bird combination particularly interesting because they are two very contrasting ways of relating to things. Very often, it feels like a tug of war between the heart and the head for the person who has this mixture of types, and I've noticed the most common consequence of this is doubt: 'Should I change jobs, or stay where I am?' 'Should I commit to this relationship, or should I run for the hills?' You'll often hear this variant saying things like, ' . . . part of me wants to do it, but part of me doesn't.' This self-doubt can have a real impact on the direction their lives take, often leading to them building an expertise in something, but being careful to stick within it rather than pushing themselves in a new direction. Because feelings are close to the surface with this type, they either tend to be more comfortable in expressing and experiencing them, which can make them highly evolved in their way of managing their emotions – open to them, but not controlled by them – while others can be extremely unpredictable. In one situation, you might be met with thinking bird calmness, and in another, a Tasmanian devil of whirling emotions.

Finally, the thinking/song bird combination. This combination will speak a lot more than other thinking birds, and what goes on their checklist will often be about noise. They won't like a lot of conversations going on around them when they're doing something because they won't be able to 'hear myself think'. If they're studying, some music will help them focus, but talk on the radio will distract them. They're likely to be strongly attracted to a voice or accent (or repelled) and, unlike pure song birds, will not learn well by being told something because of the competition between their internal voice and that of their teacher's. They learn best by reflecting on material later so that it 'makes sense' to them.

Most thinking birds will come across as quite introverted on first meetings, and those that actually are introverts can be extremely hard to get to know. They will be very self-sufficient and even solitary. Their partner is likely to be their best friend as well, if not their only one. Extroverts are going to be more outgoing, but you rarely get real party animals amongst thinking birds: although alcohol can sometimes cause a Jekyll and Hyde-type transformation, they're not that into letting go.

There are many good things about thinking birds. While they might tend to make friends slowly, they're extremely loyal once you've got under their defences. They might not feel the urge to ring you from one year to the next, but they'll drop everything the minute you need them. They're also good to have in a crisis because when all around them are losing their heads, thinking birds are busy inside their own working out a solution. They tend to be less stressed than most, most of the time, but suffer from it quite acutely if they have a situation that is out of their control or without an answer.

A big downside for thinking birds can be the nature of their internal voice. I often say that thinking birds' voices are either their best friend or their worst enemy. For example, in a job situation, does the voice in their head say things like, 'This is going to go really well, I'll be great!', or does it say, 'What was I thinking? This is going to be a disaster.' We tend to get the future we expect, so it's important that thinking birds are on their own side on the inside (of their head).

I also have thinking birds coming to therapy with a kind of generalised dissatisfaction with life in general, and their love lives in particular. I've listened to many thinking birds who are in a great relationship, yet still wake up in the morning, look at their partner, and ask themselves, 'Is this the best I can do?' It can even drive them out of it, on a perpetual hunt for 'the one'. My best guess is that it's because they're not adept at measuring their emotions, so never trust that a feeling like love is ever as strong as it should be. And, of course, the problem is they often leave something great for something that only seems better because of its novelty.

A final word: make sure the internal self-talk is positive. Male or female, think about how you want something to be, not how it isn't.

Kingfishers

'It's the little details that are vital. Little things make big things happen.'
John Wooden, motivational speaker

Owls and Kingfishers are a special category. Where all the other birds are grouped according to whether they pay most attention to what they see, hear or feel, these guys are all about thinking. This can lead to them appearing a bit self-contained or withdrawn, as they'll spend a great deal of their time absorbed in their thoughts: it's fair to say that it's rare for them not to have some kind of conversation going on with themselves, and often that can render them oblivious to what's going on around them – including your attempts to have a deep and meaningful talk, or just to ask them to pass the salt.

Kingfishers, being ground-birds, are interested in the detail of things; they'll often find strategic thinking a stretch and be more comfortable organising things and making sure that everything works the way it should. Which is usually *their* way.

It's all in their head

Kingfishers like things to make sense. It can really bug them if they don't know or understand what's going on, and often they won't be able to rest until they've got what they need to satisfy themselves. Most of my insomnia clients are either Kingfishers or Owls because they can't let something go until they have a solution, so it can rattle around in their heads into the wee hours. Kingfishers often take needing to know how things work to include dismantling stuff to see what makes it go, or absorbing themselves deeply into a single activity. Many great geeks belong to this particular bird tribe, like Bill Gates and Mark Zuckerberg. They will often accumulate huge amounts of material on things that interest them, and their hobbies will range from tinkering with Swiss clocks (they'll probably know the makers' marks for every manufacturer from the sixteenth century onwards) to building their own aeroplane.

If you're in a relationship with a Kingfisher, you have to be prepared to lose them to their interest every now and again. That's a fib – I actually mean a lot of the time. Even if they're with you physically, it'll feel sometimes as if they're locked in the hobby room that is their head. Don't make the mistake of thinking this means they don't care about you – you're in their head with them too, it's just that they can forget to say on the outside what they're saying to you on the inside. You'll both need to work on getting them to stay on the outside more, and that's hard because we've only got one auditory channel, which means you can either listen to the outside world or what's going on inside your head, not both at the same time. This can mean that something you say may cause them to go off on a little thought journey and you've lost their attention without either of you realising it.

Kingfishers can often feel like they're observers of life, rather than being a part of it; that they don't fit in like other people or belong as others seem to. I think it's because of the way they've learned to filter what's happening to them through the sieve of their thoughts, which will often keep their feelings and emotions from making it through the holes. Without a flow of feelings between people, there tends to be less of a feeling of connection: this absence of connection is almost certainly not there on the part of the people the Kingfisher is wanting to connect to (unless they're a thinking bird too), so it's only a perception she or he has. Due to this, however, Kingfishers can sometimes feel alone, even in a crowd, but the upside is they're never lonely because they always have a voice in their head.

Now, whenever I mention people having voices in their head, others tend to get a bit antsy. I remember giving a talk once to a group of financial executives – all men, in fact, all Yorkshiremen (and you can tell a Yorkshireman, but you can't tell him much). I was teaching them about the different ways people think, and said that I belong to the type who have a voice in their heads. I asked them who shared that experience. There were twenty people in the group, but for the first and only time in my career nobody put their hand up – normally I can depend on at least five. There was a pause, and then one piped up in his inimitable Yorkshire manner, 'Well, you're just f****** mad, aren't thee.' It wasn't an easy morning.

Whenever I ask this question of a group, the Owls and Kingfishers always look a bit reluctant to put their hands up because people have an ingrained idea that talking to yourself is a sign of going mad. For thinking birds, it's actually just a normal way of experiencing their thoughts, and they'd be lost without it.

Plan to succeed, in detail, and in the right way

Kingfishers like a plan. In fact, from the moment they wake up they'll have an idea about how the day should go: often it'll be in some detail and will be marched through like a military manoeuvre (and that's just the relaxing days off). The upside of this is that their partner's life will work very smoothly; everything will have a place, and be in its place. Including the partner. Or else.

Which leads me onto the rules. All ground-birds have rules,

but Kingfishers tend to live by theirs to an even greater degree, which means that if you're in a relationship with one of them, you'll be expected to as well. In fact, many of them will take you respecting their rules (i.e. slavishly following them) as a sign of your love, so bear that in mind as an explanation when they look so hurt at you failing to follow the clear colour coding of kitchen utensils.

As a sky-bird, I've always found this to be the most challenging aspect of any relationship I've had with a ground-bird. I've discovered that calling their strict adherence to the rules they consider simply to be the way the world should work for everybody, their 'little madnesses', really doesn't work, so now I just do my best to learn what they are and remember to follow them whenever I'm not distracted by something more important. Like anything. By way of an example, a client of mine had this to say about her Kingfisher partner: 'I tried to help out in the garden, but apparently I didn't put things in the composter in the right order. Until I met him, I didn't even know there *was* such a thing. I tried to help him out in the garage, but all his tools have a special place on the wall, and only he knows where that place is, but it's supposed to be obvious to me. I tried to help him cook. You guessed it – I put the ingredients for a sauce in the wrong order. And there were only two ingredients. I gave up.' For Kingfishers, rules matter, and their unrelenting efforts to train you in their adherence is only for your own good.

Being ground-birds, Kingfishers thrive on the little things in life. Detail matters, so they won't shirk over the minutiae of the day. If they open up to you about *anything* you'll get *everything* – and they'll expect the same from you or they'll think you're hiding something. Along with their love of plans this makes them natural organisers and the one in the couple who really should run the finances. They miss very little, and the only downside to this is that they can take so long to work through everything they think they need to know to make a decision that the boat has sailed before they get to yes.

Feelings? What feelings?

I mentioned before how many Kingfishers developed their self-talk as an effort to dissociate from things that made them feel bad when they were younger – such as loneliness – while others didn't get enough opportunities to engage socially. Unfortunately, in adulthood this can continue as a reluctance to engage with their feelings, leading to Kingfishers remaining uncomfortable with emotions, whether that's experiencing them, someone else having them, or having to express them. In situations that call for emotions their thoughts act as a kind of safety buffer; something that lets them observe feelings rather than be catapulted into them. The standard tactic for a Kingfisher in the face of an emotion is to run from it or to shut down by going inside and distracting themselves. Losing emotional control feels threatening to them, so they mistrust experiencing feelings to any level in case they escalate. (Which is why Mr Spock from *Star Trek* would feel very much at home at a Kingfisher convention.) If they do lose control, it's likely to be spectacular, and not usually in a good way.

In intimate relationships, this can clearly be a problem. Kingfishers are likely to lack emotional expression, even though they'd die for you, while somehow expecting you to 'just know' that they love you. They might be incredibly romantic in their head but forget to act it out in the real world – after all, it's the thought that counts. They have to learn that it really isn't. If you like the strong, silent type, this is the person for you.

The dissociation can even extend to their relationship with their body. It's as if they spend so much time in their heads that the connections below the neck have withered. This can mean that they can carry an injury for a long time without noticing or, at least, not keep their attention long enough to do something about it. I've known Kingfishers get cold enough to be borderline hypothermic, hot enough that they got heat stroke, uncomfortable enough that they put their back out and ill enough the doctor needed to call an ambulance, all because they were so immersed in their thoughts, and so badly connected to their bodies, that they didn't respond to the signals it was sending. If you're living with one, you'll probably need to spend a bit of time watching out for them – throwing them a jumper because they didn't notice they were cold, or telling them to take something off because they're on the point of fainting from the heat.

Having put all that, it's only fair to point out that there will be Kingfishers who have learned to connect to their emotions – mainly they'll have Dove as their second type in quiz 2. If that's so, they can actually be very emotionally flexible people, capable of being in touch with their feelings, but also able to control them where appropriate. It's just that they're a distinct minority.

How they love

As I've said, Owls and Kingfishers are a little different to the other bird types because of the fact that they're made rather than born. In that respect, their way of knowing themselves to be loved won't be based on their Lovebird type – i.e. their Kingfisherness – but on what type came after Kingfisher on quiz 2, taken at the start of the book. So, if you're an Owl or a Kingfisher, whatever was your second strongest type, read that entry, too – it's likely you'll see that you're a mixture of them both. For example, if a Kingfisher has Peacock as their second type, then they're likely to share visual things – like the looks their partner gives them – as important. If Swan came second, then they'll probably be more tactile than other Kingfishers and either be more comfortable with their feelings, or have a harder time controlling them. Kingfishers can be better understood if they are seen to have begun life as one bird type, but developed into a Kingfisher later, with their original type still informing some of the things they like or dislike.

I've spoken about how much of the world a thinking bird lives in comes from their own head: well, a client of mine recently gave me an interesting insight into a particular way this can impact on a Kingfisher: 'When my wife left me, the hardest thing I found was not the fact that the physical her had gone, but the fact that the her I had carried around with me all the time we were together (obviously with all the best bits embellished) was still very much in my head. This was quite an eye-opener to me, to suddenly feel that jolt that the physical her had changed and moved on, but the one in my head was still the same. I think this is why I found it so hard to let go. There was nothing wrong with the relationship I had with the wife in my head, just the wife who left me, and my brain had a hard job differentiating.' This is why thinking birds really need to check in with their partner on occasion about the reality of their relationship, by asking questions like, Are we happy?

In the bedroom
I've just said that the second Lovebird type will be a strong guide here for thinking birds – so read that, too – but there are also some things specific here to Kingfishers (and Owls) that are worth noting.

Don't surprise them when they get home from work with the vision of you in a feather boa or a diving suit. Kingfishers generally don't respond well to spontaneity – they've got a plan, and *your* attempt to seduce them in a snorkel probably won't sit well with *their* plan to appear spontaneous by appearing in the bedroom dressed in whipped cream and wellies at 9.07 p.m. precisely. They have it all planned, see?

It might feel a little bit sometimes as if it's more about sex than making love with Kingfishers. It's likely to be a bit romance-lite, except perhaps in their heads – which is why they should be encouraged to say out loud what they're thinking. Thinking birds tend to love words, so talking dirty is often a turn-on: they'll probably be talking themselves through what they've planned to do to you all day anyway, so if it doesn't inhibit you, encourage them to tell you as they do it. It will also prevent them from allowing their internal dialogue to get in the way: Often thinking birds treat sex as a performance, so they can be quite critical of themselves. The minute they begin to question the level of their arousal, or how good they look, or how much you're enjoying it, they're fighting a downhill battle (literally, in the man's case). In fact, I had a client send her Kingfisher husband to me because of his erectile dysfunction. With a bit of digging, it quickly became clear that at critical moments he would start asking himself, 'Am I hard? . . . Am I hard enough? . . . Is it staying hard?' Any man knows where that conversation is headed. It was pretty simple to change the direction of his thoughts, and soon things were on the up.

Owls

'It is better to have your head in the clouds, and know where you are
. . . than to breathe the clearer atmosphere below them, and think
that you are in paradise.'

Henry David Thoreau

As mentioned in the Kingfisher profile, thinking birds are a bit
of a special case. All of the other birds have a preference for one
sense over another, while my experience over the years with
thinking-bird clients has been that some, in fact quite a few,
develop a way of thinking, sometimes by way of a defence mechanism. As a result of childhood experiences, some people go
inside their heads because they didn't like what they were experiencing through their eyes, ears or sense of touch, and talked to
themselves as a way of dissociating from it: it's why controlling
feelings is so important to Owls – as children, having them often
didn't lead to anything great. Instead, they learned to *think* about
what they saw, or heard, or felt, rather than *feel* anything about
it, and this made it less emotional for them. As adults, they tend
to stay that way. A fairly typical example is a client who was an

academic child born into a working-class family that had some weird ideas about it not being good to be clever. They didn't know how to deal with his questions or his aspirations, so they would take the mickey out of his intelligence or tell him to shut up. He went inside himself because he was the only one who he had to talk to about what he was interested in.

This withdrawal isn't always the consequence of unpleasant experiences; sometimes children who are an 'only child' or whose contact with others was limited, develop a rich inner world in which they while away the hours. This can lead to them drifting back into their own world as an adult, and having less connection with their physical senses. Emotions may be less of an issue for them, but they're likely to be less sensitive to them.

The main difference between the thinking birds is that Owls talk to themselves about the big picture, whereas Kingfishers like the detail.

It's all in their head

Owls spend a lot of time talking to themselves. For them it's not a sign of going mad, it's their way of staying sane. They can lose themselves in things they've said, things they shouldn't have said, things they plan to say, designs for a better cornflake, or wondering why there's an eject button on the remote control when you've got to get up and change the DVD, anyway. It can mean that if you're in a relationship with one it can get a bit lonely.

I confess this is my type, and there are times when my wife literally claps her hands before she begins to speak to me to make sure I'm with her. This is handy, because a common Owl experience is emerging from your head fully halfway through a conversation someone else has started with you, thinking you were listening. Early in our dating days, Bex and I went to B&Q for something and had to ask a very helpful, and old, assistant where the thing was. Have you noticed how B&Q seems to have a policy of employing older people, and isn't that so often better than trying to find a vacant teenager who's hiding behind the piles of plywood, squeezing a zit? Anyway, that's what I was thinking when I realised my wife had stopped talking to me and was looking for a response. I took a gamble and said 'Yes.' Result – she looked satisfied with that. A few seconds later, I ventured, 'Do you suppose they deliberately employ old people here?' She stopped. In fact, I think time stopped. Sagebrush certainly tumbled past us. She said, 'I just said that.'

Now, I know from previous women who've left me, that this would usually lead to a, 'You never listen to me, you don't care about me, you're sleeping on the couch' kind of conversation. However, I'd talked to Rebecca about this stuff early on, so she paused and said, 'Oh, you were talking to yourself, weren't you?' and we carried on with our day. I felt understood (and that she was a keeper), and she knew my lack of attention wasn't about her.

A thing to remember is that people can only listen to one thing at a time – what's in our head or what's outside it, and with Owls' internal chat being so dominant it can be a barrier to what's going on around them. They can be surrounded by mayhem and remain lost in their book. Don't mistake this apparent distraction for a lack of interest in what you're saying. Sometimes you can lose them mid-sentence, even though they may continue to look at you and nod, simply because what you're saying has made them think of something, or they've leapt ahead of you and have already started working out the ramifications of what you're talking about.

Owls can often feel like they're observers, rather than that they're involved or belong. Also, because of the dissociation they learned as children, they can appear aloof, distant or robotic. It's not that at all; it's just that being in the present is a bit of an effort because the lure of their internal world is so strong. A thing to remember is that they're never alone: they always have some kind of a conversation going with themselves, so if you interrupt that it can be annoying. If they go quiet, or you find them in thought, give them time to come out before you launch into what it is you want them for. A clue is that most of them look down to their left when they're talking to themselves (I'll talk about this further, on p. 109).

Things need to make sense to Owls. This is vital. If
something doesn't, it'll be discounted or discarded, so you'll
find that they have little time for the trivial, but can absorb
themselves to an amazing extent in something they find
meaningful. Owls will often be butterflies. They'll get interested
in something and throw themselves into it – in some cases
becoming quite obsessive about it – then, overnight, they can
take to the skies again in pursuit or in favour of a new passion.
It means they'll often know quite a lot about quite a lot, and
if they find something that fires their curiosity for life, they
can achieve remarkable things – it just means that often their
partners can feel somewhat abandoned in favour of their other
love. If you're with an Owl, you know why you love them;
allowing them time in their head, and time with their passion,
is just part of the deal.

One of the things that will need to make sense to Owls is their
partner. They are likely to want to know what their partner is
thinking at any given moment, and they won't like their partner
keeping secrets or anything, really, from them. Knowing is security for them, so an Owl's partner might also find the Owl wanting
to analyse the relationship, checking out with their partner how
things are. For the partner, it can feel like they're pinned under
a microscope at times, so strong is the Owl's need to know their
partner's thoughts, and yet Owls can be quite blind to their
partner's feelings unless they express them.

Plan to succeed

Owls are big on planning; in fact they won't get out of bed
without having the day mapped out. It doesn't mean they need
to stick to it – they can adapt as they go – but they'll rarely just
let things happen, as they'll want to know how everything fits
together. Saying, 'Let's not go to work today, let's go to the beach,'
is worth it every now and again, just to see the look on their face,
and the frantic efforts they go to in their heads to reconcile that
against what was in their mental diary. Cruel but fun – and good
for them.

Feelings? What feelings?

I said earlier that it's my opinion that Owls and Kingfishers often develop their way of thinking as a way of insulating themselves from negative feelings that were present, probably strongly, in their childhood, or from a lack of exposure to experiences where emotional connections were learned – which is mainly through contact with others. This dissociation very often leaves them with a poor connection to their bodies, and their emotional life.

Let's start with their body. Owls can live in their heads so much that they can be quite oblivious to what's going on down-stairs. It can mean that they're unaware of whether they're hot or cold, comfortable or uncomfortable – in fact, they can even be ill for a while without noticing (but if it becomes a head cold they'll complain that they're dying – yes, female Owls, too). My wife is the very opposite of this (she's a Swan). To me, her life is a constant search for comfort and sensory perfection. It leaves me perplexed, because most of what she cares about I don't even notice. I can have a bruise that would put her in intensive care and have no idea where I got it. I can sleep on a plank comfort-ably, but have to pretend that the hotel mattress last night really was an outrage when she starts to rant – the princess with the pea was a beginner in comparison. And that's what I find with Owls a lot; they feel like they're having to play at being 'normal' in responding to what other people are physically experiencing because they don't want to show out as some kind of robot. To do this they'll listen intently to someone's comment on anything sensory, from the great taste of a cookie to the softness of a fabric, to the sadness of a film, and do their best to respond appropriately, while feeling a little bit anxious in case they're getting it wrong – and they'll rarely be the first to volunteer an opinion on something like this in case they're completely out of sync with those around them.

And then there's the foreign world of emotions.

The most common reaction to an emotional situation for an Owl is either to run from it, or to shut down. The fear, you see, is that if they don't have complete control over their emotions then they don't have any control at all, so whenever something begins to stir feeling up within them they'll dive for cover – and the thickest cover is in the forest of thoughts. Watching films involving love, sadness, loss or tragedy will be avoided, or they'll keep disappearing for more popcorn during the tear-jerker moments, or just stare blankly at the screen while they disappear inside and have another stab at redesigning the cornflake.

Clearly, this can make intimate relationships difficult. They usually won't think to cuddle as a way of expressing emotion (unless perhaps a feeling bird came second behind Owl in quiz 2) and may actually stiffen up when you do, in the early days at least. They will expect you to know you love them. I remember with my first wife how I came home from work one day and told her that I'd seen some flowers that I'd thought of buying her . . . Whoever said it's the thought that counts was talking rubbish; it clearly wasn't, and I've learned over time to say on the outside what I feel on the inside. And if Bex says, 'I love you' I'll say 'I love you, too', rather than just think it in my head. Strangely, I've found that makes a difference.

There are exceptions to this, of course; there are Owls who have learned to connect with their feelings – and they're usually the ones for whom Dove would be a second type in quiz 2. They can be both sensitive and able to remain in control in emotional situations – a rare combination – but you don't come across them very often.

The devil's in the lack of detail

Owls often have big ideas. They love to discover patterns between things and many are brilliant strategists. This is all about the big picture. Owls will avoid having to involve themselves in the detail of anything if they can avoid it – their boredom threshold is very low, especially for anything they consider trivial. For moment-to-moment awareness, this type is probably the worst on the planet: they can be so wrapped up in their inner world, floating along in the pursuit of a new idea, that they could walk unnoticing through a tornado and wonder later why their hair is messed up. One of the consequences of this is that they don't tend to be great at remembering to do things, even if the need for them is obvious. I've been known to step over piles of washing, waiting to be taken downstairs, multiple times (before a pair of pants, thrown with some venom, hits me on the back of the neck to gently remind me).

How they love
Owls and Kingfishers are made not born, so things are a little different for them. I find that overwhelmingly they love, and know they're loved, through the second bird on their list that came from quiz 2, that you took earlier. An Owl with Nightingale as a second type, for example, is going to talk more than most Owls and be most tuned to sounds as a way of making sense of things.

In the bedroom
While the second Lovebird type will be a strong guide here also, there are a few things specific to Owls and Kingfishers in this area.

Spontaneity is probably not going to be a strong suit, unless it's planned. Owls will like to prepare for romance – I've known Owls who actually schedule it – and may create elaborate seduction evenings that work like a Hollywood production: five minutes into the kissing the oven timer will ping for some nibbles, the champagne will be thoughtfully placed beside the couch so you don't have to stretch, and ten minutes into the foreplay the gypsy guitarists will ring the doorbell.

Partners of Owls should be aware that their internal dialogue will probably continue into the bedroom. This can work positively, if they externalise it by telling you how they're feeling – what you're doing to them in terms of their arousal, that kind of thing. If they keep their chat internal then it can be a source of problems. For example, if a male Owl is talking to himself the following can happen: 'This is going well. Great, she's come. Ooh, she's stroking me. Am I hard enough? Does that feel hard enough? Is it getting softer? Oh God, is it going down!?'

We get more of what we think about, so it's important that the self-chat is positive. I've found that the opposite being true has been the source (and solution) for many clients who've come to see me with this kind of performance issue. But let me be clear (and not just because I'm an Owl), I'm not saying that Owls and Kingfishers are more prone to performance issues than other bird types; just that where it occurs with them, this tends to be the reason. (That didn't come across as a bit defensive, did it?)

Conclusion to Part Two

So far I've identified eight different types of people, which I know you know isn't meant to be taken too seriously, or at least too set in stone. Think of each one having an elasticated waistline to accommodate the inevitable variations that occur whenever we try to pigeonhole people (you see how I'm still pushing the metaphor?).

Before we move on, I'd like you to take the time to ponder the following questions:

1. How does what you've read make sense of how you know you're loved? What did you agree with, and what didn't you agree with?

2. How does what you've read make sense of what *you* do that lets your partner know *they're* loved? Does that explain anything about your relationship?

3. What do you think your partner does to let you know you're loved?

4. What would you like them to know that you think they currently don't (based on what you've read)?

Share this information with each other and see where the conversation takes you.

PART THREE

Spotting Potential Nest Mates

I created the quizzes you did earlier so you'd have an easy way of identifying yourself and your partner, but clearly it's not going to be convenient on a first date to whip out a questionnaire before you decide if it's worth staying for the main course. (Let's face it, whipping out anything on a first date is a high-risk strategy.) Instead, there are ways you can pick up clues during a normal conversation that I use every day and that, with a bit of practice, you can too.

When a couple come into my therapy room, I'm beginning to look for Lovebird indicators from the very beginning, and they fall into roughly three categories: their eye movements, the words they use and how they say them. Let's begin with the eyes.

The eyes have it

It's long been recognised that eyes are an important source of information about a person, from the idea that they're a window to the soul or the notion that having them too close together is a sign of a lack of trustworthiness, to the belief that some people's gaze is hypnotic. Eyes attract us.

I mentioned NLP earlier (the system developed as a way of describing an individual's way of seeing the world, and the different ways they do so). It has an interesting model that, while controversial, I have found extremely useful. It suggests that when we are thinking in particular ways our eyes go in meaningful directions.

Let me use a short example of a session with a couple, Joe and Sarah, to highlight what I mean:

Joe and Sarah settle into their chairs in front of me, both looking a little nervous, Joe looking at Sarah more than she does him. She's mainly looking at the floor, to her right.

Me: 'Have you been to see someone like me before?'

Sarah keeps her eyes on the floor and just shakes her head. Joe looks up at the ceiling for a moment and then looks at me: 'Yes, we went for a few sessions at Relate.'

Me: 'Good, what did the counsellor have to say?'

Sarah blushes slightly, shoots me a glance and then says, with her eyes once more on the carpet, 'My feeling was that he sided with Joe and just thinks that I'm precious and it's all my fault.'

Joe looks at the ceiling again, and then his eyes flick to the side. 'I don't see the session that way. He said some things about me too; that I'm too demanding of your time and get jealous for no reason.'

Me: 'Jealous? What about?'

Joe looks down at the floor and then back up to the ceiling. 'Well, when other men look at her I don't like it, and I think sometimes she likes the blokes in her office a bit too much, as she always seems to be working late.'

Sarah stays looking at the floor for a moment and then looks at Joe angrily. 'You're so stupid. It's my job and it's a building company – of course there are blokes working there. I don't do anything to make you jealous, you just wear me down with it.'

And we're off.

I really enjoy helping couples improve their relationship and, as you can see, it's often in quite incendiary circumstances. (Unfortunately, couples don't usually seek help when they're at the beginning of the slippery slope to separation; they normally wait until they're hurtling at full speed.)

So, what have I noticed so far about Joe and Sarah?

If I said, 'What colour is your front door?', most people would visualise their door in order to answer the question. According to the NLP model, as you do that, your eyes will look upwards. When you think in pictures, your eyes look skyward. So far, Joe has looked towards the ceiling quite a lot, which is an early indicator that he may be a sight bird. It's too early to tell if he's a Swift or a Peacock.

Sarah, however, has looked mainly at the floor. You know how people say, 'What's the matter with you; you're really looking down?' The words we use are often more literal than we think. When people are in the grip of an emotion – and the stronger it is, the more likely this is to be true – they look down, especially for negative emotions like sadness, anger, jealousy or hurt. Why else would we say, 'Never mind, things will look up'?

When feeling an emotion, most – about 90 per cent of people – look down to their right. There is a strong correlation between this and people being right-handed, because most of the 10 per cent who look down to the left when they're feeling are left-handed. So far, it looks as if Sarah might be a feeling bird, but it's early days and I don't like to rush into labelling anyone.

There are two other directions the eyes travel that are important. At one point, Joe's eyes flicked to the side for a moment. When people access sounds, like recalling a past conversation or the words of a song, their eyes will tend to look levelly to one side or the other. Mostly this is quite a quick movement, so it's easy to miss, but some people will look away for longer periods of time.

The last direction is looking down and to your left. For the majority, it's where people go to talk to themselves: any time people are busy having a conversation in their head, their eyes are likely to be looking down at the floor to their left – unless they're one of the (mainly left-handed) 10 per cent of the population who look here for feelings, in which case they'll look down to their right for this 'self-talk' option.

The really important point I want to stress is that all of us look in all of these directions during conversation; it's just that most of us will look in one area more than the others, i.e. we'll habitually 'think' in either a visual, sound, feeling or self-talk style more than any of the others.

What this means is that Peacocks and Swifts will look upwards most when talking for any length of time, Nightingales and Robins will look sideways, Swans and Doves will look down to their right, and Owls and Kingfishers will look down to their left. It sounds odd, but bear this in mind during your next coffee break. Watch people's eyes while they talk – I think you'll be amazed how quickly you realise that people's eye patterns do have a relationship with what they're talking about.

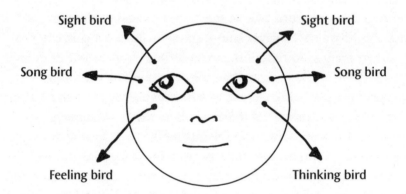

As I converse with Joe and Sarah, I'm matching what they're saying to where their eyes go to get an understanding of their style of thinking. Both might say 'I just get so angry sometimes,' but Sarah will look to the floor and Joe will look to the ceiling as they do so. What might be happening here is that Joe is seeing a picture of what makes him angry, while Sarah is focusing more on the feeling itself. This will mean, for Sarah, that the image of the event is fainter or out of her awareness – she knows Joe makes her angry, but won't be able to give examples of why as quickly as he can. She probably could if I got her to look up as she felt the feeling.

By the same token, someone who looks sideways when talking about their last argument is probably going to have a better recall of what was said than someone who looks down or skyward. It's not about who has a better memory, so much as who has a better memory for what needs recalling in that particular event.

For example, feeling birds are often poor spellers, because you can't really feel how to spell a word: you have to see it or hear it. Thinking birds will be great at working out the order in which things happened, while seeing birds will remember the face of the waiter who served you on your first date, but not their name, while the hearing bird will be more likely to remember his name but not quite be able to picture him.

There are many other interesting things to notice about eyes, and here are a few more that might just make you go, 'Oh, *that's* why they do that!'

Some people, particularly sight birds, close their eyes while they're thinking – even if that's in the middle of a conversation. It can be a bit disconcerting, not to say weird, to be on the receiving end of, but it's normal for them. Because the same part of the brain is used to process the visual information coming in through our eyes as the pictures we imagine in our head, closing our eyes often cuts down on distractions. Imagine they're using their eyelids as a projector screen to put their thoughts onto so they can see them more clearly.

Other people have a very strong 'look to talk' rule. If you had a parent who insisted on, 'Look at me when I'm talking to you', then it's likely that you'll feel it's rude to not do so. This can involve having to follow your partner into the kitchen to continue your conversation or, worryingly for the passenger, turning to look at the person sitting beside – or even behind – you while you're driving. Taken to extremes, these can be the people who look at you throughout a conversation without ever breaking eye contact or blinking. If it feels as if they're looking straight through you, they are, in a way: if they don't feel okay to look away while they think, they'll usually defocus as they look at you and project the picture they want to think about somewhere in between you.

It can make them seem a bit spaced out or inattentive. Most will be sight birds, but some may just have been taught this as children.

Many hearing birds find looking at something blank helps them to hear better. Sounds bizarre, doesn't it? Years ago, when I was an instructor at the police college in Hendon, I noticed that some students would either stare out of the window, or at the wall or the floor while I was teaching. Naturally, I assumed they weren't paying attention, yet when I tested them they invariably demonstrated that they were – just not in my way. It taught me that 'Look at me when I'm talking to you' doesn't necessarily lead to the person hearing what it is that's being said.

Listen very carefully . . .

Words are the things we use to communicate our thoughts to others, so it's not surprising that there might be a link between the way we think and the words we choose to describe our thoughts. Let's go back to Joe and Sarah to show you what I mean:

Me: 'Joe, tell me a little about what's going wrong between you.'

Joe: 'Where do I start? As far as I can see, I can't do anything right. I try to show her my feelings by bringing her flowers, or buying her something she'd look nice in, but I can tell by her face that she doesn't like them.'

(I'm deliberately condensing the phrases he's using to demonstrate my point, which is, if you read what he says, how many words relate to seeing, looking, or in some way, using his eyes to know things.) Many words describe information using particular senses, and there is a great range of choice. For example, asking Sarah the same question, she responds with:

Sarah: 'He's just really dragging me down. Nothing I do for him is right and at the moment being with him just feels like wading through treacle.'

Notice how she's describing what's going on in physical terms? A sight bird might say, 'We really see eye to eye'; a sound bird might say, 'We're on the same wavelength'; a feeling bird, 'We just clicked'; and a thinking bird, 'We just make sense as a couple.' Again, I want to stress that someone saying any of these phrases doesn't automatically place them in a particular Lovebirds nest; all of us use phrases from across the sensory board. What I'm listening for, however, over a period of five to ten minutes, is whether someone uses more from one type than another – and does that correspond to the way their eyes are going? The more the two support each other, the more confident I can be as to which type I identify them as.

This knowledge can be a fantastic help in gaining rapport, because people respond to people who are like them. If Joe talks to me in seeing-bird language, I respond using the same types of words, and swap to feeling-bird expressions with Sarah. With her, I hope to get her to feel that 'we're connecting', while for Joe, that is 'I can see where he's coming from'. I teach each couple these principles so they can begin to incorporate them into the way they relate to each other. If your partner says to you, 'I can't see what you're saying', in my opinion they're usually being literal – they can't translate your words into a picture. You just repeating what you said, but a bit louder, really isn't going to help: you need to change what you're saying into words that will suit them. Everyone knows they think, but most people don't think about *how* they think, and beginning to recognise these differences can make a huge difference to the quality of your communication.

I haven't mentioned Owls and Kingfishers yet. They will tend to use words from all sensory systems, perhaps favouring those of the Lovebird that came second in quiz 2, but they do have certain words that they use more than other people: 'That makes sense' is a common one, because that is core to their thinking. They'll often talk of concepts and notions and systems, because how things fit together is important to them, but overall I find watching where their eyes go to be a stronger indicator than the words they use.

Here are some phrases that are most commonly used by particular types, just so you can start to get to grips with them (which is obviously a feeling-bird phrase).

Sight bird	Song bird	Feeling bird	Thinking bird
see	hear	feel	sense
look	listen	touch	experience
view	sound(s)	grasp	understand
appear	make music	get hold of	think
show	harmonise	slip through	learn
dawn	tune in/out	catch on	process
reveal	be all ears	tap into	decide
envision	rings a bell	make contact	motivate
illuminate	silence	throw out	consider
imagine	be heard	turn around	change
clear	resonate	hard	perceive
foggy	deaf	unfeeling	insensitive
focused	mellifluous	concrete	distinct
hazy	dissonance	scrape	conceive
crystal	question	get a handle	know

Nor is it only the words a person uses that can be an indicator of their Lovebird type – it can also be the pace at which they speak. The stronger their type, the more likely the following is to be true:

Our eyes take in over 70 per cent of the information processed by all of our senses, so the visual part of our brain has to work really quickly. As a consequence, you'll often find that Swifts and Peacocks come across as quite wired and speedy: in their movements, in their energy levels and even in their pace of speech. If they are talking about something that's engaged them, words can fly from their mouths like machine-gun bullets, and can be quite hard to keep up with. If you think of F1 race commentators or auctioneers you'll get the idea.

Nightingales and Robins tend to speak more flowingly and can be very pleasant to listen to – many almost seem to use their voices as instruments and take pleasure from the words themselves. Their pacing and enunciation are likely to be clear: newsreaders often come from the ranks of these particular Lovebirds.

Have you met the kind of people who seem to have a time-delay between a question you ask, and the answer they provide you with? Like you're talking to someone on the moon? Or who seem to struggle to find the right words, often starting a sentence several times, or leaving it half-finished while they begin another? Chances are they're a Swan or a Dove. Words are a long way from feelings, and it can take them a bit longer than most to connect the two together. Once warmed up they're fine, but if they have to say something new or on the spur of the moment they can struggle to be articulate. They're much better speaking about familiar things.

The exceptions here, again, are the thinking birds: you can't really spot Owls and Kingfishers from the way they speak. They're a little chameleon-like in that they can vary according to the voices around them, or have the characteristics of the Lovebird that would be second strongest if they were to take the second quiz at the beginning of the book. The way their eyes move remains a better indicator.

Once again, pace can be very important in gaining or keeping rapport. If a Swift launches into a conversation at full speed with a Dove, it's likely to overwhelm their capacity to keep up and they'll just shut down and stop listening. In the reverse case, a Dove might take so long to get to their point that the Swift loses patience or gets bored and stops listening. It's vital that you listen to the speaking style of your partner and do your best to get close to it, at least at the beginning of a conversation, to get it off to the best possible start.

Hopefully, the way their eyes move, the words they use and the pace they speak at will give you a good idea about whether they're a sight, sound, feeling or thinking bird. And when you've achieved that, how can you divide them into a sky-bird or ground-bird? This bit's pretty easy; you just listen to them.

★　　★　　★

Here are two in action:

Ground-bird: 'I just got back from Majorca. Two brilliant weeks with the family. Have you ever been?'

Sky-bird: 'Yes, once I think.'

Ground-bird: 'We loved it. The food was great – we went to this lovely restaurant that served the most delicious seafood, their paella was to die for. And I went parascending. Have you ever done that?'

Sky-bird: 'Yes, I have.'

Ground-bird: 'Did you like it?'

Sky-bird: 'Yes, it was good fun.'

Ground-bird: 'Amazing! I was really scared but Paulo – he was the driver of the boat – was ever so good. It was a bit like a parachute jump I expect, but you get towed . . .'

As you can see, ground-birds go into much more detail than sky-birds and will always volunteer information. It's not that sky-birds are reticent or reluctant to talk; they just don't naturally infer that any greater level of detail is required. Plus the nature of what they want to know is different, too:

Sky-bird: 'So, what will upgrading our satellite package bring us?'

Ground-bird: 'Well, we'll get thirty extra channels.'

Sky-bird: 'And what do we need those for?'

Ground-bird: 'Well, we get five extra sports channels, some great documentary channels and I think there's a new comedy channel. And it's only £5 extra.'

Sky-bird: 'But we don't watch the channels we've got, and

we're both going to be really busy over the next few months. I don't see that we'll get the value.'

Ground-bird: 'But it's a limited offer . . .'

For ground-birds, more of something is usually a good thing, and they often don't pull back and look at the big picture; they'll make a decision based on what's in front of them. As sky-birds are generally looking for the purpose of something and the use it can be put to within the great scheme of things, having something because it might be useful to have doesn't really work for them.

It will take some practice to get used to watching and listening to people and picking up these clues, but if you're a people-watcher I think you'll find it fascinating. People are telling you more than they think, all the time. And it can be a lot of fun to realise that you're helping yourself get along with someone without giving away how you're doing it. It will also make it easier to spot when sales people are doing it to you . . .

What we'll go onto next is to look at what the Lovebird types can tell us about how different combinations will act and interact within a relationship.

PART FOUR

Lovebird combinations

Robin and Dove

Robin: 'She's always giving me a cuddle and wants to hold my hand when we walk – which is nice, but she rarely tells me how she feels about me, or even pays me a compliment, come to that.'

Dove: 'Of course I love him – do you think I squeeze just anyone's bum? He says some lovely things, which is nice, but sometimes I just wish he'd show his feelings more. I can't remember the last time he cuddled me.'

This couple can develop a great relationship with just some attention paid to their major difference. Sure, Robins like to talk a lot and Doves are addicted to things that are snuggly, but that's not the big deal. The challenge comes from Robins being ground-birds, so liking rules and details, and Doves being sky-birds, and therefore being more attracted to the big picture. Where Robins like hard facts and evidence, Doves are much more into gut feelings and hunches. That's going to take some work but, used properly, this difference can make for a really productive relationship. Just not always harmonious – but where would be the fun in that?

Cuckoos in the nest

Robins need to talk like they need to breathe. Did you see the film *Castaway* with Tom Hanks as a man marooned on an island after a plane crash? After a while, he drew a face on a volleyball to give him someone to talk to. Robins would do that after an evening on their own. And sometimes their partners are going to feel like that volleyball, as the Robin talks at them to get their thoughts straight, words gushing from them in a torrent that your contributions get lost in. Best to let them empty. The good thing is that you're going to know that they're happy, and they're going to let you know when they're not. There's no stopping them. Doves, on the other hand, will often keep what is nagging at them to themselves. They let their frustrations fester and ferment, often because they don't want to cause an upset. Eventually, however, the final straw will break their silence and they'll let you have it with both barrels. (Did I just switch metaphors midstream?) Anyway, move to a safe distance when they lose their temper, because when they let go, they are nobody's peace symbol. The good news is that they don't usually hold onto this feeling for long.

Doves tend to be big on comfort, and a lot of their effort will be spent on creating a bubble of perfection around the two of you, but especially them. This can make them feel a little high maintenance, because a strange bed will rarely be as good as their own (as years of research went into finding that one), food won't be quite seasoned enough, or be seasoned too much; the cinema will be too hot or too cold – and the seats are never comfortable, are they? Going to the shops can sometimes feel like you're going for a short holiday, because several options of clothing will need to be taken to accommodate the local weather fluctuations – that only they will notice.

Robins will want to share their day with you, in detail: who said what to who and what they said back from the beginning to the never-ending end. Interrupting them will only cause them to go back to the start. Get a cat or dog so at least you've got something to stroke to help you through it. Don't EVER ask them how the book they are reading is, as you'll get it read back to you without them needing to open it. When all the Dove wants is to sink into the sofa with a glass of wine, a cuddle and the telly, the Robin will want to download their day – and then probably tell you about yours. It can be exhausting.

Robins will tend to have rules: there are certain things that need to be done in certain ways, or you'll hear about it. Repeated infringements could lead to a workshop on it, and it's likely there will be repeated infringements because Doves tend to be 'in the moment' people, and are not rule-sensitive at all. They can accept them as guidelines, but whoever said, 'Rules are for the guidance of the wise and the blind obedience of fools' was a sky-bird.

Doves tend to trust their hunches and intuition more than the stuff Robins label 'reality'. Doves are going to be particularly strong in this regard, because feelings are what they're all about. While Robins will want to sit down and work things out – weigh the pros and cons, debate the evidence – Doves will, by comparison, give things a brief glance and just take a punt. That will drive the Robin mad. It's best that they do the planning, organise things and pay the bills. (It gives them a chance to chat to the call centres, after all.)

Doves can be incredibly sensitive to the emotions of others, and will often work really hard to keep harmony within their network of friends and family. They are often worriers in this regard, because they can see the impact of discord beyond just that of the individual. In this respect they'll need the support of their partner, and the Robin's love of discussion could be a real help – as long as they recognise that often discussion for a Dove is an opportunity to air their feelings, or to let some of the emotional pressure out. If they're subjected to a Robin's five-point plan for the situation then you can end up with them feeling worse than when they started – which, of course, will lead to them keeping things to themselves even more. Robins just need to remember sometimes that listening to others is part of a conversation, too.

Feathers for the nest

What Robins need to know about Doves
Do:

Doves will know they're loved by the way you make them feel. Physical sensation is one of the most important ways, so touch needs to be an everyday part of your conversation. Casual touches, affectionate pats and strokes, gentle kisses and the odd squeeze all communicate, 'we're connected, I'm with you and I'm into you'. In psychology, practitioners talk of a thing called 'stroke deprivation', where strokes are any kind of positive exchange between people, from a nod to a smile to a hug. An absence of such strokes has been proven to increase sickness rates and can lead to depression and anxiety – in anyone, not just feeling birds.

Doves need a lot of physical strokes; any kind of distance between you when you're together can feel to them like an emotional gap, so connect regularly. They will almost certainly love to be pampered with a massage, or a warm bath or a foot rub.

They will often be putting a lot of effort into making your life comfortable. It's good to let them know you appreciate it – with a caress more than a speech – but it will also mean a lot if you reciprocate. Pay attention to the things they like related to their comfort, and do them for them. It can be as simple as you getting up to make the evening cocoa (gravity is heavier for Doves than other types, so they tell me) or doing one of the jobs you know they hate. You don't need to make grand gestures; sometimes it's the small kindnesses that count.

Being so into sensation, Doves will often love things that make them feel. I just can't predict what feelings they love to pursue most – you live with them, so pay attention. Do they love the gentle feelings they get from watching comedy or love films? Do they cry at the opera? Do they shriek like banshees on a roller-coaster and drag you on for a second go? Is bungy-jumping on their To Do list? Feed these feelings for them and they will love you for ever. And join them in these occasions as much as you can, as being with you to hug, hold hands with or cling onto for grim death is part of the bonding.

Don't:

Try very hard not to overwhelm Doves with detail. Seriously. Listening to a full-length recollection of your talk with the boss is going to make their will to live weaken. They may even cry. Think 'abbreviated version' with everything. Think, 'What do I need to say?' and halve it at least. All Doves ever want is the pass-notes version of life.

I know that rules are important for you. I'm going to ask Doves to do their best at following yours, but the truth is they are probably going to suck at them. It's hard to believe, but not following your way of doing things will not actually change their life for the worse in any way they'd recognise, so do your best not to go on about them. It's not about them not caring – don't hit them with the, 'If you loved me you'd humour my need to put the remotes in size order', because it's just not a good look on you (okay, I'm sorry, I just gave myself away as a sky-bird, didn't I?).

Don't make Doves feel bad about liking things to be the best possible experience they can be. You can eat a meal without caring that it's not quite salted properly as long as the chewing doesn't interfere with your talking, but they can't. Be patient, and be in their corner when the waiter comes over. (After all, it's not your food they're going to spit in.)

What Doves need to know about Robins
Do:

Your partner feels loved by the simple act of you telling them, and that's about all, which is simple, isn't it? You just have to remember to say things you appreciate about them as they occur, like: 'You look really nice in that', 'I love what you did for me' or 'Nice bum!' It's likely that if you say 'I love you' after they say it, it won't be seen to count. (A Robin friend of mine told me that a standard for him in his marriage is that if his wife says, 'I love you' after he's said it, it doesn't count. She has to say it first, and when she does, only then does he have the little 'Ahhh' moment.) Also, make sure you mean it. Robins are incredibly sensitive to tone, so if your words don't match your tone – they'll believe the tone. Ringing them out of the blue just to hear their voice will be the equivalent of you having your feet dipped in smooth, warm caramel (that doesn't stick), so do it once in a while.

Robins love rules. They will tell you what they are. They will expect you to follow them because they are rules. You're going to forget them. Do your best not to. Apologise with words when you do. They won't abandon them, you won't care about them: it will be one of the signature challenges of your relationship.

As you know, Robins both love and need to talk. It's as essential to them as touch is to you, so you need to meet in the middle here. They are going to say more words about something than you'll ever want to hear. You need to honour that need and shout, 'Enough already!' as rarely as you can manage. I've told them to do their best to cut down the word count when describing things to you, so meet them halfway on this one, yes?

Don't:
Accusing Robins of being boring just because the details of things matter to them more than you is a no-no. In fact, it'll come in handy as they take over more and more of the things you find boring, like paying bills on time. Don't forget that they find your trust of the intangible, your gut instinct, is as weird as their insistence on evidence and facts.

Don't think Robins don't care simply because they think that buying you a talking birthday card somehow trumps a day at a theme park or spa. Don't hate them for thinking listening to the boxed set of Monty Python, and then reciting back the Parrot Sketch for the next week, isn't the most fun you can have. Comedy for them is going to be based on clever one-liners and catchphrases, whereas you might like people falling over a little more; it's just a difference. Neither should accuse the other of a lack of a sense of humour just because different things tickle you. Ooh, tickling – that'll be one of your things . . .

Swift and Swift

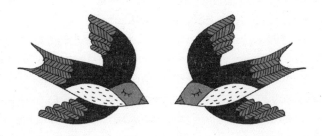

Swift 1: 'The trouble is, we have so many ideas that we can never agree which ones to pursue, and if we do, we never seem to see them through because we get distracted by something else.'

Swift 2: 'I know what I look good in. I don't need her telling me what to wear. Who is she, the style police?'

You two sky-birds are alike in all the ways this book is measuring and, as my basic premise is that it's differences that cause most of the problems between couples, what could possibly go wrong with your relationship? Well, there are more differences out there than I can cover in one book, and they might be contributing but, also, similarity sometimes can bring its own pressures: I'll do my best to give you some ideas about that.

The key things are the way both of you value what you see, and your preference for keeping away from detail by soaring in the world of ideas and the big picture.

Cuckoos in the nest

Seeing is believing for you two, and so much more. Everything is judged by its appearance; including you and who you hold hands with when you walk out in public. I would expect your house to be full of pictures of you both, mainly in situations where you look your best. Obviously this can be a nice way of remembering happy times, but sometimes it almost feels like it's laying down a standard that forms part of your relationship contract: 'This is how good we look, this is what I've signed up for.' It can be a pressure. I've heard many pregnant partners of sight birds complain about how they're hearing, 'Just because you're pregnant doesn't mean you should let your looks go.' Because you're similar in this respect, it's possible that you evolve a kind of 'looks arms-race', where the pressure is applied to each of you equally so neither of you ever takes your eye off the mirror. It doesn't sound very relaxing, but if looking good for each other is that important, it could be something that binds you rather than drives you apart. But if it's more important to one than the other, or if a life-situation like pregnancy or illness makes looking good difficult, then things might get a bit tense. I actually heard from a wife whose Swift husband's first response to the news of her cancer was, 'I hope you don't lose your hair, you'll look awful.' That makes him sound heartless, and maybe he is, but each of us has something we value highly, and for him, rightly or wrongly, it was how his wife looks on his arm.

You're both likely to have strong opinions about anything visual. I imagine you can pass many pleasant hours sipping coffee in a café and demolishing the fashion choices of passers-by. If your tastes match in regard to interior design, art and fashion, then I envisage a world where you live in visual bliss. If your tastes clash, then it could be a bit of a dirty war, where favourite ornaments fall victim to the vacuum cleaner; pictures are smashed by a weird earthquake that was limited to your living room; and clothes get chewed up by the washing machine. One thing that's unlikely is that a Swift could live in a space full of things that offend their eyes, so if you love Art Deco and your partner comes home from a flea market with a bargain piece of modern art that resembles a coat hanger sprayed with muesli, I don't see either one of you letting the other's choice stay on your walls for long.

It's going to need some careful negotiation, but it's difficult to compromise with you two because both of you would hate living in the blandness of something that falls between your taste differences, as much as you'd hate living in your partner's vision of what's lovely. Challenging.

One thing you two will find difficult is separation. Swifts feel that out of sight is out of heart, so being apart can feel threatening to the relationship: indeed, if either partner appears to make a choice of doing something apart when they could be with their lover, it can seem like infidelity – which seems a stretch if you're into train spotting. Nevertheless, a Swift will tot up in their head the time their partner could spend with them, and the time they actually do, and if the discrepancy is too big there'll be tears before bedtime.

What this can lead to is a situation where you become joined at the hip. Again, this is only a problem if it's a problem: some Swift couples will love it. A few individuals might begin to feel a bit confined, however, and it's important that if this is the case their desire to explore new horizons isn't taken as a sign of a weakening commitment. It could actually shine some new light into the relationship.

As both of you are sky-birds, your strength is in seeing the big picture, in having ideas and brainwaves. You can have immense fun pursuing a new passion before discarding it for the next. It means that, collectively, your garage is going to be full of stuff you've accumulated from hobbies and interests, although most of it will be coated with dust. Many domestic projects will be half-completed, unless they make the house look a mess, in which case you'll probably get someone in to finish it.

The only downside of this is that your life is going to look pretty messy and disorganised to many people, i.e. the people who aren't like you. Both of you are going to avoid detail and have a low boredom threshold for anything small or repetitive, which means you're almost certainly going to get those annoying calls from credit card companies about missed payments, forget to book dentist appointments, and probably make a spectacular cock-up over holiday arrangements that leaves at least one of you in tears at the airport. I really wish you'd sit down and work out responsibilities and stick to them, but I also wish for world peace, and that's not going to happen either.

Feathers for the nest

What Swifts living with Swifts need to know
Do:
With your eyes being your main window on the world, it's no surprise that you use them to decide whether you're loved or not, and you do it in one of three ways.

The first is something I've touched on already. You weigh your partner's commitment by the amount of time they spend in front of you. If something takes them away from you there's a danger you view that as them expressing a preference, and if what takes them away involves someone else, however innocently, then the green-eyed monster is likely to enter stage left. If life keeps you apart, then I suggest you invest in Skype, FaceTime or whatever technology brings you face to face again. If work stretches your working day, then make sure the time you spend together is quality time – sharing experiences, looking into each other's eyes, shopping: that kind of thing.

The second thing you use to know your partner's feelings about you is the way they look at you. You'll both recognise a special look that says, 'I love you', so make sure you remember to use it. Also, you know that saying about 'If looks could kill'? Well, if they could, it would be Swifts who'd be the victims. The wrong look from their partner could wound a Swift deeply, and be remembered for ever. I remember one Swift coming home proudly in a new jacket he'd picked up. As he walked through the door, his partner gave him a look that he took to be completely derisive. The jacket went in the wardrobe, he hasn't worn it since and he refuses to discuss it with his partner. But it sits as a silent accusation. (So if you've just smelt something bad, for heaven's sake don't look at your lover until you've had a chance to adjust your face.)

The final way a Swift will know they're loved is by the gifts they receive. This doesn't mean that they're grasping or materialistic; it just means that presents and tokens have a particular meaning for them. I've never been one for sending birthday cards, well, cards of any kind actually, and my mum moaned about it for years. Then the penny dropped. Even though Mum must know that a card from me is meaningless, she still values it as a sign of something only she can properly understand. (So now she gets them.) So it is with Swifts. They'll put a premium on such things, and on the appropriateness of a gift. Anything you buy each other needs to be something that says, 'I know you.' Buying your Swift something that doesn't fit their taste, or their wardrobe, or their interests, is saying to them, 'I don't really get you.' It feels like an insult. Happily, another Swift will know this. You'll know to buy presents, remember anniversaries, buy cards, and make them all meaningful to your partner.

Don't:
Okay, I'll have one more stab at it: don't let things slide. Your dislike of detail can be such that, even though you know you should be doing something like paying a bill or checking a booking, you somehow let it go until it's too late. You might both be happy with the chaos, and be able to laugh at the occasional disaster, but it wouldn't take much organising to sit down once a month with a glass (or bottle, if the going gets tough) of wine and force each other through the agony of making your life work more smoothly. It'll be worth it. Honestly . . . you still won't, will you?

How you look is important to you. How your partner looks is, too. On some level, your mind treats their appearance as a judgement of you, and with you both seeing the world the same way, there is likely to be a balanced interest here. But it can become a bit of a competition, with both of you vying for who looks sharpest, who gets the most comments, who's the most hip. (Is that still a word? If not substitute groovy.) Anyhow, call a truce or take it in turns to dazzle, or you'll eventually fall exhausted in a changing room somewhere, overcome by fashion fatigue.

On the same note, don't be overcome by your need for other sorts of appearances to be kept up. One couple was under enormous financial pressure because the husband had been made redundant from his job in the City – something to do with ruining the economy I think – but he still insisted on looking his best by buying expensive suits for his interviews. If you're not careful, the two of you could over-extend yourselves through your desire to make life look perfect, and your love of adornment.

Finally, don't drift. You both focus on the big picture and are probably great at coming up with good ideas or brilliant new projects – in your careers too, you'll be great at strategy. Where you'll both probably fall down is in implementing your schemes, as you're much better at the inspiration part than the perspiration part. Over time, this can mean that you don't get very far. You'll have a great time starting things, you'll have fun beginning to move in a new direction, but – look over there, it's a squirrel! – you'll probably get distracted or get enthused about something else, and all you'll be left with when you look back on life is years of motion but no progress. Stick with things, or find someone to do that bit for you – i.e. a ground-bird friend. All sky-birds need one somewhere, even if you have to pay them for their services.

Nightingale and Dove

Dove: 'I love to hug them, but sometimes I'd prefer to smother them, just to get a minute's peace from their wittering. The one place they never suffer is in silence.'

Nightingale: 'I don't understand how they can get so much from a massage, and so little from a conversation. How else are you supposed to get close to someone?'

Doves feel the world around them through every contact they have with it, whether it's from an emotional connection or from a scratchy pair of trousers. It's the *feelings* that will dominate their world far beyond what they see or hear. Nightingales, on the other hand, could sit on a chair of razor blades and not notice, if they were engaged in a conversation; which means that sometimes they can be so immersed in what they need to say that they'll be oblivious to the emotional state of the person they're talking . . . at. This is a difference that will bring some challenges.

A similarity that binds you is that you're sky-birds, avoiding detail wherever possible and paying little attention to rules. You'll probably be happy in a cosy chaos but there will be some down-sides, which I may be able to help with.

Cuckoos in the nest

Nightingales depend on the words they say to know what they think. This can sometimes make their conversations rambling, circuitous – even seemingly endless. It's a characteristic of them that if you seek to end their sentences for them, they'll just start over. They need to work their thoughts out verbally to know what they are; they don't seem to be able to do it in their heads. If you're in a relationship with one, you're going to be used as a talking post: they're going to need to tell you what's going on in their life – and they'll want to hear about yours, too.

The thing is, though, that Doves can be quite wordless. Because they prefer the big picture, they'll tend to be quite sparing of the detail of anything, and because they communicate so strongly through their feelings, often all you'll get is a hug – although to them they're speaking through their skin. Clearly this can lead to misinterpretations, where their Nightingale partner takes their silence for something else, and the Dove mistakes their partner's talkativeness as a device to avoid contact – 'We can hug in a minute, first I have to tell you something.' Half an hour later, they still are and the Dove is suffering from cuddle deprivation. Not good.

Doves can take a lot of satisfying. They notice every imper-fection in their environment, from draughts to lumpy pillows to coffee where the milk hasn't been warmed first. These imper-fections impact on their wellbeing far beyond other types, and they appear to be in a constant battle to either remove these imperfections, or, once they have, to use this level of hard-fought comfort as the springboard to the next level of nirvana. For their partner, it can feel as if it's a never-ending search for a place called Satisfaction, but no sooner have they arrived than it just turns out to be a stop along the way.

Nightingales can't abide silence. They'll switch a radio on and then leave the room; they'll always have the TV on 'in the back-ground' or, if all else fails, fill any space with a whistle, a hum or a song, however tuneless. A friend tells me that she has to put up with a running commentary of what her Nightingale partner is doing in the kitchen, put to song: 'I'm cooking the carrots . . . tadada . . . draining the spuds . . . doobydoo . . . pouring you a drink . . . badabing . . .' You get the idea. This need for sound means that enforced silence, like in church or a library, can be torture for them. They won't go out for a fag break to smoke; they'll just want to chat with the smokers (in fact, this can be a major obstacle for Nightingales who want to stop smoking). When it comes to shopping, they'll always want someone with them to talk through their choices – if they're alone, they'll soon make a friend out of a hapless assistant. Within the relationship, their partner needs to accept that peace will be in short supply – or else create a space for themselves within the house where they can find it. Then put a bolt on the door. And lean a chair against it.

One thing you two have in common is that you both prefer to think of things in big-picture terms, rather than get bogged down in detail. You'll be full of ideas and trust your gut instincts rather than plough through all available evidence. The upside of this is that you'll bounce along happily together, sharing the same mistakes. The downside is: you'll keep making mistakes, from not paying bills or parking tickets, to getting the dates wrong for wedding invites. You might even sometimes miss flights or booked train journeys. It's not that you're disorganised – although that's how it will look to others – it's that you don't spend enough time on the detail of what you organise to avoid making those kinds of errors. You really need a PA for your relationship. It can mean that you begin any number of projects, or point yourselves towards a host of different goals, but never seem to get very far before being distracted by something else, or failing because you didn't take action on the little things that were necessary. Something to be aware of.

Another thing you share, for the same reason, is an absence of rules. You'll both be quite slow to adopt a common way of doing something, and fail to identify rules that might make your life simpler or more straightforward. Again, this might make you appear disorganised, but it's more a case of not being particularly focused on efficiency because your mind will be on some big idea, rather than on the detail of whatever it is that you're currently involved in.

Feathers for the nest

What Doves need to know about Nightingales
Do:

Nightingales will know themselves to be loved because their partner tells them. Words are the things they believe in, often even if they are contradicted by actions – which is why they can be hurt on multiple occasions by people who sound plausible, even though you can see by what they do how untrustworthy they are. Nightingales are suckers for a silky tongue, so make sure you tell them of every positive feeling you get for them. Compliment them about anything they deserve a squeeze for – in addition to the squeeze. Ring them out of the blue just to let them hear your voice: it will mean more than you know – and be aware that saying 'I love you' won't count for much if you only say it after they do.

Get comfortable when they want to talk to you. It will probably take a while and for them is a vital part of intimacy. They feel you need to hear what is happening with them. And they probably want to hear from you what your day has been like, too – although almost certainly they'll keep interrupting and talking over you. Speaking to a Nightingale can feel like a bit of a competition for airtime!

Both of you need to hear this (but probably neither of you will listen): sit down regularly and work out who needs to do what to take care of regular relationship business, and then meet again to make sure the other one's done it. If you don't, don't blame me when you find your holiday was cancelled because neither of you remembered to pay for it, or arrange a visa.

Don't:

Do your best not to shut Nightingales up because they're going on too much, and be careful with the words you use. Nightingales can be incredibly sensitive to criticism or a harsh tone, and are brilliant at storing instances of these up and regurgitating them – even years later – so do your best not to shoot from the hip. Don't get drawn into an 'I said, you said' argument. Not only are you likely to lose, they won't let you win, because memory of conversations past is so much their territory that they won't accept anything less than a recording of what you're claiming they said. Even then, they'll claim you doctored it.

Don't expect them to care about sensation in the way you do. They won't necessarily be able to tell the difference between faux fur and the real thing – and it almost certainly won't bring them out in a rash. In your pursuit of perfect experiences you are, to no small degree, on your own: while they'll be happy to have something to talk about, don't have any hope that they're invested in it the way you are. And if you want a massage, expect to have a stroke-by-stroke commentary all the way through – just remember to 'Ooh' and 'Aah' throughout to show your appreciation.

What Nightingales need to know about Doves
Do:

Your partner will know they're loved by the way you touch them, and also by the things you do for them. Just recently I had a text message from my lovely Swan wife: 'I just went to the fridge to get a drink and found a new bottle. You did that for me, you did. And I love you for it.' I had noticed that the sparkling water she likes was nearly empty so simply replaced it with one from the cupboard – no big deal you might think, but to a Dove or Swan (both are feeling birds) that kind of thing says, 'I LOVE YOU!' as loudly as if someone said to you, 'I LOVE YOU' . . . er . . . loudly. Look for things that make their life more comfortable, pleasurable or easier, or give them experiences they can physically savour, like a hot bath, or a massage or a spa trip.

Do your best to make what you have to say more concise, and if you see your partner fidgeting, have mercy and give their ears a rest. You've probably noticed that they don't need to say as much as you – that's actually how much they'd like you to say, too. That's never going to happen, but try working on thinking some stuff through before you share it. Or get a dog and take it for a walk – let it share the burden. Hell, buy a goldfish, they're good listeners.

You probably phone your partner quite often, and that's fine. Doves tend to be in-the-moment people so probably aren't missing you the way you do them, so it doesn't mean anything that they don't call you as much. Pay attention to what they do when you do see them – they can turn into a Labrador, face-licking and all. That's how you know they love you.

Don't:
Touch means a lot to Doves, so don't forget this. Hold their hand when you're walking out with them, stroke their hair or their bum; become more aware of how often they physically connect to you – and begin to match it. You might be amazed at how much response you'll get from a simple, loving, hug. (Probably a lot more than you'll get from the love poem you so painstakingly wrote for Valentine's Day.)

Words are not the Dove's domain, and you'll find it easy to dominate conversations, win arguments and belittle them with sarcasm. Don't. What they lack in a connection with words they gain through their connection to feeling. They have an innate emotional intelligence that will often enable them to connect more with one touch than others can with a thousand words. Honour this difference. Use your talents to nourish theirs, and you'll have a wonderfully rich relationship.

Kingfisher and Peacock

Peacock: 'I don't know what it is with him. Sometimes I could parade around naked in front of him and he wouldn't notice.'

Kingfisher: 'You know, sometimes thirteen choices of colour for a living room isn't a good thing – it's a torture. I don't know which is better, I don't care which is better, I just want him to stop going on.'

For Peacocks, the world is a rich tapestry to enjoy, and maybe even add colour to. For Kingfishers, it's often something that gets in the way of enjoying the world in their head. This is a combination that works well together, in that both are ground-birds so value the details of life, and the usefulness of having rules: all that's left to agree on is who does what. The greatest challenge is learning to understand that while Peacocks thrive through their connection to the moving world around them, Kingfishers spend a lot of time blocking it out to allow them to think better.

With Kingfishers, it's important to know what their second Lovebird type was in the second quiz they took at the beginning of the book, as this can have a real bearing on how they behave in relationships. For example, if Swan came after Kingfisher, it would be a good idea to read that section as well as this one.

Cuckoos in the nest

Peacocks have a thing about time. They think you can weigh love in minutes spent with them. The flip side of this is that they also weigh the minutes you choose to be somewhere else as a debit against your love account. This can be a problem, because Kingfishers are often people who get absorbed in things, whether it's their business, hobby, sport or children. Without it having any impact on their love for their partner, they need some 'me' time. Sadly, the Peacock will think of this as their 'not me' time. That's going to need to be worked on.

Similarly, Kingfishers spend more time in their heads than they do paying attention to what's going on around them. You'll regularly catch them staring into space, or blankly at a telly, while they think big thoughts. Kingfishers might get away with this with some other types, but not sight birds, as they're all eyes. Peacocks notice everything there is to be seen around them – and that will include you only being with them in body. 'I might as well be here on my own,' is a Peacock telling you that, as far as they're concerned, these minutes aren't counting in the love weigh-in, so you'd better come outside and start being present with them. This can be an irritant for a Kingfisher. People only have one auditory channel – you're either listening to yourself on the inside, or something from the outside. Talking to themselves is a fundamental part of a Kingfisher's existence – I'd go so far as saying it's necessary for their health – so being dragged out of their heads when they're in the middle of a thought can be annoying and frustrating.

Peacocks are likely to be more vocal than the Kingfisher – unless you hit the play button about the Kingfisher's hobby or passion – and, being ground-birds, they will often feel the need to give chapter and verse on any story they're telling. If it's the Peacock who is talking at length, it'll be hard on the

Kingfisher who needs to go inside and talk to themselves about anything they're experiencing. You can bet that any conversation that extends further than a few minutes will lose them periodically as they make sense of what they're being told. This can be mistaken for a lack of interest, and you're back in quality-minutes-deficit world again.

Kingfishers might care a lot about their appearance if fashion happens to be one of the interests they get absorbed in but, otherwise, it probably won't matter much: clothes just stop them getting arrested for streaking or turning a funny colour. This could drive the Peacock to distraction. They may not expect you to be a fashion icon – that's probably more their job – but they believe that how you look is a reflection on them, so mixing spots and stripes and silk and something crocheted is tantamount to the Kingfisher wearing a sign saying: 'My partner has no taste whatsoever!' Moreover, your turnout says something about how much you care for them. Have you seen those people who dress up to go to the supermarket? That'll be sight birds. Ever turned up uninvited at someone's house and found them perfectly turned out, but going nowhere? Same again. There is no slob-mode for sight birds: to them the concept of dress-down Friday is a step towards the collapse of civilisation.

Kingfishers don't feel the cold much, or heat come to that, so clothes barely register as a survival need. Ask them what they're wearing without looking down and it'll take some thought to remember. (Peacocks can tell you down to the washing labels.) So slob-mode can often seem to be the default setting for a Kingfisher's wardrobe choice. I know one who turned up at a wedding in a morning suit and slippers. He just hadn't noticed he wasn't wearing shoes. I also saw a woman on the tube once wearing an odd-looking head band. On looking more closely, it was the sleep mask she'd shoved onto her forehead when she'd woken up. Kingfisher or Owl, I guessed.

Both of you like rules, so that's a good thing. Your life together is likely to be well ordered and regular, with jobs assigned, and probably a year planner displayed in the kitchen. You'll both take comfort from knowing where you are with all your payments and plans. Just be careful not to get so bogged down in the regularity of things that you don't let anything fresh or novel into your relationship.

Feathers for the nest

What Peacocks need to know about Kingfishers
Do:
It will really help, as a Peacock, to embrace the fact that your Kingfisher partner has a rich inner world that they are drawn into, often without realising it. If they see, hear or feel something that grabs their attention it will often cause them to go inside and talk to themselves about it – thereby cutting themselves off from what happens next. Often in conversations they'll lose track at some point while they think of something, and then play catch up when they realise you're still talking. They are often bad at remembering people's names when they're introduced because they're so busy thinking of what they're going to say that they don't hear the name spoken to them. As a consequence they call a lot of people 'mate' or 'sweetie'.

Kingfishers aren't great at the fine detail of *sensory* information, so you asking which one of four shades of apple-green they'd prefer for the bedroom walls is going to be a tough one. In fact, Kingfishers often get anxious at these kinds of questions, because for them, it's like trying to guess Ali Baba's magic word: 'Which answer will make me not look as odd as I feel right now for not being able to tell a difference – or caring about it?'

Do understand that time has little meaning to a Kingfisher. They can lose hours playing a computer game, or be bored in moments by party talk they consider trivial. It's all about the meaning of what they're doing for them, not the length of time they do it for. Learn to give them the space they need to pursue their interests without seeing it as a rejection of you, because it isn't. If you trap them in your company, they'll only retreat to the wrong side of their skull, anyway. By giving them time to be absorbed in something else, they're more likely to give you quality time when you are together.

Don't:
It will probably amaze you how a Kingfisher can sit surrounded by what you consider a visual apocalypse without noticing or caring, whereas you have to get up to straighten a picture before you can settle in a room. Don't accuse them of being a slob – most of the time they're just not seeing what's around them as they're too busy looking at the pictures going on in their heads.

Don't expect to see something that moves you, and expect your Kingfisher partner to reach for a tissue. What you see is directly connected to your emotions, so I'd expect you to react strongly to sights of beauty. A friend recounted how, on an Australian beach towards evening, several couples had gone for a walk to see the amazing sunsets the area was famous for. Most of the couples held hands or cuddled as the romance of the evening surrounded them. She looked around to do the same, and for a moment couldn't see her partner. When she looked down, however, there he was on his knees, admiring the tracks a stingray had made in the shallows! Romance does not spring readily to a Kingfisher's breast, at least not when it might with other people.

What Kingfishers need to know about Peacocks
Do:
Make an effort to ensure that when you're with your partner, you pay attention to them. They will feel themselves to be loved by the look you give them, and if that look is a glazed one because you're thinking of something else, they're going to tell. Unless you're a world-class poker player with a pokerface to match, they will read your thoughts in your face.

Another way they feel loved is by how long you spend with them. Quality time is the key here. If you spend time doing something else when you could be with them, there's a very real chance they'll take that for not wanting to be with them. This is something you'll both have to work on. The solution isn't to not have time away; it's for them to understand what it doesn't mean, and for you to work hard at getting the balance right – so, the time you're with them, you really need to be with them, in mind and body.

The way things look is likely to be important to them. Keeping the house to their standard of tidiness and cleanliness will make them happy, so why not make a habit of looking around a room before you sit down. If it looks like a weapon of mass destruction has gone off in it, do some clearing up first.

Don't:
It's a mistake thinking how good your partner looks without saying so. *They can't hear you unless your lips move.* Anything you see about them that you like, tell them – it will really help your communication. When it comes to gifts, don't fall for the line about it being the thought that counts: it's not for a Peacock, it's the gift that counts. It needs to be something they'll like, and that largely means something that 'goes' – with their wardrobe, their house or their life. Put some thought into it, you're good at that.

Don't throw clothes on just to cover your flesh. Think of yourself as an advert for your partner. In their world, people are looking at you and measuring you against them. If you're not looking up to much, what does that make your partner? If you really have no interest in clothes, let your partner choose them for you and follow their advice.

Don't forget to create experiences you can both share – and take lots of photographs. Pictures can really bring the past to life for your partner, so integrating them as part of your décor can create a wonderful link with your life together at all its stages. Make sure you include both of you in your pictures; Kingfishers are notorious for taking lots of snaps of where you went, but no sign that you were there yourselves. Both of you in that place *is* the memory, not the place on its own – that could be anybody's.

Finally, don't inhibit your partner's creativity. Peacocks are often creative – although they'll often feel they're just borrowing ideas from everyone else – and whether they express it in a hobby, like flower arranging, painting or customising motorbikes, letting that creativity into your life will make them happy. And, after all, hanging a tangerine Harley Davidson above the mantelpiece isn't much of an ask – you won't notice it's there after five minutes.

Robin and Swan

Robin: 'He never tells me he loves me. He'll grab and grope, but never shows real affection.'

Swan: 'Sometimes she can be a bit cold. She says some really nice things to me, but it'd be nice if she showed me her feelings more; her hugging me for once would be a start.'

Robins and Swans share the fact that they're both ground-birds, so order and detail will be things that they're both comfortable with. Like all similarities, this can bring some issues to be resolved, but nothing that normally figures as a major problem in a relationship. One of the great things about you is that it's unlikely your credit cards will incur late payment charges, or your car will miss a service. You are a Swiss watch of a relationship: precise, well-engineered, with all the cogs spinning in perfect time. It's the difference between you in how you connect to the world that is where the challenges come from: Robins are about sound, and Swans are about feelings. Here's an example of how that can create a challenge:

Two clients of mine (a Robin and Swan) had a massive row when he was hiring a suit for a forthcoming wedding. In the shop, the Robin tried the morning suit on and, looking in the mirror, felt the waistcoat was too big. He went out to show his wife and said, 'What do you think?' She looked up from her mobile and said, quite distractedly, he thought, 'It looks fine.' Remember, a Robin will know they're loved by the words you say *and* the tone you use. 'Fine' was a weak word to use and the tone communicated a lack of interest – meaning, for him, a lack of interest in her care of him. He said, 'Are you sure?' to give her a second chance at it. Her reassurance was no more convincing to his ears. He looked at the waistcoat's label and saw it was an extra-large. 'When have I ever been an extra-large?'– obvious code from his tone of voice that this was clearly wrong. Still distracted, she didn't pick up on what he considered a clear clue that he was unhappy. Her reply that, 'Different shops have different sizes,' sounded to him like, 'I don't care enough about you to care about this'.

When he looked back later he was amazed at the strength of his response. He had felt really hurt and carried the suit – including the tent of a waistcoat – out of the shop, silently (which is surprising) furious. At last her sensitivity to his mood, if not his tone, kicked in and she realised he was unhappy and suggested they return to change it. It took several minutes of her calm persuasion before he came down enough from his sulk to do so (thwarting his plan to look a muppet at the wedding to teach her a lesson). When they got home they had the matter out in a blazing row, with her failing to understand what she had done wrong – she'd said it looked fine! She was calm in the midst of his hurt anger until he said, 'You just didn't care enough to give a toss.' Looking back afterwards, she was amazed at the strength of *her* response. She shouted something at him and stormed out crying.

The row was still simmering on a low heat when they came to see me, both of them feeling unloved. It's not difficult to see why. The Robin has his wife's voice tones logged in his head. He knows her caring tone when he hears it, and it hadn't been used. The

Swan didn't recognise the significance of his tone, but that wasn't what made her angry. Swans show love by the acts of service they perform for their loved one. Accusing them of a lack of caring makes them feel you've failed to recognise the hundred things they do in a day to make your life nicer. That's what caused the storm with her. So, Robins, be aware that not all voice tones have a meaning to your partner, and Swans, that pointing out one thing you didn't do doesn't mean a lack of appreciation for everything else.

Cuckoos in the nest

Robins are likely to know they're loved because you tell them. And the more often, the better. They'll call you at work several times a day just to hear your voice and end it with an, 'I love you.' (Although really they'd like you to say it first because saying it after them doesn't really count.) They're very sensitive to voice tone, so can be cut to the quick by a thoughtless moment where something insensitive slips into your tone, however harmless the words might otherwise be, like saying, 'Of course you're the best' with a rising note in your voice that could be interpreted as sarcasm. Likewise, they'll have your sincere-voice tone recorded on their internal iPod, so you'd better remember to match it when you say the L word.

Swans aren't much for words; it's actions that count. Normally, they express love through touch, which can be a little misleading because they find it hard to say anything to anybody without touching them. Some of them are a sexual harassment claim waiting to happen, but for completely innocent reasons – touch to them is like punctuation; it's just part of the conversation. Another way they express affection is through the things they do for you. They will often go to great lengths to make your life more comfortable, to nurture and spoil you. Obviously, the classic error of communicating your feelings using how you like to receive those of others can create famine in the midst of plenty: the Robin can sing themselves hoarse in their love for Swans, and Swans will largely be deaf to it as they wait for some physical sign that it's true. Similarly, the Robin may have to wait for ever for sweet words of love, while reclining on the silk cushion the Swan has caringly placed under their head.

You'll often see this mismatch at gift time. The Swan will wait with baited breath to see the excitement on the face of their Robin when they unwrap the cashmere romper suit that will caress their skin while they relax watching the TV in the evening. They'll be waiting a while for that look, however: the Robin was hoping for the amazing wireless headphones they've been going on about, or those tickets to the concert of their favourite group – the flyers for which they've been leaving lying around in plain sight. The same goes for the Swan as they excitedly rip open their gift. The Robin will often be confused at how anyone can fail to get excited about a set of wifi headphones for their iPod. Of course the Robin could have got them that recliner the Swan always sits in and sighs for whenever they go in the department store, but it's only a chair – where's the excitement in that?

In the bedroom, this difference in expression can have a major effect. The Swan will be into sensuality: silk sheets, mood lighting, massage oils, feathers. The Robin will be about Barry White on the stereo, dirty talk, moans of appreciation. This is a two-way challenge. Words will distract Swans from immersing themselves in their arousal – often they'll be relatively quiet until the point of orgasm and then let rip. Their partner's words may pull them from their feelings and have the opposite effect to that which was intended. Silence, for them, can mean that they can concentrate, which is, of course, the opposite of what works for the Robin. I'm sure they'll find three days of aromatherapy massage as foreplay perfectly pleasant, but they'd get more from ten minutes of a dirty story, being told what you're going to do to them, or simply listening to the sound of you being turned on. So you can see, a balance needs to be struck, or a sequence where each gets his or her needs met, so that you can harmonise your pleasure.

A similarity between Swans and Robins is that you both like rules and detail. In most cases, because you understand the importance of rules you'll be tolerant of each other's little ways

– unless one of their rules flagrantly flouts one of yours; in which case, a summit may need to be called and the matter thrashed out at the highest level. But in most cases, it will mean that your world will be ordered and structured – it's a relationship made in Germany. It might mean that you become a little set in your ways, remorselessly moving through the years to a well-proven formula but not introducing much new into the relationship, and you may both be perfectly happy with that. If you're not, you may need to fly a little higher and look for new ways to do existing things: recruit a sky-bird friend to give you a big idea to work towards together that you'd never have thought of.

In the detail we have another similarity, which, again, in most cases doesn't cause many problems. Both of you are likely to share a similar desire to communicate information in the same-size chunks, i.e. you'll go large. This can make for many companionable, if long, evenings, sharing the ins and outs of everything. The only disparity might arise from the Robin's love of words. Some Robins only know what they're thinking by hearing it on the outside of their heads, so this, allied with their love of detail, can make them truly epic on the chatterbox scale. By comparison, Swans are likely to be the least communicative of the ground-birds, focusing their love of detail on the things that will make their, and by extension your, life more lovely. So they'll know precisely how many times to stir the spoon anti-clockwise to get your coffee just right, but they may not feel the need to read to you the names of the 732 different Colombian blends, or to have you read them. It's not a slight; it's just a difference.

Feathers for the nest

What Robins need to know about Swans
Do:
Learn to give a decent massage. Take a course – it'll repay you massively. The feeling of you paying attention to their body will mean a lot, let alone the feeling of the massage itself.

Give Swans time to catch up with you as you speak. They can

be a little overwhelmed by the machine gun that can be your conversation. Like a good red wine, Swans need time to get to room temperature, so pace yourself.

Pay attention to the things your partner does for you. Every one of them is the equivalent of a play list you've painstakingly put together for them. Show your appreciation by doing the things for them that they do for you; just telling them of your appreciation won't cut it.

In bed, be aware that silence does for Swans what Des O'Connor in the background does for you (okay, I took a wild stab there – replace it with *your* favourite smoochy singer). Noise can distract them from concentrating on how you're making them feel.

Don't:
If Swans are busy, don't keep ringing them. Swans will like to concentrate in the moment and a phone call can take half an hour to recover from. If you need to hear their voice, record them saying something on your phone.

Don't expect them to sit through a second-by-second recollection of your day, including the alternative route you had to take home. Comfort is everything to them, and they will start to squirm as their bum goes numb and their ears start to bleed.

Don't sing in their ear while you're getting down and dirty on the sofa, they like to put their awareness in their skin, so words can just distract them.

Don't read them directions while they're driving; just tell them where to turn and when – with plenty of notice. Swans can find their way anywhere they've been before, but verbal instructions won't mean much, and maps can be a challenge. 'Turn left back there' is the kind of instruction you get from them. Satnav has probably saved a lot of relationships.

What Swans need to know about Robins
Do:
Find some music you both like, because it's going to be playing in the background of most things that are going on. Leading on

from this, be aware that when your partner says, 'I love this song, it reminds me of us,' there is something really important in the lyrics. Listen and make a comment; don't just give them a squeeze and tell them how sweet that is.

They will adore hearing you say you love them. Surprise them with a phone call every now and again. You know the feelings you get sometimes when you look at them? Verbalise them and notice the response you get.

Often Robins will want you there to help them make a decision, but it might feel that you're someone to talk at rather than to. It doesn't mean that your opinion isn't important just because they're not listening. They need to get their thoughts straight first, so wait until they seem to have done before you contribute.

Don't:

Sex is not the answer to every bad mood, row or poor football result for Robins, so don't think it is. Physical contact does not solve the world's problems in everyone's eyes – including your partner's. They think that sweet-talking is a much better way, so learn some of their lines.

If Robins need to say something out loud to get their thoughts in order, don't interrupt them or finish their sentences, even if you know where their thoughts are headed; they'll only go back to the start.

You tend to be an in-the-moment person, so whether you're missing your partner or not can depend on how absorbed your attention is at that particular time. Don't get annoyed by their need to hear from you, and do be careful with your voice tone.

Don't tell them to shut up when you're making love, and don't forget to make some noise yourself. The sounds of your appreciation are their equivalent of a sensuous massage for you.

Owl and Swift

Swift: 'He's so intense and moody. He can go quiet for hours and then try and tell me nothing's wrong. And everything is an inquisition. He wants to know the ins and outs of everything.'

Owl: 'He's a bit superficial. It's all about how things look on the surface, not about what really matters about something. Sometimes I leave the cushions messy, just to annoy him. And it does!'

As a pair, you two can have a lot going for you; there're just some things you need to be aware of. The first is that you're both sky-birds, so are unlikely to run a very tight ship. Neither of you are going to want to do the organising of anything, or take care of the boring everyday stuff. As long as you're both okay with a bit of chaos, you're probably going to manage. The other thing is that Owls tend to seek meaning in everything, whereas Swifts are much more about how things look. This can easily lead to name calling, with the Swift feeling their partner is a killjoy, while they get the label of 'shallow' thrown at them. Owls are a bit of a special category, in that the way they connect with the world, from reading a paper to falling in love, will be strongly influenced by the bird type that was their second in the quiz they took at the beginning of the book. So, if Swift came behind Owl in quiz 2, for example, I'd advise also reading that section too, and how Swifts get on with Swifts.

Cuckoos in the nest

Owls live in their heads. A lot. They can spend hours not watching a film, apparently absorbing it in front of the TV while actually miles away and deep in thought. For every moment they connect to the world outside, they spend ten exploring the world inside. Sometimes the difference between the two can blur. I don't mean they're crazy – I'm one of them, so I wouldn't suggest that, would I? – it just means that they can say something in their head and think they've shared it with you, or they can work out a situation and begin to act as if you're a party to their solution, without actually mentioning it to you.

Owls like to know the inner workings of things that take their interest – from radios, to computers, to you. They are likely to want to know your thoughts – and sometimes it can feel a bit of an inquisition, but it's just an expression of something you should prize, because if an Owl loses interest in you or stops finding you interesting, it could signal the beginning of the end of the relationship.

Emotions are something most Owls work hard to avoid, unless Dove came a close second in the second quiz they took at the beginning of the book, in which case they might be okay. Most can feel uncomfortable just watching a chick-flick – even if they're a chick. This can make them hard to get close to and their partners can sometimes be left feeling that they're the only one connected to an experience they should both be sharing. Some Owls wear this control as a badge, which, in my opinion, is a limitation and one I work with clients a lot to remove. As the trust and intimacy grows between you, your relationship can provide a safe environment for them to blossom emotionally, but they'll need support and encouragement. What mustn't happen is for them to use their control of emotions as a sign of superiority and undermine the more emotional connectedness of their partner by labelling them soft, weak or flaky. To do so would create an even greater barrier to intimacy, as well as damaging the self-esteem of all but the most resilient of partners.

Both of you are sky-birds so detail will bore you, and it will take an effort to make your house run without the regular hassles of failing to put the bins out, forgetting to pay bills and remembering to do the shopping. It's also likely that you won't pay attention to things you should, which could end up with you deprived of the vote or imprisoned for not paying your council tax. As long as you recognise that you're as bad as each other, you can avoid this becoming a reason for name-calling and blame. You both need an organiser, for a start.

Swifts depend on what they see. If something is hidden from them, they can question its existence – like knowing they are loved. One of the ways they know they're loved – which is likely to be particularly important with this combination – is the way you look at them. With Owls often being a bit of a closed book, this can be a problem. Along with Kingfishers, Owls tend to be the poker players of the types contained in this book, so Swifts can be left confused by an apparent absence of evidence as to an Owl's feelings for them. Another important thing for Swifts is the amount of time you spend together. Choosing to spend time away can be taken as a sign that you'd rather do something else than be with them. Owls will often be people who spend time – mainly on their own – involved in an interest or hobby, or involved in something going on in their head. Either way, their partner can be left feeling unloved through this perceived lack of attention.

Appearance is important to Swifts, too. They'll often have an interest in design or fashion, but even if not, they'll have a feeling for how things should be to look 'right'. If it's personal appearance then this might become a bit of a battlefield. Owls probably won't care that much about what they wear – they'll often buy more of one thing they like to save them the trouble of shopping, and stick to the same colours and styles for years – they'll have a strong sense of what works for them and be resistant to change. Swifts, on the other hand, are likely to be swayed by what's 'in' and so be in a state of perpetual wardrobe refreshing. Because the appearance of their partner is taken to be a reflection on them, this can lead to fine tussles between them outside Gap.

Feathers for the nest

What Swifts need to know about Owls
Do:

As a result of this book, I hope you'll have some ideas about how your Owl expresses their love for you, so – look for them. Often they'll be subtle, but they should be observable. But they probably won't be the things you want them to do for you – unless they're reading this with you and are picking up some pointers (after all, that's the point of the book).

Give them time to be silent. It's likely that they'll need to process things after any event – when they come home from work is a prime example. If you draw them out of themselves too quickly, it may annoy them and they'll be distracted for ages afterwards. Now, this can create a conundrum because Owls quite commonly have trouble sleeping because they can't switch their minds off – if they have a problem, they'll keep thinking until they find an answer – and getting them to voice their worries can help to purge their inner dialogue, so you have to develop a sense of when it's right to get them to come out and talk, and when to leave them to it. (Good luck with that.)

You're both far more excited by big-picture thinking than focusing on facts, so you're suited in that respect. However, the Swift is likely to be more prone to flights of fancy than the Owl, who will need more of a structure, or a plan to make sense, before they'll consider it. So, make sure what you're proposing does make sense, otherwise it'll be shot down in flames.

Don't:

People often accuse Owls of not paying attention. They are – just not usually to what you want them to. They can be sitting happily in a living room that looks like a bomb site, deeply engaged in a task like reading or working on a computer. For you, doing anything surrounded by mess (unless it's related to the task) is likely to be impossible. For them, it's irrelevant because they simply won't be paying attention. Don't nag them about it because you won't change it – you'll just give yourself wrinkles.

Don't make yourself miserable trying to change them. Owls can be extremely stubborn about what they've decided is right for them, so going on about their clothes choices, food choices or fun choices will only make them consider their partner choices. The way to change an Owl is to present them with an idea and leave it with them to germinate (they'll probably end up claiming it was theirs). If the idea takes root, well done. If it doesn't, leave it be and fight another day.

Time works differently for you two. Owls can lose days if they're absorbed in something, and you might feel as if you've ceased to exist for them. You haven't, but you'll definitely be blurry. It's not about love. I should write that in upper case. IT'S NOT ABOUT LOVE. Just because you will go to huge efforts to make sure you can spend quality time with your Owl partner as a way of showing you love them doesn't mean that they see it that way, too. Don't think they care less about you because they care less than you do about how much time you spend together.

What Owls need to know about Swifts
Do:

Okay, the news is that most people will find you a challenge to live with. Absolutely worth the effort; but a challenge, nevertheless. You might feel that you're low maintenance, but that can be part of the problem. You tend to care so little about your surroundings that sometimes your partner will feel that that's all they are to you – part of the furniture. You really do need to work on coming out of your head and paying attention to your partner. Set an alarm! Anything to focus you in the moment, and give them the full focus of your care. Read this book and learn how your partner recognises love by what you do, and make sure you do those things, otherwise one day you're going to come to your senses and realise they moved out two weeks ago.

Your partner will know or feel that you love them by the looks you give them, the things you buy for them, and the amount of time you choose to spend with them. Each of these needs to be attended to. It's quite possible that you don't let a lot of your emotions show on the surface: the person you love is a great person to ease that rule with. I know how passionate you can feel about them – imagine them being able to see on your face what you feel on the inside. Imagine it, and practise it; you'll be amazed at the effect it has. The next thing you'll be good at: when a Swift receives a gift, it needs to fit. If it's clothes, that's obvious; but this is more about fitting their taste. If they receive something they wouldn't give houseroom to, they can get quite affronted because to them it means the giver of the present doesn't 'get' them. For Swifts, the way they make their outside look is representative of what the inside is like, so if you buy something that clashes with this, it means you don't see them the way they want you to. Being an Owl, I think you'll be pretty good at working out what your partner likes and what would suit them. Work at it, because it's a major points-scorer for you.

The last thing, I've already spoken about. This is probably where you'll struggle. There are likely to be things you like to do that take you away from the world: hobbies, interests, books, anything that lets you live inside your head and get absorbed by something. It's important that you realise that any moment away from your Swift partner that they don't think is necessary is seen as a vote by you for spending time without them. So make sure you measure your day or week, and connect fully and completely with them within that time. And that doesn't mean pretending to watch the TV with them while you think about stuff: Swifts are very observant; they will notice.

Don't:

Disappearing into your head for hours at a time is a 'no'. This is such an easy thing for you to do – often without you realising it. When you're with your partner, do your very best to stay in the present moment. Time together won't count if the lights are on but you're not home.

Don't forget to connect with your Swift, and share emotions with them. If Owls are single for a long time it can become quite a challenge to open up their lives to a partner. It's worth the effort, however, because otherwise Owls so often drift into a grey world where emotions are kept at a distance.

If you're an Owl who isn't comfortable with their emotions, don't make a virtue out of not feeling things – you'll come across as a robot, or heartless. A relationship is a place to begin to relax and let those things out. It's the only way for intimacy to develop.

Dove and Peacock

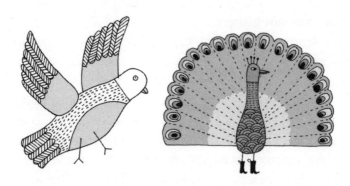

Peacock: 'She is so boring. I want to go out and do things but she is always too tired. If she makes the effort she'll moan about where we go. The chair will be uncomfortable or there's a draught. After I finish work, I have to make a real effort to be with her and all she does is fall asleep on me. She doesn't appreciate me.'

Dove: 'He doesn't understand that if he doesn't get home until 9 p.m. I'm past it. I just get to the point where I don't want to talk or do things. He is really inconsiderate.'

As a couple you have two areas of difference that are going to have an impact on your time together. The first is that one of you is a sight bird, and the other a feeling bird. This puts you at opposite ends of the spectrum when it comes to pace. Peacocks tend to live life at speed, and this is reflected in their pace of speech as well as their choice of car. Doves tend to move through life at a more relaxed rate most of the time, and communicate at a similar, measured speed. Peacocks pick ideas up quickly, Doves pick up things they can physically practise or by experience. The second is that one of you is a sky-bird, and the other a ground-bird. Which doesn't mean that one of you is airy fairy and the other tightly wound. Sometimes it might just feel that way.

Cuckoos in the nest

Peacocks are often the kind of people who are always on the go; they have to be doing something and never seem to sit down. Doves can't match them. I don't want to give the impression that Doves are lazy because they're not, but they tend to need a run-up to things and often have a smaller fuel tank of energy. They'll be happy being active, especially in bursts, but when the tank is empty the collapse can be sudden and spectacular. Push a Dove past the point of tiredness and you will see a person in pain. Peacocks will often start the day bright-eyed and bushy-tailed, going from 0 to 60 in seconds. Don't even try to bring your Dove partner with you. They need time, space, cajoling, coffee, a defibrillator. Do some small act of kindness for them which makes getting up easier to face and they will really appreciate it. Making this area work is about pacing. Acknowledging that each of you travels at different speeds is the first step to working out how you can meet in the middle.

As I explained in the individual pen portraits in Part Two, Peacocks are very particular about time. They often confuse quantity for quality, and think that living in each other's pockets is an ideal to aim for. Running a pub or some other joint enterprise might really appeal to them. They will demonstrate commitment by rearranging their diary to have time with you at the end of the day. Doves might actually get grumpy about this if they have gone past their energy threshold.

Peacocks need to be aware that because Doves are people who are very oriented in the 'now', they will not miss them in the same way. They do not appear to pine as much or as soon as Peacocks. The absence of 'Dove connectedness' tends to build more slowly than being 'out of sight' does for a Peacock. For

Doves, being out of sight is, to some degree, out of mind, but it does not mean that they love any less – just differently.

For Peacocks, 'being there' is paramount. I had a friend whose Peacock girlfriend had an affair. He discovered it only days before he was due to go on a business trip that would keep him away from home for three weeks. They talked it through and agreed to attempt reconciliation. She promised that the affair was over, and was in floods of tears as he left her in the departure lounge at the airport. He rang when he landed in America to find her still crying from how much she was missing him. Four days later, she was seeing the other man again. Her only explanation was that her boyfriend 'wasn't there for her'.

Peacocks tend to focus on detail, whereas Doves are about the big picture. As a consequence, Doves will avoid tasks they view as boring – which is anything involving repetition, a need to pay close attention, or anything fiddly. Peacocks are likely to be quite particular about how they like a lot of things done, whereas the only area where Doves are likely to be similar to them in this regard is where it affects their comfort.

Peacocks are highly visual and find it quite easy to think about the future, but being a ground-bird they tend not to place too much emphasis on planning, which is handy because the future-looking tendencies of sky-birds is reduced in Doves, whose emphasis on feelings makes the present moment more important to them. In this respect, you two are quite balanced.

Feathers for the nest

What Doves need to know about Peacocks
Do:
Make sure you keep in touch with your Peacock during the day. If you can pop in for lunch that's great; if you can't, Skype is the next best thing. If you text, send a photo – you may have changed your appearance since morning.

Gifts are likely to be quite important to your partner – not that Peacocks are materialistic; just that gifts can be a sign they were in your thoughts when you were apart. However, the gift itself can be tricky because the Peacock is likely to read a lot into it. If it isn't their taste, they're likely to take it quite personally because to them it means you don't 'get' them. And they're not the kind of people to wear a Christmas jumper to be kind – the next time you see it, it's probably going to be a dog blanket. Listen for when they give you gift clues (they will), and stick to those rather than take a chance. It's also a good idea to pay attention to what gifts they show most pleasure receiving and surprise them every now and again.

Peacocks love sharing experiences: a trip to the theatre or the dog track, it doesn't matter – the ability to talk about what they saw with you will be a bonding experience. That cuddle you shared on Ayers Rock was a great moment for you, but it's the sunset they'll reminisce about, not the physical connection a Dove would remember. It was Peacocks (and Swifts) who probably coined the term 'quality time'. Quality time is what you spend with them, the rest is just time.

If at all possible, let the Peacock feel they influence your wardrobe, and pay attention to what messages they might feel you're sending by what you wear.

If you've been together any time at all, you probably don't need me to tell you that Peacocks have 'funny little ways'. They're called rules, and are more important to them than you can imagine. For many Peacocks, there is a connection between the rules being followed and the sun continuing to rise – at least pretend that's true, and you'll get some idea of why they leap for your throat at what you feel is a minor transgression of them. As someone experienced in relationships with ground-birds – by that I mean a lot have left me – I strongly advise you to take note of their rules and follow them. It's by far the easier way. And if you can do so without taking the mickey out of them, that'll be even better.

Finally, leave them to do the planning; they'll be much better at it, and you don't enjoy it anyway. This doesn't give you permission to opt out of things entirely. Pick some things the relationship needs to keep going – like paying bills – and make it your job to do it. If you can, find a way to idiot-proof the jobs, because otherwise you'll find a way to forget. It's not your fault; it's the way you came out of the oven.

Don't:
Peacocks tend to find words faster than you, and probably pick up things they're told or see more quickly, too. Don't think they're cleverer just because of that. Your intelligence tends to be practical, and you learn best by doing something. Often your emotional intelligence will be superior and you'll see things in social situations that pass others by.

You know yourself to be loved by how much you're touched, and what is in the touch. Don't think your Peacock doesn't love you just because they don't reach out across the restaurant table to stroke your hand. Look for how they're looking at you – that's their equivalent. And don't get jealous if you see them touching someone else in conversation – you do it all the time, and realise that the person they touch probably isn't responding the way you would.

What Peacocks need to know about Doves
Do:
Give your Dove the time to warm up – in everything. If you pressure them with your pace, they'll eventually feel inferior. It's not uncommon to find the feeling birds feeling the lesser partner in their relationships, which takes an awful lot out of what the relationship should be. You could really help them realise their potential, so nurture your Dove's strengths, just as they probably spend a lot of time nurturing yours.

You will have ways you like doing things, which sometimes can get in the way – I know Peacocks who would rather be late for something important than leave the house untidy. Realise that your way of doing things is just one way, not THE way, and try to be flexible.

Remember that doing things for your Dove, like cooking for

them or giving them a back rub, is the same as them buying you a gift or taking you somewhere nice. Your partner will know that they're loved by you by the acts that show you care. Pay attention to what they seem to value you doing – sometimes they'll seem quite trivial – and just do more of them. Astonishing as it may seem, making your Dove a drink before bed could be more important to them than that lovely bit of bling you bought them.

Your partner is probably very tactile; it's an important way of exchanging information, and they'll infer a lot from your touch, so if you stroke them, do it with thought. Sometimes a pat can seem condescending or dismissive; always communicate love and affection through your fingers, whether it's taking their hand as you cross the road, to patting their bum as they reach for the peas in the freezer.

Hopefully, you've read your partner's profile, so you know what I mean by a 'self' or 'others-referenced' feeling bird. Observe them for where you think they stand within this continuum, and adjust your behaviour accordingly. If they're an 'others', make sure you show lots of appreciation for the effort they put into making you happy. If they're a 'self', treat them to a back rub with something that smells nice on a regular basis (I don't mean roast chicken). With 'selfs', they probably won't give you much choice, but at least now you know why they're so demanding.

Planning is likely to be both more important to you and something you're better at – so make that your job. Doves have the attention span of a goldfish when it comes to details, so anything that requires form filling or repetition is likely to be done badly or too late. You may not enjoy it any more than they do, but you will be better at it, so it's probably healthier for the relationship that you suck it up and do it than use it as a thing to beat them up over (you might score some points over them forgetting to send a cheque, but it's both of you who are't going on that holiday).

Don't:
Just because Doves don't get as excited as you about the future, it doesn't mean it doesn't matter to them. They just don't see

what's ahead as clearly as you do. What matters to them more is what is happening now, so don't put off all enjoyment now for a later pay-off, as it will make them despondent. With a Dove, you always need some nice things in the present and near future to tide them over until they get to the big thing you've been planning all year.

Don't think that they're less clever than you just because they take longer to understand something. Their style of learning is very different to yours, but they have ways of knowing things that may seem a mystery to you. Trust their instincts, even when they lack the evidence to prove something on which you usually base your decisions.

By the same token, don't crush all their dreams with your need for detail. Doves love playing with ideas and trust possibilities more than you do. By letting them have their head, sometimes it can inject something into your life you would otherwise miss – and that would be a loss.

Finally, don't judge them too strongly on their appearance: comfort often matters more than style. How they look is not actually about you. Oh no, it isn't.

Swan and Kingfisher

Kingfisher: 'He always seems to make such a fuss over everything. A bump in the road makes him yelp, banging his elbow seems like a reason to go to A&E. He's so damn sensitive – he needs to man up a bit.'

Swan: 'She has got to be the most unemotional person on the planet. I can be sobbing my way through something on the telly, and it's like she's watching a party political broadcast. I just don't get how she stays so detached – even from me.'

There's no doubt this combination comes with a few challenges. Swans belong to the bird types who connect to the world passionately through their senses – sometimes being overwhelmed by their feelings – and always aware of theirs and yours. Kingfishers, on the other hand, are of the type who sit and watch; who filter their experiences through their thoughts and approach any emotion with the caution of someone considering sitting naked on a snake. With one of you ruled by your heart, one by your head, there are some things you need to know. On the plus side, you both prize order, detail and rules, so while you might see the world in very different ways, you probably won't make a mess when you do disagree.

Cuckoos in the nest

Swans like things to be cosy, both physically and emotionally, wherever they are. They hate bad atmospheres and are often the diplomat of the family – although, on occasion, they can also be the fire that needs putting out. Kingfishers are very different. They can be quite oblivious to what is going on around them, to the extent that they'll be happily reading a paper in the midst of a Christmas day family row. With the Swan's propensity for smoothing the feathers of others, and the Kingfisher's ability to ignore the need, you can have two people living in two very different situations, with the Swan probably feeling unsupported because the energy they're expending isn't even faintly matched by their partner.

On the comfort front, Swans rule. It can often seem as if they're never quite comfortable enough, so life appears a never-ending series of adjustments to cushions and mattresses (my wife is a Swan and we've tried at least four mattress toppers – before her, I didn't even know such things existed); a daily series of costume changes to reflect the minute changes to their personal micro-climate; and the pursuit of the perfect coffee machine or waffle toaster. For a Kingfisher who just wants to watch the TV, this constant fidgeting and interruption can distract even them, especially as they'll be regularly invited to play the game of, 'Where's that draught coming from?' The draft could freeze the Kingfisher to their recliner and it wouldn't interfere with their viewing. (And sometimes, it'll feel preferable.)

Kingfishers spend a lot of time thinking. They can look as if they're with you, but actually they're miles away, deep underground in their mental bunker working through what's happening in their life, or just, well, thinking. As Jackie Chan said in the recent version of *The Karate Kid*: 'Being still and doing nothing are two very different things.' Thinking for a Kingfisher is like a hobby. (Unless they have a hobby, in which case thinking about *that* can be their life.) You know those people who lock themselves away with their collections of Victorian dog-food tins? Probably Kingfishers. If something interests them, it can consume them quite obsessively, and either last a lifetime, or blow itself out in a hurricane of passion, before being replaced by the next thing that captures the Kingfisher's interest. For the Swan, unless they share the passion, this can be quite displacing, with the feeling that the emotion that should be pointed their way is being lavished on something else – or someone else, if the hobby is a community thing.

I mentioned earlier how Kingfishers avoid their feelings – unless they're expressed via something 'safe', like their hobby or their football team. As a therapist, my opinion is that many Kingfishers learned in childhood to avoid feelings they didn't like by filtering them through their thoughts, or that they simply didn't get much chance to use them because they didn't interact with others much – which is why it's important for them to look at their results from quiz 2 at the start of the book, and read about their second type, because that's often where you'll find the clues about how they love. It's as if they began life as one bird, and changed into a Kingfisher later, but their original preference still drives some of the things they like or dislike. This means that a Kingfisher with a Robin as a second type might behave quite differently to a Kingfisher with Peacock as the second.

The reluctance of most Kingfishers to engage emotionally can be a critical difficulty in this relationship, because for Swans, feelings are where they live and how they connect to the world. My prediction is that this is where the relationship will succeed or fail, in the degree to which the Kingfisher avoids emotional connection, the degree to which they're prepared to risk opening up, and the degree to which the Swan can tolerate living in an emotional desert if they don't.

One similarity that can help is that both of you like to deal in facts and to base decisions on tangible things. You'll also have rules for how things should be done. This can usually be a good thing because you'll evolve a way of running the relationship with clear boundaries about who does what, and how they do it. The only difficulty arises if the two of you have rules that run counter to each other's, and which you believe really strongly in. Both of you can be incredibly stubborn if you find something to dig in about, and for ground-birds, their rules are one of those things. This can lead to a kind of cold war, where each party seeks to exert their rule on the other. I stayed with a couple once where one had a rule that the house should never be left in a mess, and the other felt it was the rudest thing in the world to be late. I watched, smiling, as one of them was literally still wiping a surface as the other one was pulling them out the door by their foot.

You will need to thrash these things out, because the world won't actually stop spinning if a rule is broken – it just feels that way to you. It can be a good thing to try other people's ways of doing things, just to recognise that your rules are not the be all and end all, and to help you become a little less set in your ways.

Feathers for the nest

What Swans need to know about Kingfishers
Do:
Read the Lovebird type that came second when your partner took quiz 2 at the start of the book, as often that will give you clues about how they love and know they're loved: e.g. if their second type was a Peacock, then it's likely that some of the sight bird areas of their life will be important to them, like your appearance, or how much time you spend with them. Without this, it is difficult to predict what they need because they keep so much inside them. There will be times when they'll be loving you deeply without you knowing it, because their internal world can be so strong that they forget you're not in there with them. You might give them a squeeze to show you love them, and they'll reciprocate, but only in their minds. If they're reading this book with you, point out to them what they do that makes you feel loved.

Actually, even if they're not, tell them anyway. Hopefully they'll take the hint.

Swans will often show they love their partner by the way they look after them. Unfortunately for you, you're living with someone who won't notice much to do with their physical comfort, so a lot of your effort will seem wasted. Kingfishers will live seemingly oblivious to the heaven that surrounds them – obviously your version of it – and you just have to trust that they love you when you don't find them reciprocating. Listen and watch instead for how they love you.

Leave them time to think, and don't overwhelm them with requests for feedback about your feelings; for most Kingfishers, that's like someone speaking Klingon. You live in a very rich world of feelings, sensations and emotions. Do encourage them to explore that world with you, but you are walking a tightrope because such things make most of them feel uncomfortable. Patience is going to be the key.

Don't:
Don't be satisfied with a partner who makes a virtue out of not feeling things. Long-term, this will just drag the fire out of you – and there is so much more in your partner that is worth bringing out. So if they have an idea that they're unfeeling, don't pander to it or join in creating it. And don't make the mistake of believing it yourself – you need to believe they feel, however buried it is, for you to have the hope of the emotional intimacy you dream of. It's there, but with many Kingfishers you just have to dig with a very delicate spoon.

One of your compatibilities is that you both like to know where you stand before you make a decision – in other words, you'll only commit to a plan when there is evidence to support it; no flying by your instincts for you two, you like hard evidence. The one thing this can lead to, however, is a relationship that over time settles into a predictable rut with few surprises, novelties or new experiences. This might suit you both, but it might be worth just occasionally throwing in something spontaneous to shake things up a bit. Even if you have to plan the spontaneity!

What Kingfishers need to know about Swans
Do:
Say 'I love you' out loud. Like you, I'm a thinking bird (Owl) and in the Lovebird quiz my second strongest bird type was the Nightingale – so I show my love through what I say. What I learned from hard experience was to remember to say 'I love you' out loud when I think it – and also, if I have a moment of appreciation for my Swan wife's body, say, to do what she would recognise as appreciation, by touching her. What I strongly recommend is that you pay attention to what your Swan partner does to express their love for you, and what they show appreciation for you doing – and do lots of it, *outside* your head. Thinking 'I love you' or imagining stroking your partner is not the same as actually saying or doing that. People are not mind-readers.

Swans know they're loved by touch – notice how often they touch you. Take any opportunity to reciprocate; just holding hands means more to them than you'd imagine. Giving them a massage at the end of a hard day will score you massive points. But be aware that how they're feeling is everything to them in terms of intimacy, so if you're interested in getting jiggy with it, make sure you've paced their mood.

The other way Swans know they're loved is by the things you do for them. You know how sensitive they are to everything? Well, there's an opportunity in their high maintenance-ness. As often as you can, remember to look around you and ask yourself, 'Is there something I could do here that would make their life more comfortable, special, or make them feel pampered?' They're like cats – look for what makes them purr and do more of it.

Don't:
It can feel as if the task of getting your partner to a place where they're satisfied with life is never-ending. It is. You can put up with a far greater range of environmental challenges, like draughts,

temperature fluctuations, peas under the mattress or itchy labels in a shirt, than they can. And if they reach a moment where everything is perfect, it'll just raise the bar for what they want more of more often. You'll just have to get used to that, and avoid making it something you ridicule them for. Kingfishers can be inclined to wear their lack of sensitivity as a badge and use it to make Swan partners feel like they're being precious, or whingy. Do your very best to avoid this, because not being able to express their experience of the world to you will make Swans unhappy and drive a wedge between you. If they don't feel they can mention something they're uncomfortable about without you accusing them of being a princess – or prince – it'll be something else that makes them itch – and they are unlikely to wait seven years to scratch you out of their life.

So, on the theme of sensitivity, if you do have problems expressing your feelings, avoid making yourself even more emotionally withdrawn by kidding yourself that it's a better way of being. Don't run from the feelings your partner offers you – embrace them, because it will enrich both your life and the life of your partner – and give your relationship a much greater chance of success.

Owl and Robin

Owl: 'Sometimes I'm screaming in my head because I can't hear myself think. He goes on and on, even when he knows I've got the point. He's like a broken record.'

Robin: 'It would be nice if, once in a while, I felt I was sharing her life and she was interested in mine. It's like talking to a brick wall, sometimes.'

My dear grandfather used to say that things are not supposed to be easy, just possible. He may have had you two specifically in mind, because you've probably wondered on more than one occasion what on earth keeps you together. (Unless you only met yesterday, in which case you've probably only wondered it the once.) You are fundamentally different in two ways, both of which I've found to be important factors in relationship difficulties. But there's hope, because clearly something is on your side or you wouldn't have got as far as you have.

Cuckoos in the nest

When it comes to the sounds we pay attention to, they come in two ways: they're either coming from the outside world, or we're creating them ourselves inside our heads. The thing is, we can only pay attention to one of these ways at a time. Robins listen to what is coming from the outside – in fact, many of them have little awareness of any thinking done on the inside, so they'll often talk out loud to *themselves* in order to sort their thoughts out. Owls, however, pay great attention to a near constant dialogue that they generate inside their heads about what's happening on the outside. (You can probably already see where this is heading.) If an Owl is busy talking to themselves and their Robin interrupts, it blocks their thinking and can frustrate or annoy them. Whereas if a Robin isn't able to use their partner as a sounding board for their 'thinking', they're left talking to thin air and if the Owl glazes over, the Robin feels unloved.

Owls have a reputation for being 'deep' because they rarely share what is most important to them unless they feel really safe doing so. Most also feel vulnerable in the face of emotions – their own or another's – so usually do their best to avoid them. They'll avoid rows – their partners will call it sulking – because strong emotions scare them, and will just withdraw into themselves unless they're strongly provoked, in which case their temper can be awesome. The idea of losing emotional control is often quite frightening for them, and they tend to see it as a dichotomy: feelings will either overwhelm them, or not exist, so the appearance of one to any degree is mistrusted in case it's the herald of some kind of feeling-quake that will destroy their world. This can make Owls seem distant and reserved, and that's how they usually feel themselves.

Robins can seem the complete reverse, in that they'll often be found sharing intimate details of their life with complete strangers. It seems like anything that comes to mind is expressed on the outside without any filtering – which can make for some funny moments where they put their foot in it by loudly blurting out something inappropriate at dinner, for example.

The second big difference is that Owls are sky-birds and Robins are ground-birds. Owls need things to make sense, have great curiosity and tend to be very creative in problem-solving and coming up with ideas. The downside to this is that they have a low boredom threshold and details are one of the primary things that bore them, so they'll come up with a plan but often won't see it through properly. This is a potential area of strength for you both because Robins are good at details: many successful business partnerships are based on this combination, with the Owl providing the inspiration, and the Robin the perspiration. For that to work, the Robin has to give the Owl their head sometimes, and not drag them down with a need to evidence their hunches or work out precisely how their idea will work. If they don't, the Owl can feel undermined and suffocated. On the other hand, the Owl needs to recognise that Robins need to be talked through the plan in stages, because the big picture will probably overwhelm them.

Both in business and in relationships, one key thing is that the Robin needs to put the brakes on their sharing of detail, because it will drive their Owl mad. Robins have no 'news headlines' version of events; more than any other bird type, they will give you chapter and verse on everything. Robins need to learn some verbal précis skills or their Owls will need a place of refuge they can retreat to with a lock on the inside, or a hobby that doesn't involve or interest their partner. (In this instance, don't think of it as a hobby – think of it as a life preserver.)

The thing about ground-bird Robins, other than their love of detail, is that rules are very important to them. Robins will run their lives with a number of 'laws' that guide them. And, like all ground-birds, their rules are THE rules and the world would simply be a better place if everybody followed them. Big problem. Huge. Sky-bird Owls are so busy thinking that half the time they don't pay attention to what they're doing, plus they don't find rules necessary in the first place. A Robin's response to this flagrant dismissal of what makes the world go round is to remind the Owl of them, over and over again – 'If I've told you once . . .' is their likely refrain. To the Owl, it's like living with the rule police, and it will cause them to disappear even deeper into their heads, or leave them feeling like they're about to be ambushed in their own homes over any and every lapse from some invisible perfect standard. (That made me sound like an Owl living with a ground-bird, didn't it? Ahem . . .)

Feathers for the nest

What Robins need to know about Owls
Do:
Your Owl partner lives in a world of their own that doesn't always mesh with yours. You've probably noticed that they can stare into space for ages, and realised there are many times they haven't heard a thing you've said. They need silence. I expect you walk into the quiet kitchen and turn on the radio. There was a reason they'd left it off. Respect their need for quiet; they're as busy with the thoughts in their heads as you are when you're in a conversation.

Break what you have to tell them into smaller chunks and give them time to digest what you've said. If they glaze over make the chunks smaller. It's not that they're not interested – in fact, it can be the opposite and what you're telling them is so interesting they need to think about it, so give them the chance.

Most Owls are uncomfortable with feelings: even watching a sad film can send them down the shops for something they've suddenly remembered that they need. As a Robin, if you are upset about something, it's likely you're going to want to talk it through with them, and your main need is just to express it, to be heard. Because Owls are going to want you to stop being upset as soon as possible, they'll probably go into problem-solving mode and suggest solutions. We both know this is a waste of time until you've vented. Just remember that they're doing this because they love you and want you to feel better, and this is their way of doing it.

Don't:
In terms of how Owls know that they're loved, it really depends on what their second strongest type was when they took the

Lovebirds quiz at the start of the book, so it's a good idea to read what I've said about that type too, and how it combines with the Robin. Between this and that one, you should get a good sense of your partner and how best to work with them. For example, if your partner's second strongest Lovebird was the Nightingale then, like you, they're likely to find some things related to sound important to them – and may be more talkative than most other Owls. The key thing to remember is that they guard their feelings and will see losing control of their emotions as weakness. Hold onto the fact that they love you, even though they'll often only be expressing it on the inside and will be leaving you guessing.

Don't waste your time taking them shopping, especially if you don't have a clear idea what you're looking for. To be any help at all, they need a target to aim for, but even then what *you* really need is a friend to bounce thoughts off. Owls will research what they need before they go into town, want nobody to help them or talk to them, and try not to have to try anything on. Does that sound like your idea of fun shopping?

What Owls need to know about Robins
Do:
Robins know they're loved by being told it – and they like to be told it a lot. That's easy, isn't it? But it doesn't count if you only say it in your head. It probably doesn't count if you don't say it before they do. Set an alarm on your phone (vary the times each day) and for heaven's sake let them know. You might be amazed how strongly they respond. Work on catching yourself in those moments when you appreciate them, fancy them or just plain love them, and turn it into words.

Your voice is something they're intimate with: they'll be pretty good at knowing if there is something going on with you just from how you say that everything's fine. Your voice will soothe them, comfort them or excite them. That's why it's important that you let them hear you, and not spend every waking hour listening to yourself in your head.

Let Robins talk. I know there are times when them saying something for the third time makes you want to leave the room, but it's just their way of getting their thoughts straight – and repeating something is sometimes just because they haven't yet had the response they're looking for. They don't have the ability to think inside their heads and so they need to hear what they're thinking by saying it. As the person they love, you're the sounding board of choice.

Don't:
Robins need the details of something before they trust it, and hard evidence before they'll support one of your ideas. They're not trying to drag you down with their questions; they just don't trust their instincts as evidence in the way sky-birds do – so pace them. I know you hate detail, but do your best to give them what they need – it'll help you get what you want.

Any loving relationship is the opportunity to take the chance of intimacy, of sharing our inner feelings, so fight any resistance to forming a connection to your emotional world, as this connection will enrich everything. Start with small things and build up until you have the confidence to know that getting emotional won't actually cause an earthquake.

I've advised Robins that they'll get old quickly trying to get you to follow their rules, so not to try. I'm going to reverse that advice for you: learn what matters to them, from the way to hoover to how to cook pasta, and follow their rules unless you actually do have a better way. It doesn't make Robins right, but it does make your life easier.

Nightingale and Swift

Swift: 'She thinks she can just ring me from work and everything is fine. If she'd rather work late than spend time with me, that's her look out.'

Nightingale: 'The thing is, I get in from work and want to tell him about my day, but he'd rather sit and watch something – and then he moans if I interrupt. I might as well stay at work.'

There is a difference and a similarity with you two that are likely to form the focal points of your relationship challenges. Swifts focus mainly on the evidence of their eyes, whereas for Nightingales what they hear and say is much more important. Your great similarity is that you are both sky-birds, so detail is not your forte. Your relationship may appear a bit messy and disorganised to some outsiders, but you're likely to be happy with it, most of the time.

Cuckoos in the nest

There's a good reason why Nightingales are famous for their song – they have a voice that's hard to ignore. With a human

Nightingale it's impossible: they'll just wear you down until you listen. In many respects, Nightingales talk as part of their thinking process, so words will often spill out of their mouths before they've been considered – they're brilliant at putting their foot in their mouths – and then trying for the other foot as well – and they'll often do so at inconvenient or inopportune moments. Having someone to act as a sounding board is vital, whether it's to talk through a problem at work, or whether their bum looks big in something. Often it's not actually your opinion they're after, it's the affirmation of theirs (or just someone to make them not look odd talking to themselves in a public place).

Swifts can often get their reaction to this Nightingale behaviour wrong. They think quickly and are usually very good at future pacing – going to the future to see how things turn out – so they can jump in halfway through the Nightingale's word-dump with what they see as a solution, only to find the Nightingale goes back to the beginning and starts their narrative again, or just carries on regardless. It's difficult to remember that they haven't finished processing the information they've got, so they're not ready to take on board anything more – including a solution. Wait until they're finished – you may need to paint eyes on your eyelids – and then say your piece.

Sight birds measure time differently to most. For them, the quality of a relationship, and the amount of love in it, is expressed best by the seconds together the couple spend. Any deliberate decision to be somewhere else instead of with them can be taken as a vote against the relationship – a preference for being somewhere else other than with them. If that preference involves spending time with other people, it can be especially hard.

Nightingales are much lower-maintenance in this regard. They'll probably like to ring you several times a day – sometimes just to hear your voice – and by doing so tolerate any absences that life throws their way. What will matter to them is your voice tone. They can be incredibly sensitive to the way things are said, so it doesn't matter how smooth your words, if they don't sound sincere, loving, sympathetic (or whatever else you may be trying to fake at that particular moment), you'll feel a cold wind blowing your way.

Something else that matters to Swifts is appearances. They like to keep them up, and they expect you to as well. If you start to relax your dress code because, you know, you're together now, they may well see that as you caring less. You don't see them not making an effort for you, do you? For a Swift, looking at you is like looking in a mirror at themselves; how they see you is how they think the world sees them. That might be a pressure for you, but you'll probably have to live with it. It might just be easier for them to pick your clothes – it depends on how closely your tastes align – but just be aware they will always think their choice is better than yours. (It's a bit like how you feel about your taste in music.)

So far, this has all been about differences between you, so let's move on to a similarity. Both of you are likely to be more comfortable with the big picture than having to wade through life's details. This can mean that you live in a world of missed credit card payments, lost passports, late appointments and untidy kitchens. But you probably won't mind too much. Both of you will probably avoid like the plague the things you consider boring, and those things will usually be anything the latter you need to focus on for more than thirty seconds that you don't enjoy.

Nightingales and Swifts are often seen as Life's butterflies, flitting from one interest or hobby to another. As a shared trait in a couple, this can give you the opportunity to share many different and varied experiences; or it can mean you send each other postcards from different ends of the globe as one goes deep sea diving and the other climbs mountains. With one of you being a Swift with issues about the meaning of time spent together, the latter isn't going to work too well.

As a couple, you'll make some great decisions based on your gut instincts, and sometimes you'll make bad ones using the same thing. Logic won't hold much power over you; neither will rules, instruction manuals or the long version of anything.

One of the drawbacks of being a sky-bird couple is that you might under-achieve; either as a couple, if that's possible to do, or individually in your careers, because at some point in time you need someone to organise your life and give you some stepping stones along the way to the vague but happy future your gut tells you awaits. Hire a butler, or ground-bird friend, or step up to the plate yourself and be more aware of this as a possible short-coming.

Feathers for the nest

What Swifts need to know about Nightingales
Do:
Nightingales know what they know by what they hear, so share your life with them through your words, not just what you show them. If they do something that reminds you of how you love them, or that deserves praise, encouragement or consolation, say what's in your head: don't think that a look will do.

Let Nightingales speak. I know that sometimes it can be irritating to have to listen to a seemingly endless stream of consciousness about something you might consider trivial, but it's a vital way for them to sort their thoughts. Give them the room to do so and don't contribute unless asked, or when they've concluded. Believe me, it will save time in what will probably seem a long run.

Nightingales will remember everything you say, so don't promise anything you can't deliver or say something you don't mean. It will come back to haunt you. Similarly, pay attention to your voice tone. Your partner will have a recording in their head for every emotion you express: if your words don't match the tone, they'll find you insincere.

As neither of you is likely to be well organised, don't leave it to your partner to run things. Sort out tasks between you and give each other permission to check up on each other – even schedule a monthly meeting to go through the jobs that needed doing. (Like you'll stick to that . . . ! But do at least try.)

Don't:

Nightingales can be incredibly sensitive to verbal criticism, so be very careful how you give feedback about anything. Your words can wound them, and with their ability to recall past conversations, those wounds can take a long time to heal. Never say anything you don't mean, and swallow anything personally unpleasant even if you mean it in the moment.

Don't think that appearance will ever matter as much to them as it does to you – or that it means anything about how they feel about you. They probably feel about music as passionately as you feel about fashion, or the look of the living room, so hold that equivalence in your head.

You also tend to process information very quickly, which could leave your partner behind, especially when you're painting a big picture of the future. They'll get what you're talking about; you just need to pace them a little. Slow down.

You know you're loved by what you see as evidence of it – the way your Nightingale looks at you, or maybe sometimes what they buy for you. Also 'quality time' together is going to be key. Their quality time is likely to be the chance to 'catch up', i.e. to talk long into the night. Don't think that them talking over the film you've rented for a nice evening in is a sign they're not appreciating being with you: it's a part of being with you. Also, don't take them somewhere noisy if you haven't been together much. Not being able to talk to you is going to kill them, no matter how pretty or visually stimulating the place is to you.

What Nightingales need to know about Swifts
Do:

Make sure that you organise yourself so you can maximise the time you spend together. If you have things that take you away from the relationship – whether it's work or a hobby – be aware that that is likely to be an issue for Swifts that you'll have to manage carefully. Make them aware of how much you miss them: if you're physically absent for a few days, send them things they can open from you that symbolise how much you miss them.

They will love presents – especially if seeing something made you think of them. Swifts have an abiding fear that 'Out of sight is out of heart.' Demonstrate to them that this isn't so – but not by a phone call alone: hearing your voice is not for them what hearing theirs is for you.

Be aware that your appearance is likely to be as important to your partner as theirs is to them. It may not matter as much to you, so go shopping with them. Listen and value their opinion – they'll often be right – and just notice how much positive feedback you get from making an effort, compared to when you . . . er . . . relax your wardrobe.

You know how you like to talk? Swifts don't actually need to hear anywhere near as much verbiage as you give them. This is going to be a big challenge for you but, wherever possible, give them the condensed version. Watch them when you speak, and when you see them glaze over, stop. If they start snoring, you'll know you missed the signals.

Don't:

As a Nightingale, you will know that you're loved by your Swift partner telling you this, and the tone of voice in which they say it. Swifts will know that they're loved by the time you spend with them, the looks you give them, and sometimes the gifts you get them. Don't forget this. Serenading them down the phone will not make up for the third late night at work in a row, so organise a special night out doing something they'd like. I know that sitting in a cinema might seem a strange way of making up for absence – certainly in comparison to a good chat over a meal – but sharing visual experiences will mean a lot to them, with the chance to talk about it later, of course.

If you buy your Swift a gift, be careful that it matches their taste in things or expect to find it in the local church raffle when they think you've forgotten about it. Listen to them for present opportunities and surprise them later, they'll love it – the presents Swifts have chosen for themselves are always safer than you taking a stab in the dark. If you want to really be ahead of the game, keep a notebook and write down your listening-inspired ideas as they happen throughout the year.

It's likely that neither of you excel at organising yourselves. It will make life easier if you share the responsibilities and then police each other. As I type, I can hear my doubt about your ability to do this. I suggested to your partner that you have a meeting every month to allocate tasks and track the progress of previous ones. It would really work for you. The next best thing is to remember not to blame your partner for not paying for or booking something that you'd have forgotten as well. You can't afford for this to become a blame game because you're as bad as each other – you probably just remember their mistakes better than they remember yours.

Dove and Swan

Dove: 'I love how tactile she is, but it seems like things are never quite perfect enough. She worries about things which are bound to be fine.'

Swan: 'We get on really well, in the main, but he doesn't seem to care about things until they smack him in the face, and he settles far too easily for an easy life.'

This is a game of two halves. On the one hand you have a match between feeling birds, which can make for a passionate and close relationship. Feelings and emotions are the currency of exchange between the two of them, with emphasis on today rather than the future. The one thing you can count on in their home is that it will be comfortable, if not co-ordinated. Doves and Swans together can be a very cosy match, as long as they understand the one rather large fly in their ointment: the potential for conflict between a ground-bird and a sky-bird.

Doves are sky-birds, and so they focus on their gut instinct more than facts. They like to stay at a big-picture level and have a note from their mum to excuse them from unnecessary details – which means *all* details. Swans are ground-birds, so for them details are the stuff of safety and sanity – where would you be without them? Up a creek is where, so they'll work hard to amass sufficient detail about anything to feel safe and secure. They'll also tend to wrap themselves in rules, which, to a Dove, are about as attractive as details. There can be fireworks between these guys.

Cuckoos in the nest

Both types pay most attention to their emotions and their physical connection to the world. On the plus side, this means you are likely to be sensitive to each other's moods, attuned to your partner's needs, and caring. Feeling birds place a high premium on the caring side of a relationship – both how they care and how they're cared for. In fact, herein lies a potential cuckoo: if you imagine care-for-self and care-for-others to be two end points on a line, feeling birds tend to be placed on different points of the continuum. If both are care-for-self – where the focus is on how comfortable they personally are – then it can be a battle where neither feels loved by the other, and people looking at their relationship would see two apparently self-absorbed people waiting to be waited upon. Conversely, with two care-for-others, where their emphasis is on the comfort of their partner, the relationship can seem like one of one-upmanship, where each battles to be the one to cook the dinner, to do the shopping, to provide the massage. Basically, 'who loves who the most' is determined by the tasks undertaken by the other. Luckily, most pairings will fall somewhere in between, and the more opposite they are, perversely, the more compatible they're likely to be. If one is a care-for-self and the other a care-for-others type, then what people will see is two people living together where one seems to be doing everything for their partner, and their partner doing little in return, but both seemingly happy about it.

Apart from the caring continuum, feeling birds know they're loved through touch. If you've ever seen two old people bumping Zimmer frames because they're trying to hold hands as they walk, it's probably one combination or another of this type. There can be several challenges that go with this. Touching as part of talking is a very natural thing for you, but it can be misinterpreted by your partner, so jealousy can be an issue. If they see you touching someone they consider attractive while you're in conversation with them, they can make the mistake of thinking you're feeling how you do when you're touching them – and that the other person feels like you do. Light the touch paper and stand well clear! Rows between feeling birds can be a firework display of passion and emotion. And, like firework displays, they can be over just as quickly. (And the making up is usually pretty good, too.)

The difference between you is, however, a biggy. Swans are ground-birds, who like to know where they stand. They want to know the ins and outs of anything before they commit to it, and are much more comfortable with facts than ideas. Doves, on the other hand, are sky-birds who like to see how things connect: they're more interested in ideas and possibilities than facts, and are often averse to detail to the point of allergy. This can lead to the Swan feeling that they live with a flighty dreamer who never lives in the real world, and the Dove a boring, anal retentive who wants to suck adventure from the world. You can see how this could lead to problems.

On the same theme, Doves are so involved in the big picture that they often don't see things that are under their noses. They'll make the same mistakes over and over: tripping over the same shoe rather than pick it up, or repeatedly taking longer to do a household task because they haven't thought through the most efficient way of doing it. This can drive the Swan crazy, as they'll have worked out 'how to do' everything. And once they've found 'the best way', that's it: it's a law. And you know what happens to people who break the law, don't you? I have yet to be given a task by my ground-bird wife without some instructions on how best to achieve it. The constant clash of having one partner who thinks there is one way of doing something – their way – and the other partner, who really doesn't care how things get done as long as it doesn't bog them down, can be both exhausting and a relationship killer.

Feathers for the nest

What Swans need to know about Doves
Do:
You don't need telling how important touch is to your relationship, but perhaps it might be beneficial to look at the balance of giving and receiving so that the benefit flows both ways in the way it needs to.

Swans and Doves are both likely to be 'in the moment' people, although the Dove might be a bit better at seeing ahead because of their sky-bird nature. In a positive sense, it means you can be happy with what you have, whilst the negative side means you can drift and fail to move forward with things you'd like to, and also that, in bad times, you can both get quite down because you don't see beyond the moment. What I suggest is that you sit down and work through goals, both as a couple and individually. Again, the Dove is probably going to be best at pointing in the right direction, and the Swan at actually putting a plan into action (and seeing it through). In this respect, the Swan is probably going to be the person who runs the relationship.

Cut your partner some slack on the rules. I know how important they are to Swans, but your Dove is not ignoring them out of spite – most of the time, it's just that they don't notice them. You could waste a lot of time and energy trying to teach them – for their own good, obviously – but probably all that will happen is you'll make both of you grumpy.

Don't:
You can be so close that you forget about the outside world. A cosy night in snuggling up on the sofa or canoodling in a bar; either way, your physical connection can be a barrier to the world. I'm talking to both of you now – don't let it. Let some light between you; allow some fresh air to circulate. Do some things

apart, spend time with other couples – and pay attention to them, rather than playing footsie under the table.

Don't swamp your Dove with detail: think 'version-lite'. If you're looking to buy a car, you'll probably want to test-drive it so often that the garage invites you to its Christmas party. Your Dove partner, however, will probably sit in it, say, 'Vroom vroom', a couple of times, and buy it. You like facts to support your gut feeling; Doves just use their gut and some weird internal divination. Don't try to understand it, just learn to honour it – because actually their intuition is on the money more often than not, and can really enrich your relationship.

You can both probably deal with separation quite well – 'Out of sight, out of mind' tends to be your way, as long as you're happy with what's happening in the moment. If you do have to spend protracted time apart, don't forget to connect in some way. Because both of you put such emphasis on caring=loving, gifts that fulfil that purpose could help a lot. Think of the food parcels the Red Cross used to send to prisoners of war. A box of chocolates or a boxed set of a favourite DVD series that arrived out of the blue could really give your partner a boost.

What Doves need to know about Swans
Do:
Some of what I've written about your partner will also be true for you – you'll know what bits when you read them – but there are some things I want to aim at you specifically.

Listen to your Swan. Sometimes it's going to be hard, because they'll want to tell you so much about something that all you'll be able to focus on is how numb your bum has gone. The thing is, they only feel safe when they know everything about something, and so they think the same holds for you. The fact that all you want to do is skim over something seems like insanity to them, so I'm afraid you're going to need to endure. (Make sure you're sitting comfortably, with sandwiches, before they begin.)

Comfort is important to both of you, but you're likely to settle sooner: no sitting on every sofa in the shop for you. My advice?

Send your Swan out to scout for what you're after and then go with them when they've got a shortlist.

The following goes for both of you, too: pay attention to what your partner likes you doing for them, and what they like doing for you, as that means you're both loved. Create opportunities to fulfil both these stipulations: if running a bath and eating Chinese food in it with them is their idea of quality time, surprise them with prawn toast and bubbles. If they think their head massage is the best way of relaxing you, even though they've got all the finesse of the Hulk, learn to fake gooey. (Arnica is good for bruising.)

Don't:

Don't needlessly flout your Swan partner's rules. I know that often you don't even notice them, and I've talked to them about that, but do your share and follow the ones you can. If it matters to them that their pants are ironed, play along when that chore is yours. Nor will it kill you to stack the dishwasher their way. Play nice and you'll get less nagging.

You will tend to see future directions for both of you better than your partner, and they're likely to be suspicious of anything that isn't a gold-plated certainty. Don't think of your Swan as dull or uninspired; just recognise that they need to be paced towards your vision – and it wouldn't do you any harm to add a bit of flesh to your ideas before you commit to them.

You two can have a very productive partnership. With problem solving, for example, you are likely to be good at moving problems around until you've found a solution, but it will be your Swan partner who will take your inspiration and make it work, because doing so will usually bore you and you'll get diverted. As the advert used to say, together, you're stronger.

Kingfisher and Robin

Kingfisher: 'Sometimes she talks just for the sake of it. When I point out to her that what she's saying doesn't make sense, she gets in a huff and drags up every grievance she's had against me over the last century.'

Robin: 'Well, he deserves it sometimes. I just want to talk something through with him and he makes me feel stupid for asking.'

This pairing has one main challenge. In terms of listening, we have only one 'radio channel', so we're either listening to what's going on outside our head, or we're listening to what we're saying on the inside. The problem here is that Robins focus predominantly on the outside, whereas Kingfishers spend a great deal of their time having conversations in their head – the challenges that this can lead to I'll go into in a moment. You also share a strong similarity that has consequences but, ultimately, at least you're in it together when it comes to causing them.

Cuckoos in the nest

Robins talk. They talk as a way of thinking, they talk as a way of noticing what they're looking at, they talk as a way of savouring what they're eating. You could torture a Robin with a simple bit of sticky tape over their mouth. If they're on their own for long, they'll pick up the phone, even if it's just to a call centre. In complete contrast, Kingfishers are often very quiet, reluctant to share their thoughts and can appear quite distant. This needs to be understood by both parties. For example, Robins will want to get home and unpack their day with their partner, often in detail. They'll want to hear about what their Kingfisher's been doing, which will then remind them of more things they planned to say to them. This is relationship heaven to them. To a Kingfisher, however, it's all seven levels of hell. They'll want to get home and think about their day, maybe while pretending to watch TV or playing something on the computer. That thinking might spill over into a quiet dinner and, on a bad day, continue into a disturbed night. When Kingfishers have their thoughts straight they'll be ready to talk or listen, but until then, engaging with them only frustrates them.

Robins need to give their partner space, and recognise that silence doesn't mean something is wrong – as it would be for them – while the Kingfisher needs to honour their lover's need to think on the outside and use them as a listening post, even if it means postponing an internal chat for one for a while.

Robins can also be like the lady on a white horse at Banbury Cross – they like to have music wherever they go. At least when they're plugged into an iPod they might stop talking, but if it's coming from a radio or blasting in the house, then the type of music could have an impact on the Kingfisher. Other voices will distract them, so Kingfishers will tend towards music that stays in the background – unless they actually want to listen to it – whereas Robins will love good lyrics and will often belt the song out along with the singer, irrespective of whether they sound like Lady Gaga, or just plain gaga.

In my opinion, Kingfishers become the way they do mainly as a defence mechanism to what they didn't like in their child-hood, or because they weren't exposed to contact with others enough to give a lot of experience of connecting to the world.

This means that they're often quite divorced from their feelings (unless their second type in quiz 2, at the start of the book, was Swan, in which case they might be more connected) which can make them difficult to get close to, and they'll often avoid anything too emotional. This can be hard for a Robin because they are likely to share their emotions quite openly, and love to have a late-night dig into respective feelings over a bottle of wine. That's unlikely to happen with a Kingfisher. They'll watch a film and get up and make a cup of tea when it gets to a sad bit (which will look odd in the cinema) – anything to avoid having a feeling.

Robins know they're loved by being told it, but in many cases they'd need to be mind-readers to hear it from their Kingfisher. If a Robin says 'I love you', the Kingfisher will usually respond appropriately – but probably only in their head. They have to learn it's not the thought that counts, it's the words that are spoken.

How Kingfishers will know or feel that they're loved will very much depend on which Lovebird was their second strongest when they took the Lovebirds quiz at the start of the book, and it would be a good idea to read that one (and that type in a relationship with a Robin, too) as well, because Kingfishers will probably recognise aspects of themselves in both descriptions. For example, if your second type was a Robin, then there'll be a number of similarities between you and your partner, and it would be useful to read the Robin and Robin combination as well as this one.

Both of you are ground-birds, which means that you're much happier with your feet on the ground, dealing with facts and details and certainties. Not for you the heady world of the sky-birds, with their vague ideas and their 'going with their gut' decision-making: you like to work things out sensibly. I always imagine ground-bird couples' lives to be more organised than they can possibly be – and then I meet another such couple and find I wasn't so wrong; there is a place for everything and everything really does have its place. If you have a project, like a holiday, part of the fun for you will be in the planning. Kingfishers will thrive on creating an agenda and investigating the options:

Robins will love talking through the possibilities. It's probably a great source of bonding for you, and it's good for you two to always have something to plan ahead of you.

The only downside to this is if your need for detail, and the Robin's need to talk about it, slows your decision-making down to a crawl, or means you miss opportunities because the moment passes before you feel you know enough to act. Sometimes it's going to be good for you to take a leap of faith about something, to flip a coin over a decision, or do something spontaneously. Seriously, the world won't get tilted from its axis, and the experiences this might open up to you could breathe some extra excitement into your life. As ever with couples who are similar, however, if you don't feel it's a problem, then it isn't.

Feathers for the nest

What Kingfishers need to know about Robins
Do:

Do your best to externalise all the good things you think about your Robin partner. Every time you recognise your love for them, say so. Every time they do something you appreciate, say so. If they need commiserating with, join in. Words in their ears are like strokes on their body. Pamper them with them.

There will be occasions where you will just have to sit and listen, or at least pretend to listen. Robins need to talk out loud to hear what they're thinking, so they're only doing with you what you do on your own, internally. Be there for them, even if you're secretly writing a great novel in your head. They don't necessarily need you to solve their problem, just listen to it – the truth is they probably wouldn't even hear what you were saying until they've finished speaking. Just be careful to keep track of what they are saying: if you admit to missing a bit, you'll probably get the whole lot over again.

Be careful with the words you use. Kingfishers can be quite brilliant at wordplay and verbal put downs, but you must be careful how you use this super power with your partner. Robins can be incredibly sensitive to criticism or harsh words. A simple rule of thumb is to never say something that you know will hurt their feelings because they'll still be nursing the hurt of it long after you'd have liked to have forgotten it – only they'll never let you; they'll bring it up for years. Sprinkle your feedback and observations with kindness – it'll benefit you both.

Don't:

I'd really recommend that you don't make a virtue out of your suspicion of emotions. If you dare to share more with your partner, you'll find a lot of good things happen. Kingfishers often feel like they're on the outside of life looking in because of their emotional disconnection, so take up things that get you more involved with your body, like yoga, golf, or tennis, anything that gets you to connect with your body and recognise how it's feeling moment-to-moment. Watch a few weepie films and notice the world doesn't end if you get a bit misty.

It's probably very easy for you to shut your Robin down, either by pointedly ignoring them, being dismissive or even rude about their word count. The fact is, if they can't share with you, they will find someone else: they have to. Or, over time, the person you fell in love with will become someone else – someone less, and nobody should make that happen to their partner.

Kingfishers need to know things. Nothing can remain meaningless and everything is part of a pattern they might not have figured out yet – but they will. This need to know can become quite inquisitorial to your partner. In some respects, the Robin can welcome this, because at least you're listening to them for a change, but it's very easy for you to tilt into negative interpretations of innocent things, so be careful that you're not seeing problems where none exists.

What Robins need to know about Kingfishers
Do:

It is imperative that your Kingfisher gets the chance to be quiet. If they're looking at the floor, the chances are they're deep in conversation with themselves, not admiring the carpet, so starting to talk to them is like interrupting. Rude. Let them alone and wait until they return to planet earth.

Bear in mind that, unless you get their attention, you might be halfway through your conversation with them before they realise they should be listening. I'm a thinking bird and my wife will literally click her fingers before she says something important to get my attention, and if she sees me about to do something stupid (which happens more often than I'm comfortable with), she'll keep saying the same thing until I respond, like, 'That'll burn you, that'll burn you, that'll burn you.' (She doesn't let me do much cooking.)

Things need to make sense to Kingfishers or they won't give them much credence. This can make your way of making sense of things – talking them through – quite difficult for them, because they won't say anything until it makes sense, not in order for it to. If there's any chance of improving on your ability to think before you speak, work on it.

You probably talk a lot. Silence for Kingfishers is like coming up for air; listening to you speak is like holding their breath. Keep that in mind when you listen to how long you go on for.

Don't:

Just because you catch Kingfishers not listening to you, don't think they're not interested. Robins often make the mistake of connecting people's attention to what they're saying with how much someone likes them. You're often wrong. In your Kingfisher's case, it could be that what you've said has interested them so much they've gone inside to talk to themselves about it for a bit.

Kingfishers may sometimes seem robotic in the control they have of their emotions (except for the occasional meltdown). Don't mistake their lack of emoting with a lack of love for you. There's no doubt you're going to have to work on them to verbalise more about what they feel (some pliers and a cattle prod would be handy), but don't settle for feeling alone emotionally. They're in there somewhere.

Kingfishers are the kind of people who can get deeply absorbed in a hobby or interest, and often it will be one they can do on their own. If you can genuinely join them in it, great: if not, support them. By spending time in their head collecting hub-caps (or whatever), they might just come out to play with you more often. But set time limits if it gets too absorbing.

Owl and Peacock

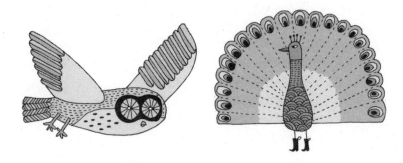

Peacock: 'Honestly, sometimes it's like living with a zombie. We're meant to be having some quality time together, but it's like I'm on my own half the time because she's zoned out somewhere.'

Owl: 'He's so bloody vain. The number of times a day I'm interrupted by being asked how something looks on him. If it's not that, it's having to come and look at something out of the window, or on the telly. I never have time to think.'

This couple can work out very well as a couple, with one key difference often being at the root of most of the challenges they face. Owls like to make sense of things – everything has to be for a reason or have some meaning. So, while they're sky-birds, preferring the big picture to detail, this need to have their world make sense, and for things to fit logically within it, usually means that they can cope better with their Peacock partner's ground-bird need for rules and details. There will probably be some working out (by which I mean rows) about which rules make sense and which don't, but nothing that can't be ironed out by your silver wedding anniversary.

Cuckoos in the nest

Owls spend an awful lot of time contemplating. They spend so much time standing staring into space, in fact, that people sometimes hang their coats on them. It's because they tend to be curious about things and how they fit together, so literally anything can set them plunging off into a thought-stream that can have them swimming enjoyably for ages. This can be a real problem for any partner, but Peacocks tend to take it particularly personally because for them, time together is one of the cornerstones of the relationship. 'Quality time' is their mantra, and that won't include their partner sitting next to them staring out of the window instead of into their eyes.

On the topic of time, Peacocks will treat any rival for their partner's as a threat. I don't mean anybody, I mean anything: extra hours at work, any new interest or hobby you do without them, any trip away without them – all these can have them feeling you're making a choice between being with them or with someone or something better. This can be important to you both, because Owls are great ones for interests, often flitting from one to another as their passion in them waxes and wanes. Getting a balance between an Owl's need to feed their curiosity, and a Peacock's need for time together to feel loved, is going to be a major challenge.

How things look to Peacocks can be hugely important; only *what* things are likely to vary. For some the house, garden or car may be paramount; for others it could be their and their partner's personal grooming. If this passion coincides with the Owl's interest or hobby then this could form a joint pursuit that features as a strong bond between them for as long as the Owl maintains their interest in it – which can vary from a lifetime to a couple of days. Obviously, if your interests don't coincide then this'll be a difference that could divide you if you let it.

Peacocks like detail and will like to share the minutiae of their life with their partner. This can drive an Owl crazy. Not only do they dislike detail – having to attend to it keeps them from the important business of thinking about anything else – but being subjected to a blow-by-blow account of their partner's day can feel like torture and will, almost certainly, cause them to run 'indoors' and slam their brain shut. When the Peacock notices this, it will tend to lead to a, 'You never listen to me, you're not interested, you don't care' situation.

Also, Peacocks like things done the way they should be – their way. As I mentioned earlier, because Owls like things to make sense, they're probably more likely to be able to accommodate this need than any other sky-bird – who don't usually notice rules often enough to stick to them. At least, this will be true if the rules make sense. Often some of the rules ground-birds have – and hold to most fervently – are ones they have picked up from childhood and which don't actually make much sense: it's just how things have always been done.

It reminds me of the story of a little girl watching her mum cook the Sunday roast. After a while she asks, 'Mum, when you roast a leg of lamb you always cut the end off. Why do you do that?' Her mum thinks for a moment and says, 'It's just the way it's done – it roasts best that way.' But it leaves her wondering, so she and her daughter go to her mother's house and she asks, 'When you taught me to roast a leg of lamb, you got me to always cut the end off. Why do we do that?' The grandmother thinks and says, 'I'm not sure; I think it makes it roast better. It's how we've always done it.' But, all intrigued now, they make the journey to see the great-grandmother. The grandmother says, 'You've taught us to always cut the end off the leg of lamb when we roast it. Why?' The old lady thinks for a moment, smiles and then says, 'I'll show you.' She goes into her kitchen and they hear the banging of doors and the slamming of drawers. Finally, she emerges triumphantly with a battered old roasting tin. 'This is what I used back then, and look – if you don't cut the end off the leg, it won't fit in the tin!'

Owls won't let you get away with those kinds of rules, so there will be some friction as an amendment process is enacted. Owls simply won't follow a rule that doesn't make sense or matter to them; and they may risk sacrificing something more important in their stubbornness. Let's not make it your relationship.

Feathers for the nest

What Owls need to know about Peacocks
Do:
Peacocks will know themselves to be loved by the time their partner chooses to spend with them (and the quality of it), by the looks they are given and maybe the things their partner buys for them.

This means for Owls that, as much as you might be drawn to immersing yourself in a new hobby or an existing interest, you have to balance things with spending good, attentive time with your partner. You need to share experiences and let them know that being with them matters more than anything.

Do your best to stay on the outside when you're with them. We both know how easy it is to catch yourself having not moved for the last fifteen minutes while your mind went off on one of its thinking expeditions, but when your Peacock is looking at you is not one of those times to do it – they'll interpret it as you not being interested in them or wanting to be with them. (And, let's face it, apart from other Owls or Kingfishers, who wouldn't interpret it that way?)

Do recognise that the look of certain things will matter to your Peacock. If those things happen to be your and their appearance then listen, and maybe go along with what's important to them about it. After all, you don't notice what you're wearing half the time anyway, so where's the harm?

Do work at avoiding cutting them off when they're telling you something, even though you think you've heard enough to get the gist. There is no *gist* for Peacocks, there's only *everything*, so they'll feel that until they've given you that, they haven't shared. I'm going to ask them to cut back on that, too, but I'm asking you not to run away from them when you hear them say, 'Wait until you hear the day I've had!'

Don't:

Peacocks trust facts and evidence, whereas Owls are much more into hunches and intuition, so don't think that Peacocks see how things are going to work out the way you do. Nor will they trust the path you think is best unless you can show them good reasons to support your argument. Saying, 'It'll be fine' cuts no ice at all. You might see that from your lofty perch, but they can't.

You are bound to contest some of the rules they have for running the house, or your life. If they don't make sense, say so if it matters to you, otherwise just go along with them. Again, you won't notice for long, and it matters to them.

You're not big on showing your emotions, but your partner seeing them is a big part of them knowing you have them. Loving your Peacock on the inside isn't enough: *show* it. Don't make being unemotional an unreasoning strength. In the right circumstances, it can be useful – like any behaviour – but as a default it can make you look aloof and uncaring. Work on sharing your feelings more, not to mention *feeling* your feelings more: they're not as scary as you believe.

What Peacocks need to know about Owls
Do:

Give your Owl time to themselves. I know that can be hard, but they have a big life in their heads, and they need to live it in there for them to feel okay. If you notice that they've disappeared from you, don't automatically think that there is something wrong; they're just as likely to be thinking about something that's good. Most people may go quiet when something is on their mind, but thinking birds go quiet for most things, whether they're happy or sad, worried or excited. I'm asking them to share their feelings more – not something they're comfortable about – and you should encourage them to do the same. If you can't tell from their face how they're feeling, ask them to tell you. It might remind them to let their emotions reach their skin.

Do cut back on the detail a bit. All right, I mean a lot. Owls get bored very quickly when given too much information. They're great at hearing enough to get the idea and then working with that. If you go on too long, they'll just stop listening and go inside their heads. Do it too often, and they might forget to come back out.

Owls will mainly know themselves to be loved according to the bird type they are that came second in the quiz they took at the start of the book, so go and have a look at that because an Owl for whom Swift came second, for example, is going to be different to one where a Dove did. In this instance, I suggest reading the Swift as well as the Owl – including the combination with you – and you'll get a clearer idea of how they know when they're loved.

Don't:
As a Peacock, you will probably worry more about what's going on in the present, while your Owl will worry more about the future. Owls can suffer from insomnia if what's on their mind isn't resolved – it'll just keep bouncing off the inside of their skull until it is. During this process, they may seem very withdrawn. Don't immediately assume that there is something wrong between you both, and don't nag them to tell you what is wrong: they'll tell you when they have it straight in their heads. At the same time – and this is the delicate bit – encourage them to share, because often hearing their concern on the outside of their head can blow a little air through it.

Don't expect your rules to mean much to them. If they make sense they'll have no objection to them – they'll just forget when to follow them because their mind will probably be elsewhere. If, however, the rule doesn't make sense to them, you have no hope so maybe – brace yourself – you should let go of it. Either way, your Owl won't do something that makes no sense or where something seems meaningless, so always be ready with a reason for the rule when you ask something of them.

Don't make too much of a fuss about the appearance of things – or at least, don't expect your partner to make a fuss. Owls can sit comfortably in what you consider a tip if they're occupied with something (which is always), and won't be that great at telling the difference between how a room was before and after it was cleaned. If you want a home that sparkles, you're pretty much on your own.

Swan and Nightingale

Nightingale: 'How can she say I don't love her? I tell her every day!'

Swan: 'Oh, yeah, but talk is cheap. What was the last thing you did for me? You won't even get off your backside and make me a cup of coffee.'

Swan: 'The thing that winds me up is that you talk all the time, even when we're making love. It really puts me off.'

Nightingale: 'But I'm only telling you how good I feel. How can that put you off? I'd love you to do that to me.'

There are some major differences between these two, but nothing that need get in the way of this being a great relationship. It's true that Swans will be able to remember the tog value of every duvet they've ever known, just as a Nightingale can recall the play list from the party where you first met, but the difference between a feeling bird and a song bird isn't going to be the real challenge; the challenge is going to be the fact that the Swan likes facts, evidence and lots of detail. Oh, and rules – did I mention those? Swans live by rules, which is a shame, because Nightingales will usually be too busy with the big picture to notice them. Nightingales trust their hunches, love ideas and look for the way things fit together in order to understand them. If you can make this difference work for you, it can be a very productive relationship. If you can't, it could be a lifetime of niggling annoyances.

Cuckoos in the nest

Welcome to the difference between talk and action. Nightingales like words. They like the sound they make, the rhythms they can weave with them, to the point where it can be disconcerting to them to find someone who is quite unmoved by their rhetoric. I'm sure many of the great poets were this birdtype. For Swans, words are fine, but what they want is action:

Swan: 'Precisely what is it you have done that makes me feel loved?'

Nightingale: 'Well, erm, I wrote you that note the other day, and I told you how lovely you looked last night, and I, er, rang you from work just to say I love you. What more do you want?'

Swan (yawning): 'Yes, they were nice things to do but, I don't know, they just don't make me feel that you care *that* much.'

The problem works in the opposite way for the Swan. If the Nightingale makes an effort to look good when you go out, make sure you *tell* them. Enthusiastically and verbally. Straightening their tie, giving their arm or their bum a squeeze might be your way of saying, 'Boy, what I could do for you!', but for them it may not be associated with the message they want to hear from you (which is, of course, 'Boy, what I could do for you!').

Swans often have a weak spot for absorbing things they're told. If you rattle off a problem to them at fifty to the dozen you may notice their eyes go blurry. They get confused, then worried that they don't understand, then think they're stupid, and then either switch off or try to change the subject. If this happens repeatedly over a period of time, the Swan might instinctively begin to turn off to what you are saying in order to avoid feeling stupid. Then you start accusing them of not listening and . . . bang! – there goes another nail in the coffin.

If you are in a conversation with a Swan, keep the sentences short, pace your speech to them, and watch them for any sign that they are not keeping up. You are 100 per cent responsible for getting Swans to understand what you are saying. And remember that this is not about their intelligence. Some of the people I know who give the best advice and who are brimming with common sense are Swans. They can be brilliant listeners with marvellous intuition and a sense of empathy if they feel comfortable with what they're listening to. So if they appear to be tuning out to what you are saying, it may be that you are overloading them, not that they aren't interested.

Rhythm can be a strong bond between these two types. Many of the best musicians are Nightingales, but many are also Swans – somehow they 'feel' the music. Whether it's through dance or listening to music, they will often have common tastes. Music can be a strong anchor to bind them to positive experiences, so having 'your' songs can often be a way of bridging any distance you feel building between you. The flip side of this is if tastes clash. Music, particularly to the Nightingale, is likely to be a very personal thing, so if they really get into a performer or band, that music is likely to be on in the house pretty much all the time. If the Swan really isn't that into it, you can see that this could get old very quickly – and the Nightingale will often think less of people who don't 'get' their music. (Snob, I hear you say? Er, yes. But a Swan will look down on someone who can't tell the difference between silk and satin, so fair's fair.)

The following is actually likely to be one of the biggest challenges this pairing faces: Swans are ground-birds, so they like order. They have rules that need to be followed and they like things the way they like them. Here's what one Nightingale had to say about his Swan partner: 'Hanging washing is an art form to her; it feels more like a distress signal to me. I'm pretty sure I'll never notice a difference in how quickly or well something has dried through hanging it exactly perpendicular – and checking with a plumber's bob. Which of course means you can bet that if I do hang the washing out, I'll come back later to find it rearranged because I didn't do it "properly".'

Nightingales, on the other hand, are big-picture people. They tend to go by their instinctive reaction to something, and live in the moment – even if that involves not remembering to follow the Swan-imposed rule they broke the last time . . .

Feathers for the nest

What Nightingales need to know about Swans
Do:

Remember that Swans don't take in words as quickly as you do. Pace them. A lot of Nightingales need to speak out loud to order their thoughts, so they talk. A lot. When you've got the bit between your teeth about a particular topic, there is a chance you could overwhelm your Swan partner and send them diving for their ear-muffs (fur-lined, obviously). So do your best to work out what you want to say before you say it, and then say about half of what you think needs saying.

Do things for them. Your actions are what they measure your love by, not your words. Holding their hand in a queue, giving them a hug for nothing whatsoever, putting your hand on their leg while they drive (careful, tiger, I meant affectionately) can all mean to your partner what sweet nothings in your ear would do for you.

Learn their rules and follow them. It's just easier. I know this sounds defeatist, but it will save you a lot of time and aggravation in the long term. Things don't tend to matter to you that much, so learning what matters to your Swan and just doing it is a sensible short cut, and will save you a lot of 'lessons' intended to 'help' you. My wife, who is a Swan, pretty much has a way of doing everything, and most of her ways don't make that much of a difference (I ducked as I typed that, just in case she was reading over my shoulder). Okay, some of them do, but not, like, to world peace or anything.

The physical world is very important to Swans. Help them connect to it. One of the ways to do this is through their sensitivity to their comfort. Be patient with their never-ending need to find the perfect bed, the perfect coffee, the perfect . . . everything, and, insofar as you can, engage in their journey. It'll mean a lot of browsing and researching, but you'll have lots of shop assistants to talk to so it's not a complete bust.

Your Swan partner has probably been called 'precious', 'sensitive' (not in a good way), a 'prince' or 'princess' their whole lives, so to have the feeling of being understood – and not judged – by their partner can be a great experience for them.

Don't:
Don't engage them in conversation early in the day. Buy yourself a radio, instead. Swans tend to be slow starters and getting any kind of meaningful dialogue they won't deny later is really hard. Leave them to it over breakfast rather than read the paper to them. If you see their knuckles white on the butter knife, you know you're pushing your limit.

Don't drag them round the shops asking them what they think about everything you pick up or try on. Leave them on a couch somewhere and make a friend of the assistant. Swans will shop by touching and feeling and words will distract them. At best, collect what you want to have and ask their opinion in one go.

What Swans need to know about Nightingales
Do:
When you give Nightingales a hug to show you love them, remember to say those three words out loud, too. Nightingales

will know they're loved by being told, so the words are important, as is the tone. Nightingales will have a recording in their head of when you said 'I love you' and they believed you. It will be used to interpret anything else you say to them on the subject, so a carelessly thrown phrase at the end of a phone call won't cut the mustard, as probably neither will you saying it in response to them saying it first. Any time you feel something good about your partner, say it loud and say it right.

Give your Nightingale room to talk, even if it means singing a song in your head while they do it (just make sure you're back with them when they get to the point). If you try to hurry things along by finishing their sentences or interrupting, they'll probably go back to the beginning and start again. Often they need to hear what they're thinking by saying it aloud – and to somebody. They're not being windbags, it's just how they think.

Be gentle with the words you use. Nightingales are easily bruised by unkind feedback or comments, and they can stay with them for ages, so never say anything unkind in anger if you can avoid it. Besides, they'll simply throw it back at you every time they need an advantage in a discussion.

Don't:
I know your rules are important. I know they make life run more smoothly. I know it feels as if your partner is deliberately winding you up by not getting their importance, but you need to chill about them. Don't nag. Your Nightingale doesn't ignore your rules; in the main, they just don't recognise the moment when they should be following them – and they probably never will because it's not how their mind works. I've advised that they follow them, and I'm advising you not to give them detention when they forget.

Don't leave the organising to them – you're probably going to be better at it. But they will tend to have the edge when it comes to ideas. Listen to them, because every now and again they'll have a great one. Don't immediately force them to come up with the detail – I know that's how you make decisions, but they depend more on their gut feeling. If you tread on their dreams through your demand for 'How's that going to work?' it will deflate them and they'll stop sharing them with you (but they will probably need to share them with someone).

Swan and Owl

Swan: 'He's so irritating. I spend so much time looking after him and he doesn't even notice. And if I've shown him how to clean up after himself once, I've done it a thousand times. He just does it to annoy me.'

Owl: 'Sometimes it's like living with the kitchen police. Everything has to be done a certain way or there's hell to pay. And when she not only asks me to do something, but then tells me how she wants it to be done, she drives me mad.'

This is an interesting combination. Swans are all about the heart and Owls the head, so one can think the other a pink and fluffy prince or princess, the other a robotic psychopath. As you can imagine, this can lead to very different perceptions about what the relationship needs. Handled carefully, this can be a wonderful relationship, and I'm not just saying this because this is the combination of my wife and I (I don't want her getting complacent). Swans are big on comfort, order and detail and are very in touch with their feelings; most Owls avoid rules and detail like the plague, have an amazing capacity to not notice comfort, and are in touch with their feelings only if a barge pole is handy (exceptions are likely to be those for whom Dove – a feeling bird

– came second in quiz 2 at the start of the book). A match made for the divorce courts, you'd think. Not necessarily, just one that will need constant attention.

Cuckoos in the nest

Swans can be incredibly sensitive, and I mean to everything. The wrong conditioner on hair or clothes can ruin their day – so probably yours, too. They can feel very high maintenance because everything needs to be right, and then when it is, it seems like that's just a launch pad for the next level of perfection.

Their sensitivity also extends to their emotions and, on most occasions, yours, too. Sometimes it can feel like they hold themselves responsible for the wellbeing of everybody they know, which can be exhausting for you both.

One of the key challenges in this relationship is that you are such complete opposites with regard to feelings. Swans are completely open to them, often the victims of them, and will feel no embarrassment in expressing them. Nothing could be further from the truth for Owls. They will have various tactics for avoiding emotions, from keeping them as buried as possible, to keeping away from situations where they might have to feel something. Most Owls live in a world where they think they either have full control or no control and, fearing the latter, they cling to the former so their partner has their work cut out getting them to open up.

Swans can be left feeling lonely, unable to have conversations about what matters most to them, and criticised for their inability to 'just put up with things'. Owls can feel besieged, constantly asked to share things they don't want to address, and to comment on things they don't really notice – I've met many who start getting tense when asked their opinion about things like which sofa feels most comfortable, which fabric is nicest or which coffee tastes best. Owls (and Kingfishers) are not tuned in to their senses. They can bruise themselves without noticing, they can be ill without paying attention to it until reaching a point where their Swan partner would need an air ambulance, and they can sleep in a bad bed until needing an osteopath, without a word of complaint. So asking them to compare sensations is like asking them to play a game where they don't know the rules.

While Swans can be brilliant at being able to make fine distinctions between things in this way, they can take a while to marshal their thoughts, and words are often not their forte. They can sometimes seem slow to verbalise what they want to say, and the Owl, for whom words are as comfortable as a swans-down duvet is for their partner, can often make them feel belittled by taking over the conversation or finishing their sentences.

Another key difference is that Swans are ground-birds and Owls are sky-birds. In other words, Swans trust hard evidence and facts, while Owls are far more interested in, and attracted to, patterns, possibilities and their instincts. It can feel to the Swan that their partner is forever launching into projects that are simply pie in the sky or wildly speculative, while for the Owl, it can feel as if they're constantly being dissuaded or brought down by the 'realism' of their unimaginative partner. What will also happen is that the Swan will increasingly take over the running of the household because the Owl is so averse to detail that, classically, the Swan will decide that 'it's just quicker to do it myself than keep trying to get them to help'.

It's quicker for the Swan because they are very particular about how things need to be done. Swans have rules, and these rules matter. Typically, if the Owl cleans the kitchen, unless they completely reach the Swan's standard, it will feel as if they needn't have bothered, because they'll find the Swan doing it again. (It took me a year to learn how to clean the bathroom 'properly'.) It feels a hopeless situation, because if an Owl starts a mundane task it will be moments before they go onto automatic and retreat to something more interesting inside their head – and the consequence will invariably be that they won't notice something left undone that the Swan will. This can lead to a conversation where the Owl 'can't be trusted' and the Swan is an 'anally retentive nutter'.

Feathers for the nest

What Swans need to know about Owls
Do:

Your partner's internal world is a vital part of their wellbeing. If they're kept from it for too long they will begin to get confused and tired. If you see them in their own little world, don't assume there is something wrong. If it's possible, leave them to it – especially if they're looking down to the left, as this is often an indication of people having a chat with themselves.

Encourage Owls to open up about their feelings, but don't demand it or overwhelm them with yours. Emotions are a foreign country to them; they're much more comfortable 'working out' their thoughts, so this could take a while. Be patient, and trust that, while the evidence for it might be presently hidden from you, they feel deeply about you. It isn't much consolation, but if they didn't, you'd know it much more clearly – because there isn't anybody colder to live with than an Owl who has ceased caring.

Your rules are important to you, quite rightly; they make life more comfortable. Unfortunately for you, you've fallen for someone for whom rules are often just a distraction from something more important to pay attention to – their thoughts. Sky-birds don't ignore rules for the hell of it; they usually just don't notice them often enough for you to think that the times they forget aren't just to hack you off. You have the choice to either age quickly nagging, or just accept that if you want a rule followed, follow it yourself.

Don't:

As a Swan, detail makes you feel safer: to get the right feeling about something, you need to know enough about it to satisfy you. In one sense, this is similar to your partner: Owls need something to make sense before they commit to it, but they don't need piles of evidence before they get there – they'll tend to jump the minute they see the way, whether or not every step is clear.

You need to talk about this, because this aspect of difference can be tremendously useful if managed properly. Owls will have many ideas, and some of them will be good. Don't choke the life out of all of them with a need for a report from a select committee before you give the nod. It might be a rollercoaster for you, but trusting their instincts, with you providing the organisation, can create a very successful partnership. Owls point the way; Swans work out how to get there. (My wife describes it as my inspiration and her perspiration, but I'm sure she means it in an, 'Aren't I lucky?' kind of way.)

Swans are 'in the moment' kind of people, whereas your Owl partner is likely to be more future-based. That can mean that you can get overwhelmed by something – and remain affected by it – long after your Owl has moved on. It doesn't make them robots; it just takes a lot more to keep their emotions heightened. If you are bogged down in something that's having an emotional effect, turn to them. They can be great at working out solutions and going beyond the present moment to weigh the consequences of decisions you might be considering. Don't get stuck in your feelings unless they're good ones.

What Owls need to know about Swans
Do:
Your partner is connected to the world in a way that you can only imagine – and possibly fear. What you get from thinking they get from feeling, so honour their need to pursue what their senses can bring them. This is likely to involve a lot of market testing in pursuit of the perfect experience, whether it's the best glass of wine – probably a lot of fun – to the best oral hygienist – which probably isn't. Go with the flow and use it as an opportunity to connect to the physical world through your senses. Some Owls turn their disconnection to the world of feelings and sensations into a badge of honour. It's not – it reduces the richness of your life, so trust the Swan you love and dive into their world a little bit at a time. It will change your life for the better and bring you closer.

Your Swan knows themselves to be loved by the way you touch them and the things you do for them – the acts of service, if you will. Make sure there is plenty of tactile contact between you. Massage them, hug them; hold their hand when you're walking with them. Watch out for the things you do that they appreciate and do more of them. They don't need to be big things, probably just thoughtful ones. Gravity feels heavier to a Swan than an Owl, so just you being the one who gets up from the sofa in the evening to get them a drink can make you a hero in their eyes. Once you've noticed the things they like, it gets very simple.

Don't:
It's the easiest thing in the world for you to disappear inside your head for hours at a time. Sometimes a hobby or interest will give you the reason, other times you won't need one – you'll just pull up the drawbridge and have some thinking time. Don't overdo it. Your partner is a very 'in the moment person', so living with someone who always seems to be somewhere else can feel quite lonely and, actually, endless. You need to focus on connecting with them and being present.

Don't accuse them of being precious just because they like everything a certain way. It's true that Swans never seem to be satisfied – and the moment they are, they just raise the perfection bar for next time – but it's just a consequence of feeling every-thing so keenly. Because you are the opposite in this regard – it's like you're both in a tickling contest but they're naked and you're in a suit of armour – it can feel like you're living in two different worlds. You are. But as long as you both don't start thinking there is something wrong with each other for not seeing things your way you can do fine.

Pace them. Things need to make sense to you and you tend to be very good and very quick at seeing how things connect. Your partner probably lags behind you in this. This doesn't make you better or more clever. In many other respects, Swans can leave you standing, so don't use the pace of your mental processing or verbal ability to undermine them. Just as you can gain from connecting to their rich world of feelings, so they can improve themselves by being around your world of words. But they won't if you undermine them; they probably had that throughout the whole of their education.

Swift and Kingfisher

Swift: 'Honestly, talk about anally retentive. She focuses so much on one little thing that she misses everything else that needs doing.'

Kingfisher: 'If it was left to him, nothing would get done properly. It's all very well having grand ideas, but why can't he remember to put the bins out? I do everything.'

These two are going to have to work quite hard. Kingfishers need life to make sense to them, and often delve into great detail about the way things work. They're likely to have a list of instructions in their head to make the world keep spinning, and respond to any transgression from them with a domestic jihad. Or, at least it could feel that way to the Swift, who wouldn't recognise a rule if they tripped over it (which wouldn't happen if they'd only hang it on the peg provided). Swifts are much more turned on by the big picture and will have a very low boredom threshold for any task that doesn't capture their interest. They are extremely visual, so how things look will matter to them a great deal – which can be unfortunate for them both, as Kingfishers can sometimes look like they got dressed in the dark. In someone else's house.

Cuckoos in the nest

Let's start with the difference between the ground-bird Kingfisher and the sky-bird Swift. In some respects, the traits of ground-birds can be most strongly represented in this type, because Kingfishers have such a strong need to make sense of things. This can mean they become exhaustively attentive to the minutiae of life – especially when they're under stress. The benefit of this can be that the relationship is extremely organised and well run, so the partner of a Kingfisher will always know where to find things. The downside is that a Kingfisher's partner will have to watch out if they put something where it shouldn't be or misfile the daily accounts. Also, there will be rules, most of which will be sensible and actually improve the Swiss watch that is your relationship. The problem is that the Swift will neither notice the improvement, or care, and so not be that bothered about remembering which rule goes where or happens when. A Swift client told me of the panic he faces when he sees a pile of washing left by his Kingfisher boyfriend. Does that mean something needs doing with it, or is it being left at the top of the stairs for a reason other than to bring down to be washed? He reports that he can stand for minutes treating it like a suspicious package. Is it a trap laid by his partner to give him yet another chance to castigate him for living like a slob? It's an uncomfortable place to be. Unfortunately, Kingfishers will often make their partner's degree of compliance with the rules a measure of their love of them. When you understand *that*, my friend, you'll understand why they come at you with guns blazing when you transgress.

Swifts, just as weirdly, will measure the effort their partner makes to look good for them as a sign of their level of caring. Kingfishers have been known to stick to the same style, brand and colours of clothes for years, replacing a worn-out pair of jeans with another identical pair from the same shop as last time. They spend so much time inside themselves that what they choose to cover the outside with is unlikely to hold their interest – if it was good enough for them ten years ago, why change now? This could drive their partner mad. A Swift could either take this attitude as an indicator of a much deeper personal flaw, or make an equivalence between the energy put into their partner's grooming and the passion being put into them. Think of yourself as an extension of them or a verdict on them in the eyes of others. As far as your partner is concerned, how you look is a fundamental part of what people who see you will think of them. I know it's hard to see how what you wear can be seen as anything more than a handy way of walking around with pockets for your important things, but you'll just have to humour them.

It's likely that in matters of art, too, there will be differences of perspective. A Kingfisher will usually prefer paintings or objects with either a personal meaning, or one that has meaning contained within it. If a friend brings them back a nicknack from their holiday, it will probably end up in the cobwebby part of a cupboard. Why would they display something from someone else's experience? Similarly, they may clash with their Swift partner, who will carefully match paintings to the décor of the room rather than select them because of the meaning they evoke in the viewer, beyond, 'Wow, look at the pretty colours!'

The Kingfisher's lack of communication is going to be a factor in most relationships, so why not this one? It can be tough for a Swift, who prizes time together as a major requirement for intimacy, to find themselves with a partner whose attention is clearly elsewhere. Kingfishers have an amazing ability to put a shield around themselves and be alone in a crowded room, and people will often feel like they're keeping a piece of themselves back. It's just the way they are and it doesn't have to signify anything; they just happen to think about things a lot. If you want them to come out and share something you're going to have to ask them – probably at least twice because they won't have heard you the first time.

Feathers for the nest

What Swifts need to know about Kingfishers
Do:

Remember that while time together feels really important to you, it doesn't mean the same to your partner. A Kingfisher can get so wrapped up in their thoughts that a whole evening can seem to pass in a heartbeat, so how can time mean the same to them?

How a Kingfisher knows that they're loved will depend a great deal on their second type in quiz 2 of the Lovebirds quiz at the start of the book. So if, for example, Kingfisher was their strongest, and Peacock was second, then it's likely that a lot of how a Peacock relates to people will be true for Kingfishers too, so it would be worth reading about both types, and how they relate to Swifts. Taken together, you should get a more rounded sense of your partner.

Leave the organising to them. I know you were going to anyway, but at least now you can quote me saying it's for the best. However, there's a price to pay. There are ways your partner wants things done. Do them. Find out their rules, and follow them. It will reduce the number of times things are explained to you again, for your own good . . .

Your Kingfisher needs to know the detail. They won't be impressed or moved by your big ideas until you're at the spreadsheet stage. They trust in facts and evidence, not your much-loved gut instinct, so try and meet them on this.

Remember that your Kingfisher is always drawn inwards. They have an internal world they use to mull over what's happening in the outside world, so do give them time to themselves. Being stuck in the real world can actually be quite exhausting for them, and after an evening of having to pay attention to something on the outside of them – like a house party – you might find them in the broom cupboard, just having a moment to themselves. If you see them staring fixedly at anything, especially the floor, you might as well stop talking. The lights are on, but nobody's answering the door for a while.

Don't:

Swifts can get very excited by the things that they see. A beautiful sunset might move you, a special piece of art boost your mood, or a fab-looking pair of shoes get you to blow your budget, but don't expect a similar response from your partner. Kingfishers can feel things as deeply as anybody, but it's a bit like an underground atomic explosion – you might pick up a rumble, but miss the fireworks that are going on beneath.

Don't mistake their distraction for a lack of interest in you. I know it can be hard to tell sometimes, but they feel deeply about you, and to them it's so obvious that it shouldn't need any words, symbols or display. They have challenges with exposing their emotions, but over time you can encourage them to explore them without the world going up in flames. You won't do that by accusing them of being heartless, robotic or zombie-like because of their lack of emoting. If you treat their emotions gently you could nurture them back to life, but if you mock them you'll never see them again, and that would be a shame.

Don't make too big a deal about their appearance. 'Functional' and 'tried and tested' are more likely to guide their choices than fashion. Don't ask them to make choices between different colours or materials; this can feel like a bit of a test and, because they're not adept at handling sensory information, for a Kingfisher the question: 'Do you prefer this green or that green?' will probably only give you a guess as a response, with them watching you for what the right answer should be. I'm a thinking bird, and I once ran 10k in my wife's Lycra shorts without noticing – and she's a petite woman. Well, I noticed afterwards, but was oblivious to the improved, erm . . . support at the time. Like I said, we're not good at paying attention to what our senses tell us.

For you, seeing is believing. For your partner, working something out so it makes sense to them is believing. The evidence that will count for them is more detailed than you could cope with, and done almost entirely in their head. Joint decisions are going to be a hard day at the office, because you two will arrive at them through very different strategies. Remember that both ways work for the person using them, so both of you have to pace the need of the other.

What Kingfishers need to know about Swifts
Do:
You probably get tired of hearing your partner's big idea and plans. For Swifts, opportunities seem to lie everywhere, and it can be difficult to choose which thing to focus on. As a result, they don't: they fly everywhere and often end up nowhere. This is where Kingfishers can be a real help. If Swifts provide the idea, and you make it happen, your relationship can pretty much go anywhere you choose. Properly harnessed, a sky-bird/ground-bird combination can be a powerhouse of completed projects and fulfilled goals. So listen to their dreams, and filter the impossible from the possible – carefully, because sometimes your need for evidence and facts can make you see possibility only in a dim light. If their passion is what provides the illumination, I'd be inclined to take a chance on it, because it will often take you to a good place.

Swifts will know themselves to be loved by you by how you look at them (so remember to leer at appropriate moments), and by how much time you spend with them. You're going to need to establish a balance here, because I suspect you have interests that immerse you. That's fine, I know you need them, but don't forget to treat your partner like an interest too: invest time in them and remain present during it, not locked in your head while your face does its best to cover for your absence. Focus on them.

One thing you're probably good at is choosing gifts for them. Learn what their taste is, watch what excites or pleases them and base your present-buying on that. Anything they receive as a gift is weighed as a measure of how well you know and understand them. So think on.

Don't:
The biggest don't is to do with nagging. You are unlikely to change your Swift partner, but you are likely to grow old before your

time trying. It's not that they deliberately ignore the things you ask them to do in a particular way, it's just that, on most occasions when they're doing that thing, their mind will be elsewhere. I don't want you to throw this book at the wall (especially if it's an eBook) but your need for order and to have rules for just about everything can be a little . . . excessive? Lighten up. Your partner exists perfectly well without them so maybe, and I'm just putting this out there, you could meet them somewhere in the middle between your near 'obsessive-compulsive, anally retentive need for order', and their 'drown in their own mess' chaos.

Don't lose yourself in yourself too often. Face-to-face time with the one they love is oxygen to your partner's love. You being absent following a big thought while they're with you can begin to starve it. Stay on the outside and look at them while they're talking.

Don't run from emotions or treat them as unimportant – yours or theirs. For them to 'see' how you feel is vital for them to feel connected to you, and their faces are often a window to their emotional life. If you don't respond to their signals they'll interpret that as there being a distance between you. For thinking birds as a whole, relationships should be a place to dare to connect to their feelings, not a refuge to hide from them.

Dove and Dove

Dove 1: 'I'm probably just as bad, but he just seems to wallow in stuff sometimes and get stuck in something that doesn't really matter. It can be a real downer.'

Dove 2: 'We're really close, and are always touching each other, but sometimes I just feel like there's a bit of a competition going on over who can care for the other the most.'

These two really are lovebirds. Doves live in a world of feelings, where what is happening now is more important than what might happen tomorrow, and where things like comfort, physical experiences and interesting sensations will be paramount. They'll be attuned to their emotions – and disproportionately knocked off-kilter when they're not – and often be highly sensitive to the feelings of others. To the outside world, these two could seem joined at the hip and self-sufficient – in a chaotic, disorganised, have-we-arrived-at-the-party-on-the-wrong-day? kind of self-sufficient way.

Cuckoos in the nest

Let's start with the fact that you're both sky-birds. For a start, this means that detail bores you; in fact, generally you have a low boredom threshold and tend to find most things you consider dull unimportant. With you both sharing this trait, it's likely that the kind of necessary chores that keep a relationship boat afloat and heading in the right direction tend to be ignored or neglected. Things like paying bills, arranging appointments, keeping on top of repairs, car servicing, holiday planning and the myriad other tasks that should be worked out between you somehow manage to fall into the tiny crack between the two of you. It can lead to a kind of companionable mess, where you'll miss a plane, or turn up in the wrong place, and laugh or cry about it together, vow to change, and stay the same. Ground-bird friends will hold their heads in their hands at your stories.

This aversion to detail can also mean that you only skim what's going on in each other's worlds. I have Dove friends who can barely describe what their partner does for a living: '. . . something to do with . . .' is where they generally start from, and finish very soon after. This can become a problem if a partner is struggling with something and the other lacks the knowledge to support them usefully. It can also be a reason for jealousy to develop, if one partner develops an interest that involves other people and the other doesn't know enough to join in.

Sky-birds tend to enjoy the big picture, so will often have only a vague sense of where they should be going, what plans they could be making or what projects they'd like to develop. Unfortunately, they're also very 'in the moment' people, so it's easy for them to get distracted. Also, because of their lack of attention to detail and low boredom threshold, they'll often lose steam. Their life is probably going to be strewn with the debris of half-finished projects, half-started plans and that thing in the corner that they'll get around to finishing off one day.

Another key part of your Dove similarity is the way you focus on feelings and emotions as a way of communicating with the world – and having it communicate with you. Doves can be amazingly sensitive, in every way. I've known them suffer from bright light, loud noises and rough textures. Smells seem to smell more powerfully to them, and when eating out they'll send food back to the kitchen more often than most. No wonder they get labelled high maintenance. And if there're two of you together, there's a risk that you'll either be on the FBI's Most Wanted list of most pernickety if you share the same sensitivities, or in a spiralling world of compromise if they're different: 'Turn the lights down, they're too bright', 'Well, your music is deafening', 'But I've only got it that loud to distract me from the scratchiness of that awful synthetic plaid skirt you bought me' . . . etc.

One common consequence of this sensitivity is a pursuit of comfort. I don't mean in a simple, fur-and-champagne kind of way; I mean a perpetual search for a more comfortable sofa, mattress, car, bra or pair of pants. It can mean a stream of coffee machines moving through your kitchen, but never staying long, or the purchase of loads of the same items of clothing when they've proven themselves scratch-free. It feels as if there's a place called Satisfaction, but the minute you think you've arrived, you wonder if it really isn't just a little bit further up the mountain. If you're both involved in the same climb I guess that could be fun for you – it certainly fills up your time (but if you're climbing different versions of the mountain, it'll be more fun watching you than being you).

Touch is one of the key ways you express your feelings to each other, and in most cases this works out beneficially for both of you. However, imagine that there are two ways of gaining enjoyment: touching others or being touched. Place them at either ends of a line. Where it can be a problem is if both partners share the same end of the line. If both like to be touched to feel loved, then they can be left deprived because they can both sit waiting to get their fix. Conversely, if the way they know themselves to be loved is from the response to their touching, then it can turn into a bit of a wrestling match where both are so focused on the response of the other that neither actually responds. Opposites are actually better suited in this regard, because one will stroke all day long, and the other enjoy being stroked. Of course, most feeling birds (and most of the rest of us, too) will be somewhere in between, so usually the flow of give and take works perfectly well.

One last thing to be aware of is that you both tend to live in the moment. When times are good there's no better place to be, or to stay. During stormy weather, however, Doves can lose their sense of perspective and feel as if the bad times will never end. If you're both down in the dumps at the same time then you really will be living at Number 1, Gloomy Villas. Hopefully your sky-bird ability to see the big picture will reduce this somewhat, but it's something to be aware of (and not to panic at).

Feathers for the nest

What Doves living with Doves need to know
Do:

I suggest, probably with futility, that you sit down and organise yourselves. Work out the repetitive tasks that need doing and divide them between you. Arrange a time every month to go through them and chivvy each other to complete them. You'll hate doing it – it's the bit of advice you're least likely to heed – but it's the bit that would probably improve your quality of life the most.

I'd also suggest you work out responsibilities for any special projects you undertake, like a new kitchen being installed or a multi-destination holiday – or hire someone to take care of the detail for you. In your business, a life coach can be a great asset because although you'll be great at thinking strategically, your ideas will often fall through or fail to prosper because you won't follow through with the steps that would make it a success. You need a ground-bird somewhere in your life to make things happen.

A Dove pairing can be so mutually supportive in an emotional sense that it can lead to them building a bit of a wall between themselves and the world, where friends can feel they're intruding or forced into the third-wheel position. Leave some space between yourselves for others to fit into your lives – it'll enrich you both. I'd even recommend that you have some time away from each other and pursue individual interests. I know many happy Dove couples who live in each other's pockets, develop the same hobbies and share everything, and never feel the need for others. They're not the ones who come to see me. The ones who come complain of having lost the connection, a waning of passion and excitement, a feeling of flatness. Clinging to each other too tightly can starve the flame, so make room for some other people in your life and build in some absence to give the heart a reason to start pounding about how good returning can be.

If you've read what I've said about comfort, you'll know how and to what degree it applies to you both. I think the key thing is to honour the sensitivities of the other, which in most situations I'd expect you to be good at. Most difficulties I've experienced in this area are a consequence of one Dove not respecting the seriousness of what is important to their partner about comfort, while expecting them to devote themselves to their own particular needs. I remember one such couple where the wife was extremely sensitive to fabrics, and was ridiculed by her husband for being a 'princess', yet he demanded that his pillow accompanied him on holidays. Some Doves, with strong prince or princess tendencies, can, if you squint at them in the right light, be mistaken for being selfish, so maybe have a little think about your own requirements before looking askance at your partner's.

Don't:
Okay, I'll take a chance with this . . . don't get too precious. In a relationship where you both focus a lot on comfort – in the way I've defined it – it can be easy for you to slide into a world that has to be perfect to be acceptable, and where the least infringement can lead to a tantrum. That's not pretty to be around and people won't be looking at you, admiring your discernment. Take a chill pill – you'll find that making do is sometimes good for the soul.

Don't make yourselves responsible for the ills of the world. You're probably very sensitive to the needs of others, and it's not much of a stretch to find yourself feeling that you're responsible for what you notice. Couples like you can be the people who are the backbone of a community: giving time, supporting worthy causes and providing emotional support. You can also hurt your health doing too much. Find a balance. This can also be true for some Dove couples in relation to each other, as the urge to makes things right for the person you love, or keep them right, can be a powerful one, and sometimes this can escalate into a situation where you gradually switch from partner to parent – both in the nurturing role and the controlling one. In theory, it can be nice to be mothered (or fathered), but over time it'll be destructive to the development of an equal, sharing, intimate relationship if it's that way all the time.

Don't forget to utilise your talents. Doves often under-achieved at school because the educational system doesn't support a learning style based on learning by experience – one of doing rather than watching and listening – resulting in the fact that you can often underestimate your talents. Within this relationship is a wonderful opportunity for you to explore just what you're capable of doing with the support of someone who loves you. Generally, your gifts will be practical ones – your intelligence lies in your hands more often than not – so whether your gift is something that can be applied literally, like building your home, or one that builds your career, doesn't matter; just dare to explore doing the best you're capable of, and don't forget to support your partner when they attempt the same thing – or even give them the occasional push.

Don't get stuck in the moment. Things pass. If you forget to look beyond a present problem then it's easy to believe that it's going to last for ever. Doves can be accused of being drama queens because the feeling they have now is the biggest thing in their life, and it tends to both absorb them and dominate them. Things are rarely as bad as they seem, but they're always as bad as you make them. So give each other permission to kick the other out of their bad moment and dose them with a spoonful of perspective.

Nightingale and Robin

Robin: 'We can talk for hours but sometimes we're at such cross purposes. He always seems to focus on crackpot schemes and gets annoyed when I point that out.'

Nightingale: 'She can be a real killjoy. Every idea I have she shoots down in flames. She has no imagination whatsoever.'

These two are both sound birds, so silence is not going to be something you hear much of in their house. They're likely to have music everywhere, or the TV on constantly as a background accompaniment to their perpetual conversation. On the whole, this similarity will suit them both, and be more of a challenge to those who come within listening range than it will for them. The difference between them is that one likes to soar and look down at the big picture, while the other is happiest grounded by facts and things that are known; new ideas need to be proven before they're taken on, rather than tried out to see if they should be. This can cause a number of problems that need working through but, true to the message of this book, by doing so, these two can be a powerful couple who can thrive in a supportive relationship.

Cuckoos in the nest

Time spent with you two can feel like an evening visiting Babel. Because both of you tend to work out your thoughts by listening to what comes out of your mouth you'll have a lot to say about things, and often at the same time, so it can sound and feel a bit cacophonous to anyone who doesn't share your bird type. It can also seem like you're not giving others a chance to be heard.

At home, it's important that both of you give the other room; it's easy sometimes for one to become the dominant voice – finishing the other's sentences or stories, talking over them, telling them what they should do or think. This browbeating can lead to unhappiness for the partner, a feeling that they only have an opinion if their partner tells them what it is. As you both need to talk to think, it's vital that you allow the other the space to do so.

One of the things that's likely to be a connection between you is music, or some other auditory art – like comedy or oratory. Song birds are the type who can recite comedy sketches verbatim, have a quote for every occasion or remember the words to a poem they heard once at school. If your tastes align this is great: I know a couple who live for a particular rock band and arrange their life around the group's concert dates; another for whom poetry is a consuming love, who holiday in places connected with famous poems or poets, and who love nothing more than sitting in a café hearing a performance poetry evening. If your tastes clash however, it can mean big trouble. Your taste is such a personal statement for you that anybody who doesn't share it is probably going to attract a negative label. If you love gangsta rap and your partner is more into Engelbert Humperdinck, well, your homie is risking getting capped in their crib, while you might just get . . . er . . . smothered in a cosy cardigan (I'm betting no fan of Engelbert has ever been accused of a violent crime).

If you get into an argument, do be careful of the words you use – for sound birds, they're weapons. Both of you have the capacity to cut the other to the quick with a comment, and you both know that it takes a long time to undo an unkind word. Take a moment and count to ten before you launch an attack. In relationships of these types, in any combination, words tend to be the most corrosive element in potential break-ups. When I've had song birds in my room, it's typical to have to listen to a litany of word-perfectly recalled hurtful comments, sometimes going back years. If you're not careful, words will burn through the bonds that connect you.

Song birds can seem slow in making a decision because they have to talk through all the possibilities before arriving at an answer. With two of you, it can take longer than just double the time: I'd love to be a fly on the wall when those sales people who want you to make an instant decision about double glazing come round; you'd drive them crackers and beat even their 'wear them down' tactics. There's a chance they'd give you the windows for free just to get out of your house.

Nightingales are sky-birds: they're good at seeing patterns and the way things connect together – thinking strategically if you like. They'll be the one who says, 'You *could* do that, but if you *did*, this would probably happen . . .' and be right, more often than not. Their weakness is detail; they'll avoid it like a kid does bedtime. With a low boredom threshold, any menial or repetitive task is going to get half-hearted attention, on a good day. This is bad news, because Robins organise their life according to certain, obvious rules. Theirs. If the Nightingale is given the task of cleaning the kitchen they'll do it, but without a clear idea of what the difference will be from when they started to when they finish – it'll just be generally cleaner. For the Robin, however, 'clean' is a very precise term, and if their partner's efforts fall below the standard for 'clean' by even the smallest margin, it's the same as not having done it at all. Left to itself, this difference can define the relationship, with the Nightingale feeling constantly nagged by the 'Rules Gestapo' and the Robin feeling themselves ignored, and something important to them trampled on.

Robins are good at detail and should be the one who organises the home – leave it to the Nightingale and you'll never really be sure you're going to get on holiday until you land safely in the resort, while important details like visas, passports or hotel bookings can be lost in the mix. 'How could you possibly forget that?', 'I'm sorry I thought . . .' can become a bit of a refrain unless the Robin is given oversight.

Feathers for the nest

What Robins need to know about Nightingales
Do:
Some of these suggestions are going to apply to both of you. For example, the way you will both know yourselves to be loved will be because you hear your partner telling you; and you know the way they do. Both of you can spot insincerity in the tone of the other, so you know the truth of their love when you hear it. I don't need to tell you to keep telling each other, to keep texting each other, or to ring each other several times a day. Your voice is a balm to the other, a support, and a way to connect through the ether in a way that physical touch can't.

Listen when you're together to how you're talking to each other. By this I mean two things: firstly in the balance between you and secondly, in the nature of what you say. Do you get the chance to feel heard by your partner? Do you give them the opportunity to feel heard by you? It's a common, and easy, trap to fall into where one of you takes up more of the talking time than the other. This might be fine, but check. Consider, also, the nature of what you say. Nothing is more predictive of this relationship failing than the number of times your tone towards your partner, or theirs towards you, is laced with sarcasm, disappointment, or – and this will mean the end is nigh – contempt.

Don't:
Robins like things a certain way, so you probably like most things a particular way, and you'll have good reasons for all of them. So the following statement might not make sense the first time

you read it: your good reasons aren't necessarily shared by your partner. How can they not be? you ask. They make sense. Yes, but that doesn't mean they feel important to your partner. Nightingales live in a world that doesn't focus on how things get done, that doesn't look for a 'way' to do something; they just work it out each time they do it. This can be maddening for you, because life would be so much easier if only they'd do things your way. I know, but they won't, no matter how much you nag – I mean instruct – them helpfully.

Don't trust your partner. I only mean with jobs that require attention, patience or repetition. Nightingales can have the attention span of a gnat and are bound to fail to focus on an important detail in the middle of a project – you'll just never know which one. A Nightingale friend of mine turned up at a wedding on time and with her children beautifully dressed and excited in their bridesmaid dresses. The bride agreed they looked lovely . . . she just didn't know them – they had arrived at the church a week early. Make sure that you take care of business. If you give Nightingales a task to complete, check later – but don't nag them for their oversights. As they're bound to make them, just find a way to work around it.

What Nightingales need to know about Robins
Do:
Okay, I've already said some things that apply to you in your partner's piece above – have a read and you'll know where I mean. What I'm going to focus on here is the consequences of the main difference between you both. You are best with ideas and plans and you trust your intuition a lot more than your partner. The thing is, they need facts and evidence before they trust something you want them to commit to. Give them to them. I know it's a bit boring to concern yourself with detail, but it'll be a necessary part of winning their support for your idea. It can feel as if they're constantly bursting your bubble, but that's not their intention – it's just a sign that they can't see the big picture like you can. Treat them to some detail and they'll catch

up. Robins are one-hop-at-a-time birds, so if you fly too far ahead, you'll leave them behind.

Pay attention to what matters to Robins, because it REALLY matters to them in a way things don't to you. Listen to what they moan about or criticise you most for, and do your best to address them. As you know, Robins have particular ways they like things done. My advice is just to do them their way unless it's really important to you not to. It will make your life easier, they'll appreciate it, and it won't bother you one way or the other.

Don't:

Many of these suggestions will actually apply to both of you, the first one being: don't hold onto grudges. You can both regurgitate old wrongs going back the length of the relationship – it's one of the reasons why rows between your types can simmer for days – but it doesn't move you forward. I've worked with some couples who agree to a rule that they can't refer to anything from the past to help them win a current argument. One even had a sign displayed prominently saying, 'It's only about now', and if their partner started dragging up the past the other could simply point at it. It seemed to work. The past is not a cudgel with which to beat your partner over the head.

Don't praise anyone too much who your partner could mistake for a rival. All of us are capable of jealousy. The way both of you will tend to be triggered into this is by the words you hear your partner using to describe someone else. Even being too enthusiastic about someone in a film might get you a bit of a sulk or hissy fit from your significant other. If you feel the need to say something nice to them about someone else, try something like, 'They look nearly as good in that outfit as you would.' As long as it's not Angelina Jolie or Brad Pitt, you might get away with it. But that is only a might. Praise at your peril.

Owl and Owl

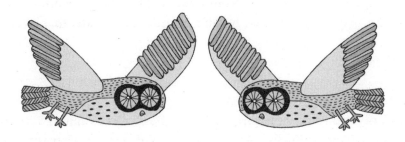

Owl 1: 'So often it's like we don't need to talk, we know what the other is thinking, but sometimes she's so far away from understanding that there's something going on with me that it's not funny.'

Owl 2: 'I know I can be just as guilty, but she can be so absorbed in something that it'll be like I'm not even there.'

As Gollum would say, you two are 'tricksy', as is describing all the combinations between thinking birds. My challenge is that, while there are very definite things that characterise your type, you're also strongly influenced by the second type you identified when you took the Lovebirds quiz at the beginning of the book. Because of that, I am going to do my best here to describe some likely things that will characterise your relationship, whilst being aware that I could get you both completely wrong. Therefore, I'm also going to ask you to read what I've written about the combinations of you and your partner's second types, and your second types and Owls. So, for example, if one of you had Dove as your second strongest Lovebird type, and the other had Nightingale, then reading about them and their combination, as well as what follows here, should give you (a lot of) information to guide you. Within all those descriptions I think you'll find nuggets that will help.

The two things that define you as Owls is your preference for ideas above concrete facts, and your need to understand things: you both hate what you consider trivial or badly thought out. You also spend a lot of time in your own heads – whatever noise your house generates won't be coming from your mouths that often.

Cuckoos in the nest

Most couples experience those enjoyable moments of companionable silence where no words are needed. You have those as often as you actually speak. Both of you have a rich internal world that you spend a lot of time in, so it can work very well for you to have a partner who allows you time in that space.

What seems to arise from this are almost telepathic moments where you know what the other person is going to say, or what's on their mind. This can be a great bonding experience for you both, however it's not infallible, and you can also be guilty of being so immersed in your own world that you mistake how you feel for how your partner is feeling. A great number of Owls and Kingfishers have been left by their partners and wailed, 'But I thought we were happy!' I've been one of them. Don't mistake your thoughts about the state of the relationship for your partner's. I made a radical discovery that you might like to borrow: I found *asking* really helped, especially when my partner wasn't as happy as I thought. Unfortunately, Owls are probably the worst of all types for bottling things up. They can let things fester for ages, having conversations in their heads, staying awake long into the night ranting about things before they finally let things out, often with volcanic consequences. Owls worry that if they can't control their emotions completely, they can't control them at all, and this can often become a self-fulfilling prophecy – they push their feelings down until finally the pent-up force explodes (unless their second type is Dove, in which case they might be more in touch with their emotional life). If both Owls gush at the same time, it can be an awesome spectacle, and immensely damaging to the two of you, because you rarely say anything you don't mean. You can be terrifyingly hurtful with your words, and can't take them back easily, because you meant them. So be careful. You're both sky-birds, which means that you enjoy having ideas and exploring possibilities. The pair of you probably flit, individually or collectively, from one enthusiasm to another, enjoying yourselves immensely for as long as the enthusiasm lasts. With you both being similar, this propensity isn't going to attract the criticism it does from ground-bird partners of Owls. The downside of this, however, is that you can be great beginners of things, but not be so hot at completing them, or come unstuck because neither of you had the attention span to pay attention to important but boring details. You have a very low boredom threshold and I'd expect the most common arguments to be about whose turn it is to put out the rubbish, clean the kitchen, pay the bills, organise the car service or any of the other scores of little jobs that keep relationships ticking over. Your relationship will tick with the reliability of a watch bought in a Bangkok market.

Your life together is probably going to be punctuated by little disasters: missed planes, turning up at the wrong place, or the right place at the wrong time. It would really help if you'd sit down regularly and plan your life a little more, even – brace yourselves – check the details of things that are coming up. It would really help, but I don't believe you'll do it. Owls don't just dislike details; it's almost an allergy. (You could get a note from your mum for it.)

Neither of you are likely to be comfortable with emotions (unless you had Dove as your second type in quiz 2) and will probably contrive elaborate methods of avoiding them – both your own, and of those people around you. This can make your life together a bit sterile; steady, but sterile. There's also a danger that each of you supports the other in their 'I don't do emotion' stance so much that it becomes a virtue you almost caricature. I strongly recommend you don't drift into this. One of the best things about being in a loving relationship is having a place in the world you can feel safe being yourself. My personal opinion is that many Owls are wary of emotion because of what happened to them when they were young; it felt safer for them to think about their feelings rather than just go ahead and have them, or they just weren't in contact with enough people to get to experience many. It's why controlling feelings is so important for them – as children, having them often didn't lead to anything great. Your love gives you a chance to change, to risk intimacy and to trust trusting. Take the chance. I've seen some Owl couples who haven't, and their relationships often look more like a business arrangement than a love match.

Feathers for the nest

What Owls living with Owls need to know
Do:
Owls will mainly know themselves to be loved in the manner that those of their second Lovebird type do. If their second is a Nightingale, for example, it'll be by the things they're told; if it's a Swift, then it's in the look their partner shares with them, or the time you spend together. If it's a Dove then you might find touch is more important than for most Owls. So while I'm suggesting some things that the two of you should do to enrich your relationship, it's heavily dependent on this secondary type; but I'll give you some purely Owl suggestions, now.

I've already mentioned how important I think it is for the two of you to engage emotionally at a more overt level. The love the two of you have for each other can be every bit as intense as any other, but you may be short on outward signs of it. If that suits you both that's fine, but often that won't be the case, at least not equally. One way of exploring emotion is by exploring physical feelings – Owls can be quite oblivious to their physical state and really not well connected to their bodies at all. Using your bodies as a means of reconnecting, first to your sensations and later to your emotions, can be a great way to increase intimacy. Give each other massages, share a physical activity like yoga or Tai Chi, or maybe learn a physical skill together. Anything that gets you out of your head and into your body, and preferably something that helps you to focus on the body of your partner too, at some stage – in a sensual rather than a sexual way. This will bring many benefits (not least among them being that Owls can be terrible at massage – many perform it like someone trying to make bread). By being more focused on what is happening through your fingers, you can get to know your partner on a whole new level.

Talk. Set time aside to share with your partner what's in your head, and listen to what's in theirs; with my clients I often suggest that the talker talks and the listener remains silent. Later, it can be a two-way dialogue, but at the beginning I want each of you to have the chance to just let out everything that's been whirling round in your brains. Say anything: talk about what you're happy and unhappy about, what you'd like more of in the relationship; what you'd like less of.

One of the great benefits of this is that you get to hear what's actually going on with your partner, while they get a chance to let out anything that might be building within. And the more trust develops from this, the more willing you'll both be to risk intimacy.

Finally, support each other's ideas – as I'm sure you mainly do – but also be prepared to provide a devil's advocate function if you don't see a particular idea as viable. Both of you can get wildly enthusiastic about a plan or idea that's come to your mind, so there's a danger that one or both of you could launch into a grand enterprise without investigating the detail and end up getting burnt in one way or another. I know you hate detail, but one of you has to do it, and you can't trust the one with the excitement in their eyes.

Don't:
Be sure to guard against cynicism. Owls have a low tolerance for things not making sense, and they're great at picking holes in other people's arguments. In fact, you can be so good, and have

so much fun doing it, that you start picking holes in everything. It doesn't lead to a happy place, so use your superpower wisely.

Similarly, I know you don't like small talk and trivia, so going to social gatherings can be really tedious and, if you go at all, you'll often spend the time stuck together either having a conversation all of your own, or just taking the mickey under your breath about those around you. Owls can be quite excluding, which may suit you, but over time this could lead to the sort of stagnation that comes from being isolated from the energy, ideas and lives of other people. Don't put a bubble around the two of you, however safe it feels, or however complete the two of you feel together.

Don't overdo the chaos. If neither of you takes responsibility for specific things, or you don't both share overall responsibility for things that need organising – and do this in a structured way with each checking on the other – you're going to get your bums bitten by your mistakes on quite a regular basis. Owls have the potential to organise, because they think in a very precise and well-thought-through way: they simply often don't want to.

Just remember my advice and keep this book handy for when something really important to you goes wrong because neither of you paid sufficient attention. (Then you can hit each other over the head with it.)

Being sky-birds, you're both likely to be reasonably flexible in your thinking, but Owls often have checklists in their heads that need to be satisfied around certain things – and each person will have their own. Take buying a new mobile phone. You'll have done your research before you even set foot in the store, and there will be certain things that need to be ticked before you can continue. And if the sales person tries to tick his or her boxes rather than yours, it's likely to be a short visit. Things need to make sense to you, your way. That can sometimes lead to you cutting off your nose to spite your face, and together it can be even worse because you'll each stoke the other's righteous indignation – especially if you share the same checklist.

Peacock and Swan

Peacock: 'He's always telling other women how nice they look and crawling all over them. What am I, chopped liver? I spend hours making myself look nice, and the first thing he does when he sees me is paw at me and spoil my make-up.'

Swan: 'I don't get it. I can't remember the last time she suggested we had an early night. She moans if I work too much, but when I get home she won't let me touch her.'

In this combination, both of you have a preference for living with what you know: you like to keep your feet on the ground, make decisions based on sound evidence and aren't prone to flights of fancy. Your life is probably well organised and compartmentalised, and in all of those things, you'll be comfortably singing off the same hymn sheet. The challenge for you both is that the Peacock is strongly biased in favour of the way things look, whereas the Swan finds how things feel much more important. It can lead to some interesting challenges.

Cuckoos in the nest

Like everybody, Peacocks measure the strength of their relationship in particular ways. One of them is through the time you
choose to spend with them. They'll accept you might need to be
apart when you're working, but will soon start to question your
need to work beyond normal hours. And when it comes to
choosing nights out with your friends, or sports practice, or going
to the gym without them, then watch out. They have a weird way
of making that become a choice between wanting to be with
them, and preferring to do something else.

Peacocks are often high-octane people, always on the go and
buzzing with energy. Swans can be a little more sedate, or at least
need to take a run-up to get to full speed. Peacocks will open
their eyes in the morning and launch into their day. Swans will
open their eyes and launch into their day sometime around mid-
morning. If someone invented a sound-proof newspaper, Swans
would buy it to hide behind at breakfast to keep away from the
ridiculous chirpiness of their mate.

Swans tend to dwell in the moment, whereas Peacocks are
more able to see ahead. This can mean that the Swan can stay
stuck in something that's been worrying both of you, long after
the Peacock has seen their way clear and moved on. Pacing is
really critical in this relationship, and by that I mean the Peacock
has to learn not to overwhelm their partner with the speed of
their thinking or the pace they like to live life. Swans also need
to learn to appreciate the gifts they themselves bring to the table,
because sometimes they can feel intimidated by their 'shinier'
partner and allow themselves to adopt a junior role. There is no
need for this to happen: Swans might take longer to come to a
decision, or they might not catch onto a film plot as fast as a
Peacock, but they tend to have common sense in abundance and
a gut feeling for things that can be almost spooky. A couple that
respects both partners' ways of thinking can be a very powerful
and successful pairing indeed.

Swans express their love through touch and by taking care of you. They can be accused of thinking that physical closeness cures all ills and can barely wait for a row to end before starting on the make-up sex. This won't work for a Peacock; they'll need some space first and maybe a bit of wooing before they'll be ready to let you close. This can be confusing for both parties, with Swans desperate to show their affection the way they do best, but with the Peacock wanting some time together first, perhaps sharing an experience, maybe a gift. Strange how a Swan could receive a present from their partner and feel rebuffed, and the Peacock be invited to 'a massage and who knows what will follow' and feel the same way.

Appearance is a big deal for Peacocks. They're likely to put a lot of effort into looking good for you – and anyone else who might see them – and they'll expect the same of their Swan. They're likely to be disappointed, however. Swans will have comfort far higher on their list than fashion, and have been known to make some strange dress choices. (They'll probably see absolutely nothing wrong with wearing sandals and socks, that's how little hope there is for them.) The root of the problem lies with the Peacock, who will feel that how their partner looks is some kind of reflection on them, so might make the mistake of trying to take over their clothes choices, just as they feel it's their job to make all decisions on interior design. The Swan needs to resist at all costs if they're not to have bunions by the time they're forty, and the feeling they've been wearing sandpaper in the cause of looking good, for the last decade . . . ahh, I haven't mentioned comfort and Swans yet, have I? It's a big deal. Swans can feel a rough label on a coat through five layers of clothes; they can tell if something is over-salted by three grains in a lake of gravy; and would detect a draught in a (by necessity, obviously) hermetically sealed space shuttle. Sensitive is one word for them; high maintenance is two. A Peacock would happily cram their feet into shoes so pointy they could have your eye out, but not a Swan. They'll walk to work in comfy trainers and do their best to forget to change them all day if they can get away with it. A Peacock will base their furniture choices on colour, how it supports the mood of the room, and the style. The Swan will just want to know if it's comfy; and it will never be quite comfy enough. As fast as the Peacock installs a post-modern razor blade of a sofa, the Swan will swamp it with silk cushions of any and every colour, as long as they're plump. It'll be an on-going war.

Feathers for the nest

What Peacocks need to know about Swans
Do:
Slow down a bit. You tend to run around at a million miles an hour, multi-tasking (even if you're a man) and still finding the time to fidget. A Peacock in harness can get a lot done, but they can also exhaust the people around them, especially types like Swans and Doves. If you overwhelm your partner, there is a danger they'll withdraw and lose confidence in the face of your relentlessness. Leave something for them. And don't keep finishing their sentences.

Your Swan will feel that they're loved by how often you touch them, and how – you'll get brownie points just from being the one who initiates holding hands when you're walking. (I know it obscures one of your fancy gloves and rucks up your sleeve, but suck it up, it'll be worth it.)

As well as with touch, Swans show they love you by the things they do for you and, because they put such a premium on comfort, that shouldn't be any kind of a hardship for you. Remember to return the favour: you might be surprised how much any small kindness you do that makes their life nicer – from running a bath to bringing them a coffee – will be appreciated.

Don't:
One of the biggest potential battlefields between you is the look of things. Left to their own devices, Swans will create a home of cosy comfiness that would be a pleasure for anyone to sink into. Colours might be a bit crazy, styles an interesting eclecticism,

but it will be a welcoming place. For you, style is likely to trump comfort. Peacock homes often look like they're show homes, and shoes always come off in the hall. Don't get me wrong, the house will look great, sometimes even amazing, but don't think that just because you have great taste that your Swan doesn't have something to bring to the house-making party.

While we're talking about appearance, and without wanting to bang on too much, you can come across as the style police sometimes. Leave your partner to be themselves, don't pressure them to dress how you think they should, and don't treat a few extra pounds gained as a breach of contract. The world is not looking at your lover and judging you, and them relaxing their appearance doesn't mean they care less about you. If you're looking for signs that they love you, notice how often you're stroked or how many times they do something to improve your quality of life. I know it can't compare to a thoughtful gift or spending quality time with you, but it is actually the same thing to them.

What Swans need to know about Peacocks
Do:
This advice actually applies to both of you because you're both ground-birds. As such, you'll value following rules and like to make decisions based on firm evidence; neither of you are ones to wing it. But, sometimes, maybe you should. There is a danger that your relationship will be so well organised and cautious that you slowly squeeze the novelty out of it. See if you can plan some spontaneity: launch a project without a three-year consultation period, and maybe even have a day where you contravene one of your sacred rules just for the hell of it – leave the kitchen untidy when you go out and see if the tidy police really *do* come for you in the night.

Swans often have difficulty seeing into the future, so your planning can be a bit short-term. When you add to this your inclination to get sucked into the moment, you can see that it could have an impact on a range of things, including your career path.

Let your partner help. Peacocks often see ahead more clearly, so could be helpful in coaching you to a longer view.

Peacocks count minutes spent together as a sum of how much you care. If they see you making an effort to be with them even though you're busy or just desperate to sink into your posture-pedic mattress, they'll love you for it. If you're working away, make sure you can Skype them – seeing your face will be important.

Pay attention to gifts they respond to positively and spot the trends. Peacocks view the gift as a way of gauging how well the giver understands them. If you give them a present that fits their style or taste, or has some connection they value, they'll glow. If you get it wrong, well, you clearly don't know them at all: exit stage left with a sniff.

Don't:

I know that appearance isn't the be all and end all to you, and that sometimes you find your Peacock partner a bit superficial with how much they care about how things look to other people, but appearance *is* important to them. You will find life a lot easier if you allow yourself to be guided a little in what you wear, or just surrender every now and again by dressing how they'd like you to. If they tell you that you look sexy in something, it's likely to mean a lot more than if most other types said it – it's practically foreplay.

Don't underestimate your worth in this relationship. Sometimes Peacocks might seem faster or cleverer than you, but that's usually just a contextual thing. If you stop to think about it, there are probably many areas where you have a competence they don't. You are likely to have a very good intuitive sense about how others feel, and you'll be in touch with your own emotions. One word of warning: just because you're really sensitive to your partner's moods and feelings, don't make yourself responsible for them, or for their wellbeing. Swans sometimes use a lot of 'shoulds' when describing the actions their partners need to take for their emotional wellbeing. Just as you don't like to be told what to wear, Peacocks won't appreciate being told what, where and how to feel. Even if it is for their own good.

Swift and Robin

Robin: 'Of course I love her – I ring her three times a day from the office just to tell her, but if I have to work late it's like I'm having an affair.'

Swift: 'Words are easy – what I want to see are the actual words coming out of his mouth. In person. If work is more important than me, he should just say so.'

Swifts are visual birds, whereas Robins are fundamentally auditory. That's going to be one of the challenges in this pairing. The other is that a Swift is all about floating up high to enjoy the big picture, whereas Robins are happiest closer to the ground soaking up the detail. Your relationship can be a very powerful mix where you create a balance between who comes up with the ideas for your life, and who makes them happen; and a middle ground where the need to see and be seen and the need to hear and be heard complement each other.

Cuckoos in the nest

When you hear a Robin sing in your garden, their rich variety of notes demands your attention. Similarly, as people, this type are not easy to ignore and often they'll use talking to get your attention – even if you're immersed in a great film, trying to avoid a pedestrian in your car, or in the middle of performing brain surgery. The two processes of having a thought and speaking it out loud often have such a short gap for a Robin that it seems they wear their brains on the outside – you can hear its workings as they occur. (This can lead to those funny moments where they realise they've said something out loud without meaning to, or say something tactless.)

Swifts can be no slouches on the talking front either, and can actually probably out-produce Robins on a straight words-per-minute basis because they tend to think quickly and verbalise their thoughts at the same speed. The difference is that Swifts will be speaking about something they wish to communicate to you, whereas often for Robins the conversation is part of their communication with themselves: they need to hear what they're thinking to get the thought straight.

For Swifts, this will mean having the patience to listen and not necessarily add to what is being said. If you expand what the Robin is saying with your own ideas and thoughts, then you just give them even more to work out and you become embroiled in a looooooooooong talk. Like a tropical hurricane, let the Robin blow themselves out, and then help with the clean-up afterwards.

Swifts can be great dreamers. They often have a brilliant capacity to visualise, so their plans, projects and ideas can be rich and creative. Properly harnessed by the organisational skills of the Robin, this can be a very successful and productive part of the relationship – this combination has been known to make great property developers, for example. The challenge is for the Swift to be able to pace the scale of their vision to the ability of the Robin to conceptualise it themselves, which will require a lot of talking, and to be patient enough to provide enough detail for the Robin to be comfortable enough to buy into the idea. Listen carefully to the objections you get from your Robin, as often they'll just be a sign that they don't have enough information to build your vision in their own words.

Swifts place great store on the amount of time you spend with them, and they'll often measure the quality time you have together as an indicator of the health of the relationship. For Robins, this isn't so important – they can usually be sustained simply by regular phone contact – but don't ever forget to ring, as that's the same as saying, 'I didn't care enough about you to want to talk' – a heinous sin. Swifts need to remember that their voice tone is being run through the sincerity detector that is a Robin's brain, so don't throw casual 'Love yous' at them, while Robins need to remember that Swifts need to be able to see you to know that they're loved – Skype probably isn't going to cut it, long term.

There exists a bone of contention for all combinations of ground- and sky-birds, but potentially Swifts and Robins could have the equivalent of a brontosaurus-neck-bone of contention compared to everyone else. Largely, it is due to the fact that Swifts are such big-picture people. They can be real visionaries, which is a good thing, right? Unless you happen to live with them. Their mind can be so full of their vision that the details of daily life pass them by. Robins tend to like order and, like all ground-birds, will have a set of rules to make life tick more efficiently. These rules are highly valued by them, so a breach is considered a personal attack. In other words, they'll probably make your adherence to these rules a personal project, from which there looks to be no escape or hope of such. This can be seriously disturbing for Swifts. Many have reported themselves 'hunted within their own homes'. Here's an example: 'I can be in the kitchen when I'll notice a stack of dishes above the dishwasher. Now that could be a trap. If I ignore it I'm going to get the lecture about how I don't do anything around the house or notice everything she does. But equally she might be about to put the machine on a self-clean cycle, or it might need more salt, or maybe today is, "Clean your own plates day". I'll literally stand there debating whether it's an ambush and get quite paranoid over an ordinary thing. And, I have to admit, I resent it, because stuff like that holds me back from thinking about better things.'

Feathers for the nest

What Swifts need to know about Robins
Do:

Give your partner the time and space to speak out their thoughts. You probably think very quickly, but don't use that to end their sentences or hurry them to a conclusion: wait until they've worked their thoughts out and then contribute your ideas.

Tell them, well, everything, really. They'll know you love them because you say so, and by the tone of your voice when you're being affectionate. Being told what you appreciate about them whenever you think it will give you a lot of brownie points, too.

Songs are likely to be important markers in your Robin partner's life, so do your best to remember what was playing when you had your first dance or kiss, and say something when you hear the song subsequently – they'll probably be waiting for you to.

Surround sound in the cinema does for them what 3-D films do for you. Let them sit in the cinema where the sound is best (often the middle).

You might like going out to places where there's lots of things to see, but if what accompanies that is a lot of competing noise, your Robin is unlikely to enjoy it as much: if it's so noisy you can't hear each other speak, it's like spending an evening in a diver's helmet to them (unless it's a rock concert, in which case they might like the volume cranked up to 11 – as long as they can talk to you about it all later).

Always remember that words are a direct line to your partner's heart. Criticism can wound them deeply, and they will have a long, word-perfect recall of unkind or hurtful things people have said to them, so be very careful of anything that threatens to leave your lips in a moment of anger. Not only will it hurt them; they'll throw it back at you for years to come, so never say anything you don't believe, or that you'll regret.

Similarly, remember that words for Robins are contracts. If

you say, in passing, 'Maybe we should go to Rome later this year', be ready for them to say, further down the line: 'But you said we were going to Rome this year!'

Don't:
Don't get so carried away with your big thoughts that you leave your partner behind. You'll need to use words to build a picture for them, and it will require more brush strokes to give them enough detail to understand your vision than you would believe necessary.

Robins like things the way they like them and can be terrible nags if you don't follow the right way of doing things – which is their way, in case you had any doubts. Honestly? You'll save a lot of time by just learning the rules and following them. You won't ever care about these rules (no need to tell the Robin that), but you'll be able to get back to your pretty thoughts a lot sooner.

Don't call Robin 'anally retentive', either – that would fall under the 'hurtful' heading I mentioned earlier. Trust me, they'll throw that kind of thing back at you for ever – '. . . and another thing, ten years ago you said I was . . .'

Which brings me to: don't ever get into a row based on who said what. Robins will beat you and, even if you are right, the fact that you remembered something said more accurately than they do will be stored up and used against you. Words belong to them.

What Robins need to know about Swifts
Do:
Your partner probably bugs you with their big ideas and dreams. Indulge them. Give them as much room as you can to at least enjoy the idea for a while. Sure, many will come to nothing, but that's often not the point of the exercise for them. Not all ideas have to come to fruition. With your help, the right ones will and you'll both benefit.

The way Swifts know that you love them will be by the time you spend with them, the way you look at them, and maybe the things you buy them. I don't mean they're mercenary, just that if you buy them something it needs to fit into their taste or interests, otherwise they'll feel you don't understand them.

Be aware that their appearance is likely to be very important to them, so make sure some of your many words are aimed at appreciating them for that. Also, they're likely to judge you by the same yardstick, so if you start to let your appearance slip, or don't 'bother' when you go out, they'll often make that personal with a, 'You don't care enough to bother' accusation. If you ever hear someone say, 'I'm not going out with you looking like that', they're a Swift (or a Peacock).

Don't:

Don't nag. I know you don't – you just offer your Swift partner useful developmental tips for their own good, but it can feel just a little bit like nagging. I know you have rules, and I know they feel important to you, but if you stopped doing them for twenty-four hours, I guarantee the sun would still come up the next day. Your partner doesn't ignore your rules – he or she just doesn't notice when they're meant to be in play because their attention is on something else. Cut them some slack. Yes, you will have to work harder to make the world keep looking like it should, but so you should; it's *your* world. And your Swift partner there is happy with how *theirs* is working, thank you very much. At least with how things look being important to them, they're probably not too untidy.

Don't shoot your Swift partner's ideas down (I know I said it nicely in the 'do' section – I'm just reminding you). You like detail and you like to know how things are going to work, specifically. Your Swift probably won't be able to satisfy you with that straight off the bat. Give it time and the details will emerge. You two can be really productive; what usually stops it is the Robin sitting on the Swift's strawberries at the beginning of an idea or project.

Allow them their flights of fancy, trust their vision, and start to put flesh on their fanciful skeleton as time passes. They need you for that, because the other thing that stops you two doing amazing things is the Swift going off in too many directions at once. You're their rock; so don't sit on their head.

Dove and Kingfisher

Dove: 'Sometimes it's like living with Hitler. He can be so set in his ways that if I do anything the way I like it instead of the way he likes, he gets annoyed.'

Kingfisher: 'The thing is, she's so airy-fairy about stuff. I don't ask for much, and everything I get her to do makes sense.'

This is one of the combinations that almost inevitably brings challenges. Doves are all about their feelings and their sensitivity to sensation, whereas Kingfishers are ruled by their heads and often display an amazing degree of desensitisation to their emotions and surroundings. Doves can find it hard to express the complexity of their feelings in words, while Kingfishers will have words for everything – if they decide to share them – but little to say about their emotions. It's a pretty big mismatch.

If that wasn't enough, Doves are big-picture people who treat rules only as guidelines and are interested in ideas and the way things relate to each other. Kingfishers, however, are big only on detail, being happier with things that are tangible than things that are just possibilities. Kingfishers will like plans and rules, often so much so that they can wrap their lives and relationships so tight in them that there is little room for a breath of spontaneity or novelty.

If both of you can work hard at understanding the differences between you then you can grow enormously as individuals within an amazingly wide-ranging world, but it *will* involve work: probably every day for the rest of your lives.

Cuckoos in the nest

Doves are lovely fluffy creatures who like to keep harsh reality at a distance, while embracing the pleasures of the moment as often as they can. Kingfishers are the exact opposite. For them, reality is the only thing to be trusted – the things that exist now are far more important than an idea that may never bear fruit. Pleasures for them are also often more cerebral: the quiet success of a crossword or a higher game level better than the sensation of a massage or a steam bath. This can make the Dove sometimes feel more like they're living in a desert than a relationship, and cause them to need to spend time outside the couple fulfilling their need for the virtues of the flesh – I don't mean having an affair: a day at a spa, or a museum or a go-kart track is just as likely. (I'd better say even more likely, so the reading Kingfishers don't panic.) Your partner's need for kinaesthetic (feeling) sustenance isn't about sex – or at least, not exclusively – it's about living in the moment and being connected to the nerve endings that face the world. Doves love feeling stuff; it's as simple as that. The fact that they'll often need to get it from somewhere else is something the relationship may need to address.

Kingfishers like silence. They talk to themselves in their heads a lot, and their internal world can be as rich to them as the real world is to the Dove. They'll often love reading books and watching films, and immerse themselves in the storylines to an amazing degree. Living in a world of their own that's so absorbing can make the Kingfisher's partner feel excluded and lonely at times.

Doves will usually fall asleep after a few pages of bedtime

reading, and see any film over two hours as a marathon involving a dead bum, a warm cola and too much noise. Kingfishers will find Tai Chi or getting their feet manipulated by a reflexologist as something their bodies are doing while they have a think, so finding hobbies to share may take a bit of worthwhile time and trouble.

Both types are big on planning, but in different ways. Kingfishers won't move out of bed in the morning without a plan for the day, and will often be quite inflexible in the face of a need to change it – if Sunday is bath night, then clearly it's not going to be possible to have friends round for dinner, unless they're quite broad-minded. Doves will like plans too, but ones that are more large-scale – they'll be looking at organising experiences, like holidays, rather than the day-to-day minutiae. Doves hate detail with a passion. They have a very low boredom threshold, so enduring a visit to a travel agent is on a level with a visit to the dentist. Ideally, the Dove will have the idea, and then the Kingfisher will make it happen.

Kingfishers are avid rule makers. Things should work a certain way – their way. Many, if not most, will be well-thought-through ways of making things work in the most efficient way, which will make life in the relationship tick along remarkably tidily and well – but so would living in a hive. It can feel quite suffocating to a Dove to be surrounded by the need to pay attention to things they don't actually notice – like which hook the door key should be left on – instead of the things they do – like whether a plumped cushion is actually more comfy than one left untouched. There can be a massive collision here between what matters to both of you. Rules simply don't matter to a Dove, especially if they are a barrier to enjoying the moment: they'll always skip the washing up if it means getting to yoga or rugby practice earlier. That can leave the Kingfisher feeling like they themselves have been trodden on, rather than just one of their rules.

Unless Swan was their second type in quiz 2 at the start of the book, Kingfishers don't feel much. That can be both in terms of physical discomfort, like being curled in a budget-airline economy seat for six hours without noticing their back has locked up, or emotions. This latter can be a defence mechanism because they fear losing control of their feelings, or their past has led them to fear the kinds of feelings they tended to have most when they were young, or just that they didn't have much opportunity in their childhood to interact with others. It means they'll keep away from situations that could trigger emotion – like watching soppy films, or violent ones. Doves, however, will like nothing more than a box set of Richard Curtis films, or a Bruce Lee afternoon (I admit, who prefers which will often be a gender divide, but not always).

Clearly, this is a difference that is likely to matter to the Dove. So much of their experience is focused within the feeling realm that it can leave them short of things to share in the face of their partner's lack of connection to their senses. One of my clients was shocked to find that their Kingfisher partner actually stores their memories as bullet points rather than as visual images, and that the best way to make sure they've reached their husband is to send them an email rather than just say it to their face (often Kingfishers will be talking to themselves during a conversation, rather than listening to you, even when they don't mean to).

Feathers for the nest

What Doves need to know about Kingfishers
Kingfishers are special types in that the way they love will very much depend on whatever their second type was in quiz 2, that you took earlier. So, if Robin was their second strongest Lovebird type, you might find the section on Robins and how they combine with Doves, as well as reading what follows here, will paint a better picture of your relationship and provide useful clues for getting on better. However, the following are key pointers about Kingfishers that most will find true.

Do:
Provide the opportunity for your Kingfisher partner to spend time in their head. Thinking time is, for them, as important as

touching time is for you. If you notice them seeming 'miles away', leave them to finish what they're doing before you interrupt them, or do so gently if your need is more immediate. Interrupting their thoughts can be as annoying for them as running out of conditioner can be for you.

Pay attention to your partner's rules and, as often as possible, follow them. I know it's a pain, and they don't matter to you, but they will feel more loved as a consequence, and you'll feel less nagged.

Meaning is very important to Kingfishers. They pay attention a lot more to things they feel have significance than things they consider trivial. They'll feel valued if you're able to tap into the things that have meaning for them – their interests, hobbies and passions – than they will by trying to force them into yours. That might mean some sacrifice on your part (how interesting can a stamp fair be?) but it'll score you a lot of points.

Don't:
The fact that your partner is not being tactile is not a sign of them not caring, so don't think that it is. Kingfishers simply don't communicate through their bodies much (outside of the obvious, and even then they can be more about performance than intimacy). Because their love for you is obvious within their own heads, Kingfishers can mistake this for being obvious to you, too. Look at their second type in quiz 2 at the start of the book for clues as to how they might be demonstrating this in their world.

Don't expect comfort to mean much to Kingfishers: there is a huge disconnect for them between their head and their body. This can be a challenge for you because often you'll show you love them by the things you do for them to make life nicer. At some level, I'm sure they appreciate just how nice their life is thanks to you, but don't expect them to settle into bed and say 'Ooh, clean sheets, how lovely.'

Finally, don't feel undermined because they pour cold water on your ideas – and don't abandon those ideas because of it. Kingfishers only trust what is in front of them: something tangible, and not a fluffy idea. This is their limitation, not yours. To get them on board, you'll need to provide them with facts and evidence. Until you have these, you might need to hide what you're doing, or develop a thicker skin in the face of their disinterest, disbelief or resistance.

What Kingfishers need to know about Doves
Do:
Work to understand that your rules are only one way of looking at things, and that, in all likelihood, the consequence of not following them won't make a huge difference to the world. Doves simply don't look for rules; they just make do or make up – and it works for them. It's not a better or worse way to live, it's just different, but if you make rules into things with which to put them on the naughty step, it's likely to make the relationship too hard for them to stay in.

Hug them, touch them, squeeze them. Doves will know best that you love them through the contact of your bodies – and that doesn't just mean sex. A casual touch while making dinner can be thrilling in a way you wouldn't imagine. Pay attention to the things they pay attention to. Their comfort is vital to them, as is the pursuit of perfect sensory experiences – like a great cup of coffee, the most comfortable mattress, the most beautiful sunset. Listen to what they have to say about them, and respond to them. Surprise them with the coffee machine they raved about after visiting their friend; book a weekend stay at the hotel with the great service (and mattress) your Dove loved last year; blindfold them and take them to a great place to watch the sunset. Cosset them and feed their senses, and they will love you for it.

Do join them in some of their interests – at least give them a go. Often your resistance to a sensory experience is only based on a past experience, and things can change. Living in a Dove world could really enrich your life and make you happier. And there is more chance of you joining them in their world than them joining you in yours, because so much of yours depends on what is going on in your head.

Don't:

Doves will seem high maintenance to you, but don't get at them for this. Often they do feel, hear, see, taste and smell things more intensely than others, so it's no wonder it takes more tinkering to get their environment right.

Don't think that their going out to do things you have no interest in is a sign of a problem. It's likely that what interests you creates little feeling in them – and creating feelings is vital for their happiness. If a pottery class, an evening paint-balling with their mates, or a night spent dancing feeds their love of sensory experience, then that love is going to flow back into your relationship. Starving it will starve you as a couple, too. Doves often have a low tolerance for emotional deprivation; the song about 'If you love someone, set them free' applies here. Let them fill up their senses anywhere they like and they'll bring the benefits home. Lock them up, however, and they'll stare at the sky and long for the freedom of it.

Nightingale and Kingfisher

Kingfisher: 'I've never known anyone spend so much time talking about nothing. They never focus on what's real – half the time I just switch off.'

Nightingale: 'Truthfully? Sometimes she's just so boring. I lose her for days when she's into her thing, and if she talks to me about it she's microscopic in the detail. I can honestly feel my will to live trying to escape.'

You two obviously like a challenge, or maybe you're working off a karmic debt. Either way, thankfully there's a lot this book can give you to make you a success. On the plus side of your relationship, the chemistry between you must be good for you to be together, so there's hope. The downside is, you're opposite in two different ways, and both I've found to be common flash points in these sorts of relationships.

There's no doubt you both bring a lot to the table, it's just important that you look at how you work around the things that will really annoy you about your partner.

Cuckoos in the nest

We only have one auditory channel: you're either listening to yourself or you're listening to something on the outside. Kingfishers listen on the inside for a great deal of their waking day, and it's not an exaggeration to say that they've always got some kind of conversation going on inside their heads (which at least means they're never on their own). Nightingales, on the other hand, often don't hear their internal voice too well – they need to speak to know their thoughts. If you're living with them, or within reasonable hiking distance, they're likely to use you as a talking post, because talking to yourself looks kind of odd. The conflict here is pretty obvious, and was captured perfectly by two clients. The boyfriend's point of view was, 'I get home from work and try to share my day with her and it's obvious she's not interested. I can see her glaze over. How frickin' rude! If she loved me she'd want to listen,' whereas the girlfriend's perspective was, 'The thing is, no sooner am I home than I get this torrent of words being thrown at me, when I haven't even had a chance to unwind. Why can't he just shut up for a while and let me think?'

Kingfishers are quite private people. They'll tend to be wary of opening up to others, and they're not great ones for sharing their feelings – in fact, they often feel uncomfortable with them and do their best to avoid having any. By comparison, Nightingales tend to be an open book. Because they do a lot of thinking on the outside, they'll often share with strangers things the Kingfisher would consider intimate. Unfortunately, the negative labels won't be long in coming: 'secretive' from one, and 'blabbermouth' from the other.

The second big difference is that Nightingales are sky-birds and Kingfishers are ground-birds. The particular relevance of this is that Kingfishers like to understand things; they hate not knowing. With that kind of curiosity, and a ground-bird's love of detail, it can mean that they are obsessive hunters of facts. If they have a hobby, it will probably absorb a lot of their life

– people who disappear into their loft to play with their train sets and only come out when the kids have left home probably fall into this category, as will people who can enter *Mastermind* and answer any question on the serial marks of Singer sewing machines from 1957 to the present day. While usually quiet, if Kingfishers are in the mood to share with you what they're focusing their current attention on, make sandwiches, because you may be some time. This will be torture for a Nightingale. Nightingales like to talk, but it's a crime to waste words on details – what they prefer as their topic are ideas, dreams, concepts, the relationships between things or people or more things, world politics . . . big-picture subjects they can hover over without getting sucked into the quagmire of detail on. For the listening Kingfisher, this sounds like airy-fairy nonsense: 'What exactly do you mean?' will be their bemused question, as will: 'How specifically is that going to work?' or 'How will that ever happen?' – which the auditory Nightingale will often hear as criticism rather than a request for specifics.

The tendency to approach subjects from different ends of the detail continuum means that discussions often turn into rows, and usually about the structure of the conversation, rather than the topic itself: 'Why is it that every time I try to talk about something you have to start picking me to pieces?' might go the 'conversation'. 'You don't have to know everything before you start anything, or need to put every thought I have under a microscope. You're so incredibly anal it's untrue' might garner the response: 'Well, that's all very well, but if it were left to you we'd get mired in another one of your airy-fairy schemes. You talk a good fight, but you never work things out well enough to actually do them properly. It's a waste of time listening to you half the time, because I know this time next week you'll have moved on to something else that you'll then want to bend my ear about. You're such a bore.'

As I say repeatedly throughout this book, ground-birds like rules and details. Sky-birds like the idea of them, in an abstract kind of way, as long as they don't have to follow the rules or involve themselves in the details. With this pairing, this is particularly important because Kingfishers focus on how things work, so their rules are likely to be especially detailed and exacting, and their policing of them constant. And while they might not go on about the Nightingale's failure to observe the correct folding of the new toilet roll so it has that hotel-style bit of origami as the first sheet, their partner will feel the full silent weight of their disapproval. Of course, this won't be met with silence by the Nightingale – what is? They like things out in the open, whereas the Kingfisher prefers to fester and leave you to guess. Think of the naughty step as a learning opportunity.

Feathers for the nest

What Nightingales need to know about Kingfishers
Do:

Respect your partner's need for silence. They're doing on the inside what you're doing when you talk on the outside. They won't share until they're ready, and neither should they have to – that's your need, not theirs.

Share your day with them. Share what's on your mind, but break it up into smaller chunks to give them a chance to go inside and process what you're saying; if you don't, you'll see them glaze over. Their switching off is not a lack of interest; it's them talking to themselves about what you're saying. Hit your pause button until you see them return to you.

Kingfishers (other than those for whom Swan was their second type in quiz 2 at the start of the book) are likely to be uncomfortable with feelings, either yours or theirs. This is going to be difficult for you because you will want to talk about yours with your partner – often just to be heard and to get a sense of them yourself. It's likely that your Kingfisher partner will quickly move to advice and solutions because it's easier for them to do that than to dwell on the feeling itself. For them, emotions are there to be resolved, not be felt. Please don't mistake this rather business-like response to your worries for a lack of care. In a

Kingfisher's world, the very best thing they can do for you is to take the feeling away, and the best way to do that is to solve whatever gave you the feeling in the first place. It's the Vulcan way.

Don't:
Don't expect Kingfishers to want to come shopping with you. They don't do well with questions like 'Which is the better colour?' or 'Do you think it will go with the brown suit I've got at home?' They don't like window shopping or aimless wandering, hoping for inspiration – if they have to come with you, give them a list of things to go for to give them a goal. Get them to do research on what you're looking for – they'll love that. Then leave them at home and take a friend. If at all possible, Kingfishers buy online, and if they have to visit a shop, they'll have researched what they're going to get before they arrive there. A helpful shop assistant is their worst nightmare – if they wanted help they'd ask for it.

Kingfishers will feel that they're loved according to the type that came second in the quiz you took, so if, for example, Peacock was their second strongest, read the section 'Peacock and Nightingale' (p. 325) as well, and you'll probably see some things you recognise in your relationship. A common trait of this type, however, is to forget to say things on the outside that they say on the inside. A classic example came from a client: 'I've realised that whenever my partner says "I really missed you today" to me, I say something similar back – but usually only in my head!' So don't think they don't love you just because they don't say it. In a way they expect you to mind-read them – after all, they're with you, aren't they?

What Kingfishers need to know about Nightingales
Do:
Nightingales will feel that they're loved by you telling them so. And telling them first is best. If they say, 'I love you' and you say, 'Me, too' afterwards, that often won't count – you have to

say it before them, off your own bat. So work on verbalising every affectionate thought you have. And if you happen to be apart when that happens, texting or phoning them your sweet nothing will get you more points than you can count. Basically, if music be the food of love, words are the flame-grilled fillet steak. (Or, for vegetarians, really really nice carrots.)

Work at expressing your feelings and listening to theirs. Sometimes your partner's problems aren't jigsaws to solve; they're just things to air, to mull over and to let out of their mouth. They will love feeling that you're letting them into your thoughts, so start with a few safe ones while you get the hang of it before dumping the real big ones on them, like should we invite Mother on holiday with us?

Do your best to stay on the outside while your Nightingale is talking. I know there is a gravitational attraction to go inside and think about anything you hear, but keep your focus on them – and let them give you the full version if you can bear it. While your heart will yearn for a 'film-trailer' version so you can go back to thinking, in their heart they will love you for the time you give.

Nightingales love having someone with them to talk through their buying choices – many will have useful shop assistants from their past on their Christmas card list. Shopping alone is not an option, so if you're not there or their friends can't make it, they'll seek eye contact with strangers until they can ask some poor schmo, 'Is this my colour?' You'll get a lot of points for going with them.

Don't:
You know the mass of detail you have in your head? Don't share it unless you're asked, and if you're asked, keep checking with your partner that they haven't gone into a coma. You can get quite carried away with the angel in the detail, but treat it as if every fact you subject your Nightingale to takes a chip out of the soul of your loved one: other people's detail suffocates them. Think about what they need to know and give them no more

than half. They have you for the rest, should it be needed. Which it probably won't be.

Don't begrudge them background noise. I spoke to one couple who waged a constant battle over the radio. Every time the Nightingale was in a room she'd switch the radio on; every time she left, or her Kingfisher partner walked in, the partner would turn it off. External noises can be a real distraction for Kingfishers, especially speaking-voices channels like Radio 4, so often they'll prefer silence. Nightingales, however, will always want to fill quiet. (If you want to torture them, make them meditate silently for thirty minutes. Honestly, they'll tell you anything you want to know after ten.)

Nightingale and Nightingale

Nightingale 1: 'Can you believe he brought up something I said to him a couple of years ago to justify what he'd done? And then he pretended he'd forgotten what he'd said before that. As if.'

Nightingale 2: 'The trouble is he likes rock music. Don't get me wrong, I love music in the house, I always have something classical playing, but his stuff just gives me a headache – and it has to be so loud. I wish he had more taste.'

A central theme of this book is that it's the differences between us that cause the challenges in our relationships, so when I'm writing about two similar people, as you'd expect, I'm a little challenged about what might cause any discord between them. Certainly I see fewer people with similar traits coming to relationship therapy than I do people with different ones, but the saying, 'They're both as bad as each other' exists for a reason. What I would suggest is that you also read the combinations of Lovebirds that correspond to the second type from your tests, i.e. if you came out Nightingale first followed by Swift, and your partner scored top as a Nightingale followed by an Owl, then read the Swift–Owl combination as well as their individual pen portraits, because it's likely that some aspects of that mixture will be present in your relationship.

Similarity can lead to great compatibility. What I'm going to attempt to discuss here is when it doesn't.

Cuckoos in the nest

Have you ever watched a couple talking, where neither seems to be listening to the other? It's almost as if they're having two parallel conversations that both are perfectly happy with. They're probably either Nightingales or Robins. Because both types need to speak their thoughts out loud in order to know them, they often use people as listening posts to talk at, rather than to. On many occasions, this will suit both partners, and an evening after work can be just a companionable babble of shared but only half-heard recollections of the day, with one person's story causing the other to spin off into one of their own, often over the top of their partner's story. This can become a problem, however, if one person is consistently more dominant than the other and leaves the less dominant partner feeling unheard, cut off or shut up. At this point, the scene can have more the appearance of a competition than a conversation. Of course, it can also be a problem if something said actually needs to be listened to, as then the 'Yes, I did, I told you all about it last week' kinds of conversation are going to arise on a regular basis.

Problems can also be slow to be sorted because it takes so long to talk the options through. Because both of you need to speak your mind to know your mind, and because you're both sky-birds, it can be easy to spend hours exploring all the possibilities, working out the different ramifications and examining the potential pitfalls before you get to a final, kind of, decision. It can be an exhausting process – not just for you, but for any innocent bystanders.

One of the key things about sky-birds is that they have a low boredom threshold for things that don't interest them, and that nearly always includes anything involving details. For that reason, a Nightingale partnership is likely to suffer from the chaos of missed appointments, frenzied last-minute surfing for holidays, frantic visa applications and punitive charges from credit card companies for late payments. But Nightingales will probably muddle through reasonably happily with the situation, with the occasional unhappy flapping of wings and tragic duets at the latest oversight.

Sky-birds make their decisions from looking at the big picture, making connections between things and trusting their intuition. Careful working out and logically structuring their plans doesn't float their boat. This can work marvellously well, and a Nightingale couple can happily float along towards an ill-defined but mutually understood future, enjoying distractions and diversions along the way. Sometimes those diversions can cause them to lose their way completely – both in their relationship and in their careers, so some strategy to help them stay focused is going to help them, like a mental ménage à trois with a ground-bird, or finding someone they trust who can act as a sounding board. At work, business coaches can fulfil this role; in relationships, I suspect it'll usually come down to a friend or close family member. And, to be clear, they're not there to tell you what to do, just to put in steps to make what you want to happen actually happen.

As we know, Nightingales are all about sound, so music is often a bond between them. They'll probably each be able to name the relevance to their relationship of a great range of songs (to the extent that picking the right ones for the wedding could actually delay it). My son is a Nightingale and created a complete playlist for the reception at his wedding, and paid a DJ a huge amount of money for, essentially, playing his own record collection. (It did work really well, though, and there were none of those moments when people stream like lemmings from the dance floor in response to the first chords of 'The Birdy Song'.) The obvious jarring note is if the couple has wildly divergent musical tastes. I know of one couple who have a quiet, on-going war where the radio or iPod is changed every time one of them leaves the room, but without either one saying anything. Nightingale is my second strongest type, and while Jimi Hendrix can bring tears (of joy) to my ears, my wife's love of opera leaves me completely cold. Richard Gere would not have fallen in love with me in *Pretty Woman*. At least not for that reason.

Nightingales have a great capacity to remember old conversations. This is a strength, if used wisely. If not, it becomes a means to knock the scabs off old wounds and resurrect old wrongs. Conversations that include, 'Yes, well, you said . . .' and 'Well, that's as may be, but what about five years ago when you said you were going to . . .' are to be avoided. Nobody wins a row, but particularly Nightingales, because they can be wounded so badly by unkind words. They'll rarely say something they don't mean, so they assume other people don't, either.

Feathers for the nest

What Nightingales living with Nightingales need to know
Do:
One of your Nightingale and Nightingale strengths could well be your inseparability. There's a strong chance you'll be best friends as well as lovers because of how much you share your thoughts. Finding common interests could really suit you, especially those that relate to your love of words and sounds. Concerts, music festivals, book clubs, choirs, learning an instrument, amateur dramatics, busking . . . (okay, maybe not busking, but you get the idea).

As a pair of sky-birds, you're likely to stumble when it comes to keeping your life tidy. The kitchen being in a state may not bother either of you, but you don't want your bank accounts to be the same way. What I suggest (with no real belief that you'll follow my advice), if you don't like the idea of having a third person in to look over your affairs, is for you both to work out individual responsibilities for stuff – take it in turns to plan a holiday; one of you deal with the household bills; the other take charge of the banking stuff. However, to make that work, you need to sit down and oversee each other's tasks to make sure nothing's been left to slide, or that vital details haven't been missed, like cars not getting insured, or passports applied for. The classic situation for sky-bird couples is to get up on the day of the holiday and only then start to think of what they need to take. An agreement for some joint foresight will avoid a lot of heartache, but I bet you won't stick to it . . . (go on, prove me wrong . . .).

Pay attention to how you communicate with each other. Are you actually listening when the other is speaking? Try an experiment. The next time you sit down to chat, have something that one of you can hold in your hand. The rule is, only the person holding it can speak. Notice how that affects the nature of your conversation. How much more listening-to-talking do you do (and vice versa)? How does it improve the quality of your chat? How annoying do you find it? My point is, simply, that in your need to understand your own thoughts, you can often block out the thoughts of your partner. If it doesn't feel like a problem (for either of you), then ignore this, otherwise maybe just practise creating a bit more of a gap between what each of you says, so you actually get the chance to listen. (Say, a couple of milliseconds.)

Remember to bring sound into the bedroom, too. Again, it's probably not something you need to be told, just perhaps reminded of. Music will have no parallel for you in mood setting, so an iPod and speakers should always be on standby by the bed (but remember that this is definitely a moment where tastes need to be in synchrony – not every partner is going to want to get jiggy to Bing Crosby). Sharing fantasies, telling each other dirty stories, maybe even roleplay, might be things you'd like to explore, even if you're British. And remember to tell your partner what feels good, where it feels good and just how good. Sound is feedback, so you'll get more of what you moan about.

Don't:
Don't hold onto grudges and use old disputes to win newer ones. Nightingales can be brilliant at dragging in old, irrelevant

grievances to distract their opponent and score points. And if the other person is a Nightingale, it's likely to make the argument into a war where words are the weapons and injury is caused to both parties – which then gets stored up for next time. Sort things out, and then leave them behind.

On the subject of words as weapons, you'll know exactly what words will hurt your partner's feelings or make them feel bad about themselves. Avoid those, whatever the situation. One thing that is never forgotten and rarely forgiven by a Nightingale is an insult. Be careful with your tone of voice as well – you'll know how to say one thing but infer the opposite by the use of your voice, and you need to remember they understand it just as well. It will do absolutely no good to say afterwards, 'I'm sorry, that's not what I meant . . .' You might get away with it being a misunderstanding with another Lovebird type, but not a Nightingale or Robin, as they'll trust their ears.

Don't forget to connect with the world. A Nightingale couple, unless they're both strongly extrovert, can become quite exclusive. They'll ring each other every few hours, text in between, sneak a quick Skype in the loo at work: they'll be in near constant verbal contact. It's likely they'll share common interests and want to share everything with their partner. It can be easy, especially in the early days of a relationship, to neglect other friendships and become a two-person band. Again, that might suit you completely, but in most cases having some time with others – even as a couple – will allow a little fresh air into your relationship.

Finally, people who are similar tend to plough a comfortable furrow together. This can narrow their horizons somewhat – just as cutting your friendships will. As the relationship matures, it can be a very healthy thing to challenge yourselves by taking yourselves out of your comfort zone and experimenting with things that don't obviously spring to mind as interests. For example, I have a friend who is a Nightingale and an excellent guitar player. His partner persuaded him to go with her on a painting holiday. He found he loved it, partly because he wasn't immediately good at it – like he had been with the guitar – but he also came to realise that it wasn't completely different to music; just a different way of expressing his feelings. He ended up painting what his favourite songs meant to him, and he came up with some really interesting images. The painting of Beyoncé's music was a particular favourite of mine. (Okay, I made that bit up.)

Swift and Swan

Swift: 'I can't believe he expects to waltz in from a night out with the lads and expects me to get all smoochy. If that's what he wants, he's got to work harder to show he wants to be with me, not his mates.'

Swan: 'She's so flighty. I spend half my life clearing up her messes – and she doesn't even recognise that the mess existed!'

The differences between these two are important, but not insurmountable. Swifts are all about the big picture, and are often very future-focused – quite happy to sacrifice the moment for a future gain – whereas Swans prefer to live in the now. Also, Swifts tend to have quite high-velocity personalities, whereas Swans need a bit of a run-up to reach operating speed. Probably the biggest challenge is that Swans like rules and to know things in detail, whereas Swifts will work hard to avoid having to come down to earth. They can live happily in the clouds avoiding their partner's rules and trusting their instincts over logic.

Cuckoos in the nest

Swifts can be a bit exhausting. They pay most attention to what they see, whereas Swans go on what they feel – on their skin and in their heart. Often Swans can feel left behind by their Billy Whizz partner in the thinking and talking stakes, but this shouldn't leave them feeling less adequate – it shouldn't, but it often does. Swans are often extremely emotionally intelligent, and they learn through practical experience more easily than just sitting and listening or watching.

Swans are likely to value comfort over style – the very opposite of their partner. You'll never see a Swan on a transatlantic flight dressed in three-inch heels, but a Swift would wear them, if that's what it took to make the outfit work. They'll suffer for the right look, which in their eyes makes the Swan really hard work. Swans are often very sensitive to things that disturb their physical comfort, from temperature or fabric texture, to whether the milk in their coffee is quite as warm as they like it. Sometimes it can seem as if they're involved in a never-ending pursuit of a silk-lined Shangri La where every physical experience is in perfect sensory balance. If you're in a relationship with a Swan, expect to be involved in many discussions about the relative merits of one experience compared to something similar. If it's your performance between the sheets, it might get a bit uncomfortable.

With Swifts being visually orientated, appearance is usually given a high value. They will often take meticulous care of their grooming and take an interest in fashion and perhaps art. They will expect their partner to do the same, especially for public appearances. If you're going to a party with them that's smart/casual, expect a lot more emphasis on the smart than the casual. Swifts can spend ages achieving the 'What, this? Oh, it's just something I threw together' look. Their taste, and their ability to put things together that others would never dream of, is often brilliant. The downside is that, as their partner, the Swan is expected to be an adornment to 'the look'. The Swan can look forward to grooming and style tips and a gentle (hope-fully) pressure to wear something for form rather than function. The good news is you'll look great. The bad news is corns, probably.

One of the big deals with this couple is the preference a Swan has for detail, and the disdain a Swift is likely to show for the small stuff, unless it's to do with how something looks. Swans make decisions based on firm knowledge and facts, whereas Swifts rely more on spotting patterns and what their intuition tells them. This can mean that the Swift can feel bogged down by their 'boring' partner, while Swans can be exasperated by their 'head-in-the-clouds' other half. Rules can be another big issue, namely that Swans run their life with them, and feel their partner should too – preferably with the Swan's rules which will always be thought best. Swifts, however, don't have much time for them; if they can see the point of rules, they'll follow them as a guideline, but not as a carved-in-stone requirement, which is what Swans expect.

Because Swans are so involved with sensation, many of the rules are likely to be about how the bed needs to be made, what angle the car seat should be left at, or how best to serve red wine to optimise its taste; none of which is likely to matter that much to a Swift. This can lead to blood on the carpet (which obviously would need cleaning in a particular way). In a relationship, it can also lead to a position where the Swan gradually takes over the running of the couple's lives, and the Swift is happy to let this happen. Be aware, however, that this will probably lead to a fairly regular explosion from the Swan about how little their partner does, leading to the Swan writing a list of duties for them to perform, followed by said Swan ripping it up because it's faster to do it themselves. (And yes, you'd be right if you think that little story has got the feel of personal experience to it . . .)

Swans live very much in today. Long-term plans will be okay, but their focus will be much more on the immediate steps that need to be taken to get there. They're not great at delaying gratification. If it's a choice between a short break now, or a big holiday at the end of the year, their resolve will probably crack and they'll start packing for the weekend. Swifts are often full of big plans and dreams, which can panic and overwhelm the Swan, both in the machine-gun delivery of them, and the scale without the detail. If the Swift doesn't pace their delivery right, the Swan will often say 'no' as a reflex and, over time, shutdown automatically in the face of the latest big idea. This would be a shame because, if they work well together, theirs can be a potent combination, with the Swift having the ideas and the Swan handling the practical details that will bring it to fruition.

Feathers for the nest

What Swifts need to know about Swans
Do:
Swifts will feel that they are loved due to the time they spend with their partner and the looks they share. For your Swan partner, it's all about touch and the things you do for them. How much effort you've made to look good for them won't count anywhere near as much as making them dinner. Remember to hug them, stroke them, any kind of physical affection – like a puppy, if you tickle their tummy they'll do anything for you.

Mood is everything to them. If you want to float an idea past them, make sure they're in a good mood first. Also, be aware that your partner feels safe with details, so put some effort into firming up your ideas. I know you have faith that all will become clear in time – you can see it happening – but they don't have that faith: if the future was a god, they'd be atheists, so give them the facts now.

I know that rules don't grab your attention, and that many of your partner's may seem trivial or pointless. That's as may be, but the important thing is they matter to them, so where's the harm in following them where you can? The advice I commonly give to sky-birds living with ground-birds is to simply learn their rules and follow them, because it costs you nothing and makes them happy.

Don't:
Just because you measure how much someone loves you by how much time they want to spend with you doesn't mean that they do, too. Don't put them under pressure to spend time with you instead of pursuing a hobby or being with friends, because it won't be quality time honestly given, and over time they'll resent it. Try to remember that each time they touch you it's the equivalent of a loving look that you'd give them. And the same is true for everything they do for you to make your life more comfortable.

Don't be a pain over what they wear. Being comfortable is a necessity for Swans in a way you can only imagine. If they feel good, it's the same to them as looking good is to you – and I mean by that that it's an equivalence. (Just remember, people don't really judge you by how your partner looks. Well, other Swifts might, but most people don't, so chill out and let your Swan enjoy looking like themselves.)

Slow down a little. Swans need time to wake up in the morning – speaking before 10 a.m. is generally a real effort – and they need to come up to speed in conversations. Many don't find words a strength, whereas you probably spit them out like machine-gun bullets. Slow down your delivery or they'll shut down and stop listening. And don't mistake this for a difference in intelligence, it really isn't. There will be ways of seeing the world that are open to them that will be a mystery to you.

What Swans need to know about Swifts
Do:
The two of you have different ideas about time. For Swifts, plans for the future are a big part of their thinking. For you, today, and maybe tomorrow, are going to be more in your thoughts. Also, to Swifts, the time you spend together is an indicator of the strength of your relationship, so potentially every trip out

with your friends, every moment pursuing a hobby and every late night at the office can be seen as a vote against them. Make sure you balance time away with good quality-time together, and that doesn't mean smooching on the sofa – that's your good time. Watch what they come alive doing with you and suggest that.

You know when you are loved by how you're touched – and how often – and by the acts of service that your partner performs. Swifts are not like you. They know they're loved by the time you spend with them, the experiences you share, by the looks you give, and by the gifts you buy.

Let me talk a little more about the latter two. A loving look, a flirty look, or an I-want-you look is the equivalent to them of a gentle stroke or a lovely kiss on the neck to you. So, practise your looks in the mirror (what you think looks sultry could actually look like you have wind). And in saying that gifts are important, I don't mean to imply that Swifts are acquisitive; what I mean is that if you buy a present that hits the spot with them, they'll appreciate it like you would electrically warmed socks. For that to happen, it needs to fit their taste, have a place in their ward-robe or home, or have some connection to you or them. I warn you now; Swifts are not the easiest to buy for.

Don't:
Don't make the mistake of thinking that sex cures all ills. Or snogging, or hugs. I know they do for you, but Swifts need to feel close to you first, by having spent a nice time together, by having had some flirty build-up, or by you hitting the mark with a well-observed present.

Don't be a party pooper. Swifts will be full of plans and ideas – a lot of them will come to nothing, but they'll enjoy the ride. Don't bring them down to earth with a bump with the reality that you bring to the occasion or they'll stop sharing things with you. This would be a shame because you need to stay open to them – some of their ideas could be doozies. Swifts are often great innovators, so your relationship could be massively changed by following some of their dreams.

Don't underestimate yourself. Sometimes a Swift's speed of thought might leave you feeling slow, but you bring plenty to the party in terms of your common sense, your emotional intelligence and your ability to focus on detail.

Don't waste any happiness by making it dependent on your partner following life the way you'd like them to. They won't stick to your rules, they won't follow your helpful suggestions that actually would make their life easier, and they won't notice the mess they make. They also won't care, so why should you? Your helpful tips can sound a lot like nagging, so contain them wherever possible.

If you use both your strengths well, you can be an awesome combination.

Dove and Owl

Dove: 'Honestly, I could be on fire sometimes and she wouldn't notice how I'm feeling. It's like living with a zombie.'

Owl: 'He is so high maintenance. There's no Goldilocks moment with him: things are either too hot or too cold, too hard or too soft. Who cares?'

This partnership is one of the combinations where, potentially, the differences can be particularly significant. Doves are led by their hearts; Owls by their heads. Doves are strongly connected to their environment, so they notice what's going on around them – especially regarding how it affects their comfort. Owls spend a great deal of their time in their heads, so they can be quite oblivious to what's going on around them and quite emotionally distant. As you can imagine, this very different relationship with the world will, in almost all situations, create a challenge to their understanding of each other.

A thing that unites them is the fact they're both sky-birds, preferring the big picture to a lot of detail or rules. This can make them more forgiving of their differences, and leave them surrounded by the beginnings of many good ideas, but not many completed ones. As long as it doesn't affect the Dove's comfort, both will be okay with this (hell could freeze over before the Owl would notice enough to reach for a jumper).

Cuckoos in the nest

It can feel quite lonely living with an Owl because they're so self-contained. Doves will put great store in doing things for their partner, so it can feel quite unfulfilling for them when they realise that their Owl doesn't notice much of it.

Doves often seem to be involved in a never-ending search for the perfect world to live in. If they find the perfect bed they'll never want to leave it. They'll pursue the perfect bed linen, the perfect snuggly sofa, the gold-standard in cashmere socks. The fact that they're living with someone who probably wouldn't spot they've put salt in their coffee, or that they're sitting on razor blades, can be difficult for both parties. A client told me the following story, which highlights the difference perfectly: 'My wife and I were staying at a hotel once. She went in the shower first and then came back into the bedroom. I picked up my towel, wrapped it around me and walked to the bathroom door. "No, darling," my wife called out to me, "that's *my* towel." Now I know she called me darling, but she clearly meant, "You f****** idiot." It is beyond her comprehension how I couldn't tell I had a damp towel on, but for me, my body is a long way from where I actually reside – in my head.'

So, Doves can feel like they're living with a sensory mute – because they are – and Owls can feel like their partner is regularly dissatisfied with what surrounds them, making them seem very high maintenance.

An important thing for Doves to be aware of is to not plague their Owl with questions such as, 'Which do you prefer?' or 'Which one is more comfortable?' Their answer is just a hopeless stab at joining in and pleasing you, and can actually make them a bit anxious, because it's like playing a game to which they don't know the rules: any comparison based on a preference between two sensory choices is likely to be a stretch for them. While I was writing this, my lovely wife (also a feeling bird) came in, looked at me (a thinking bird) and said, 'Are you warm enough?' 'I think so,' I answered after a few seconds' thought. She considered me a bit longer: 'Is that chair comfortable?'(It's a kitchen chair.) 'Yes, it's fine,' (I expect). After I say, 'It has a cushion,' she appears satisfied and leaves me again, with me not sure whether I *am* actually warm or comfortable enough. Never mind, I won't notice either again any moment now. Back to the book . . .

Which reminds me: Owls, don't make a virtue out of not feeling things (this probably won't apply to you if your second preference in the Lovebird quiz was the feeling bird, Dove). What it usually means if you do this is that you're avoiding your emotions because you're not comfortable with the idea of feeling, or of losing control. Living with a Dove can be a great opportunity to spread your wings a little and join them in their world. (I might put a cardigan on in a moment just as an experiment. Not knowing if I'm hot or cold is a tricky old business.)

Owls spend a lot of time thinking. Don't think that there is something wrong just because they're quiet – they'll let you know when they're ready to share something – but be aware that things that worry you or stay with you for ages probably won't have such a disturbing effect on them. Once they've thought something through, they'll move on. The one aside to that is that if they are worrying about something, they won't let it go until they've worked out an answer – which is probably why more Owls and Kingfishers see me for insomnia than any other type. The problem rattles around their heads into the small hours and they have no 'off' switch.

Owls can often forget that they may have said something in their heads without it necessarily leaving their lips. If, as an Owl, you have a moment of appreciation for something your partner has done for you or (heaven forbid) have a burst of affection, say it. Out loud. There is a difference, and you'll be pleasantly surprised to experience it.

Owls are great ones for plans. They don't get out of bed without one. It doesn't mean that a plan has to be stuck to, but spontaneous behaviour from them will only actually be a quickly revised revision of their previous plan. Doves are much more 'in the moment' people. They often don't see into the future clearly, and so don't value it particularly: what is more important is what is happening for them now. In terms of the relationship, this can be a critical difference. The Owl will often be preoccupied with the ideas they have for the future, and therefore miss what's making the Dove unhappy in the present. An example is where the Owl wife of a couple I saw decided to enrol in a university course to enhance her career prospects. In the moment of the decision, the Dove husband was both excited for her and totally supportive, despite the burden this would place on him – which the wife foresaw and talked him through the lens of his excitement for her it didn't feel a problem for the husband at the time but six months into struggling with the loss of connection to her; the feeling of 'growing away from him' with her new interests and study friends; the evenings 'on his own' while she sat at the dining room table writing essays; and they were in trouble. She increasingly withdrew into her head to avoid the unpleasant feelings of his unhappiness, and he began to sink into depression. Don't let your relationship move into different time zones like this. It doesn't matter how much the Owl describes how much better their life will be after she's qualified – more money, more freedom, more quality time – it won't compensate for the misery of the present, which will feel unending for the Dove.

Feathers for the nest

What Doves need to know about Owls
Do:
Owls are special types, in that the way they love will very much depend on whatever was their second strongest lovebird type in quiz 2 at the beginning of the book. For example, an Owl whose second type is Swift will often know that they're loved by the

looks their partner gives them and the time they spend with them. What I recommend is that you read this section, and also the section on Doves and your partner's second type. When read together, they'll paint a richer picture of your relationship and provide useful clues for getting on better. However, the following are key generalisations about Owls that most will find true.

Do give your partner time to be silent. When they get home from work – unless they have a long commute – they'll probably want to stare at the telly, or a wall, for a while, or maybe exercise. It's simply an opportunity to work through their day.

Listen to their plans when they share them. I know you might struggle to get as excited as they do about something that seems a long way off, but having such plans are likely to be really important to them. Owls have a particular need to know where they're going, whether in their relationship, or in life generally. If they feel rudderless and drifting they'll be unhappy, and when they're unhappy they tend to spend even more time in their heads than when they're not. If in doubt, help them find a project.

Don't:

Nagging them to pay more attention won't work; Owls can't pay attention to something they don't realise is there. Remember that they ALWAYS have a conversation going in their head, so asking them to be aware of what's going on around them is like asking you to do maths problems while you're having a massage.

Don't expect them to care much about comfort, either. Most of the richness in their life comes from their internal landscape, not from their surroundings. While they might spend a fortune on gadgets and things connected to their hobbies, home furnishings are likely to be low on their shopping list.

Don't make the mistake of thinking they don't care just because they don't show it or share it. Inside, they are likely to love you deeply – they just sometimes have an insecurity which stems from why they became Owls in the first place, which makes attaching feel emotionally risky – so for them to dare to connect with you is a testament to your bond. It might seem that they are quite independent and they are – I've heard of more than one Owl's partner leave because they didn't feel 'needed'. You are needed; Owls just won't demonstrate it much, as they'll assume you know it.

Don't expect them to focus on what's going on now. If there's something that's concerning you and you share it with them, they'll often fly out into the future and see that concern resolved, which will evaporate any concern they might have felt. They may not realise that you don't do that as easily and take more time working through the feelings you've got before you can put the worry to rest. The fact that they've got over what you feel in a crisis more quickly is nothing to do with them being unfeeling, it's about them being more 'in-thinking' than you.

What Owls need to know about Doves
Do:
Owls, more than anything else, need to come out of their heads and check on their partner. I've known many Owls sit in my office in a state of disbelief following their partner walking out on them. 'But I thought everything was fine,' they quite uniformly exclaim. Let your partner know that things are good with you as far as the relationship is concerned, and remember to ask the same of them – and listen to the answer. Hopefully, after reading this book, you'll know what to look for long before they up and leave.

Honour your Dove's need for sensory comfort. If you pay attention to the mattress when you book into a hotel and comment on its firmness, or lack of it, it'll be appreciated; it's a unit of currency in the economy of a Dove. A friend happened to see one of those things for chilling on the sofa in: a slanket? A kind of sleeping bag with sleeves. They were new on the market and his partner had never seen one. He said that when he presented it to his Dove partner it was like he'd given him Joseph's coat of many colours. Of course, he couldn't get him out of it or off the sofa for months, but he was a hero for a very long time. Look out for those kinds of opportunities.

Pace your Dove partner. For you, words are likely to be your currency. You'll like to use them, and to play with them. This is not true of your partner. Words can be a long way from feelings, so sometimes your Dove will grope to find them, especially in new situations. Give them time to work out what they mean, and don't fill in the gaps or end their sentences for them. And don't take the joke over for them when they forget the punchline: they'll get there.

Don't:
Don't keep things to yourself. Learn to share your thoughts within living memory of first having them – don't store them up or let them fester, as it disturbs your sleep and deprives you and your partner of an opportunity for connection. Do your best to be aware of how long it's been since you last spoke to your partner. I know small talk isn't your bag, but medium talk should be possible more often than you might think.

Don't treat hugs and cuddles as things that need to go on the calendar. It might take a while, but you'll probably get to like them. Things like holding hands, a cheeky squeeze of their bum in church (only joking), a spontaneous (obviously plan it secretly) little kiss in the queue at the supermarket, will let your partner know you love them way out of proportion to the act itself.

Don't accuse your Dove partner of being high maintenance. Many Doves are incredibly sensitive to the information that comes through their senses, so to them light really can seem brighter than it does to you – give them your sunglasses if a disaster of epic proportion strikes and they forget theirs. Sounds are also louder for them, and peas under mattresses really do feel like melons. Speaking as an unfeeling Owl, this looks and sounds like a lot of hard work, but I guess the pay-off for Doves is that they enjoy the good sensations that much more, too.

Robin and Robin

Robin 1: 'In most things we agree, but she has some rules that just don't make sense and it drives me up the wall.'

Robin 2: 'In most things we agree, but she has some rules that just don't make sense and it drives me up the wall.'

During many years of being a relationship therapist, what has led me to want to write this book most is the sense of how the differences between us is the thing that separates us – and cause us to separate. Most clients in trouble share less than they differ. This is not true of two Robins. You share traits in both of the ways this book measures, which makes you less likely to come looking for my services, but I hope I can give you some pointers to help you get along even better (and therefore justify the cost of the book).

Both of you place a lot of emphasis on what you hear. You will tend to need to talk a lot to order your thoughts and you've learned that having someone with you while you do so gets you fewer odd looks on the bus. Not surprisingly, you know you're loved by being told and interpreting your loved one's sincerity from their voice tone. If you've any sense, you'll be world-experts on phone tariffs because you'll spend a lot of time bouncing your words off satellites as a way of keeping up with friends and family.

The second level of similarity is that you're both ground-birds, so detail is important to you and you're most comfortable making decisions based on facts and hard evidence. You'll distrust unsubstantiated ideas and pie-in-the-sky thinking. Your house is likely to hum contentedly, so organised is it, and there'll be a place for everything that, after a while, won't dare to leave its allocated space except in emergencies. Thinking about it, you two may not even like people turning up uninvited because things would need to be 'right' for visitors.

Cuckoos in the nest

Robins together can seem like a funny couple, in that you spend a lot of time talking to each other, but not always about the same subject, and you often don't really seem to notice or respond to what the other person is saying. It sounds as if you're talking at cross purposes, but you're not: a lot of the things Robins say are for their own benefit, not that of the listener. Talking is a fundamental way for Robins to order their thoughts and work out more clearly what they think about something. I've even found that Robins who can't read exam questions out loud get fewer correct answers than when they're allowed to – it's as if they have no way of thinking in their head.

As you can imagine, this is going to make your house noisy. Tower of Babel noisy. On most occasions this is fine, as you'll exist in a mutual world where you sort of listen to each other enough to get a clue about what the other said. The challenge is when one of you really does need the other to pay attention, to listen carefully or to be supportive, which means that important bonding moments in the relationship can be missed. One thing is usually for certain – if one Robin isn't listening to the other, their partner will find someone who will. How else are they going to feel heard?

Similarly, the other consideration is the balance between you.

If one Robin is consistently more dominant and demands more airplay than the other, it can lead to their partner feeling devalued and – the killer insult – unheard.

Getting to a decision can take a while, partly because you'll need to talk things through and partly because, as ground-birds, you'll find a lot of things that need talking through. Your liking of detail – in fact, your need for the security inherent in details – can slow decision-making down to a crawl.

With you both being so sensitive to sound, I'd expect music to have an important place in your life. I know of one couple whose calendar is organised around the music festival circuit in the summer, and whatever concerts they can get to in the winter. It's a harmonious (no pun intended) and mutually absorbing lifestyle. Of course, if your taste in music differs, it's another story. I know of another couple for whom music is a battleground. They'll take a special trip to London and then split in the evening, one to go to a classical concert, another to go to a jazz club. They have also more or less partitioned their house, with each partner playing their kind of music in their areas, and neutral areas like the kitchen being music-free. (I imagine mood-setting music in the bedroom is off the agenda too, with one getting goosey over Ravel's Bolero, with the other needing . . . no, I just can't do it: I hate jazz. I can't imagine anything from that genre being a turn-on, so fill in the space yourself if you can. And I've just revealed that my second type after Owl is a song bird – a Nightingale. As such, jazz for me is just people who can't be bothered to learn to read music. It's the musical equivalent of modern art. I mention that just to give you a sense of how passionate – and unreasonable – a song bird will be on the subject.)

Both of you like life to be a certain way – your way. I would expect that, over time, you'll both make adjustments to the rules with which you run your life in order to bump along better. However, if there are certain beliefs you have about the way things need to be to avoid the crumbling of civilisation (like how cutlery needs to be stacked in the drawer in a particular sequence, or similar), then there could be conflict. If you're having problems with working these things out – and most ground-bird combinations will – then maybe you both need to sit down and write out your 'How the world needs to be according to me' list and then compare what you've written with your partner's. It's likely to reveal the source of some of your rows or snitty comments, and provide the means by which you can begin to negotiate the peace. You could even try living by your partner's rules for a day and see what happens (apart from you needing to breathe into a bag).

Feathers for the nest

What Robins living with Robins need to know
Do:

You could be one of those hermit couples who are so into each other that you don't feel the need for others. Because you talk together so often – you probably have as many phone breaks as others have fag breaks – and share so much of your thoughts, you have a good chance of being best friends as well as lovers. Find things you can share together that interest you both and give you an opportunity to go out into the world.

Pay attention to how you both communicate. On most occasions, your way of talking over each other probably suits both your needs, but it's vital that you are able to focus on your partner when they have something they really need you to hear. Try an experiment. The next time you have a chat, have something one of you holds in your hand. The rule is that only the person holding the object can speak. Notice how this changes the nature of your exchanges. Does it improve them? Does it interfere? Why? If the way you're talking to each other is working for both of you don't worry about this: my point is that your way of thinking is to verbalise it. Because you can only listen to yourself *or* someone else, but not both at the same time, it's easy to miss what the other person is trying to put across because you're too busy working out your own message. At the very least, the object you hold could be a useful symbol to your partner for when you need a deep and meaningful. (Just make it something soft, in case it gets thrown.)

Organisation is important to both of you. Chaos is unlikely to be tolerated, and your domestic life might seem almost Teutonic in its efficiency. The danger of too much order (yes, there can be such a thing) is that you might manage to squeeze novelty out of your life together. You might end up eating at the same restaurants, holidaying at the same holiday spots, and watching the same TV programmes, just because it's efficient and easy. Resist this: new experiences blow fresh air into a relationship and give you more things to talk about.

Be gentle in the words you use with each other. It's the easiest thing in the world for you to find the right words to wound the one you love – who knows their frailties better? However, what has been said is very rarely forgotten, even if it might be forgiven. Robins can bring back conversations they had from years ago, so rude or hurtful words will be a cinch to remember, in particular. Never say anything you could regret later, because in your relationship you certainly will.

Don't:
Continuing the theme of being gentle – don't hold onto grudges. Rows between Robins can be an amazing thing to witness: words come so naturally and quickly to them that it can be mistaken for a rap battle. In the heat of this, it can be easy to grab for the nearest thing to hurt with – a partner's previous mistake or error, something from an earlier row, or a personal sensitivity can all be thrown on the fire. This can lead to a situation where the flames continue to flicker for days afterwards. Apologies don't damp the fire anywhere near as well as hurtful words ignite them, so work out a way of airing disputes that avoids it becoming personal.

It can be easy to neglect other people. Robins lean on each other so much that there doesn't seem enough daylight between them to squeeze anyone else in. This can create a lovely, close, synergistic relationship, but it can also lead to a certain staleness.

Any relationship needs a degree of spontaneity and fresh experience in order to grow – and Robins need new things to talk
about, so don't raise the drawbridge on the world just because
you have each other. I'm aiming this point mainly at introvert
couples, extroverts will naturally maintain a larger set of friends.

Robins are more comfortable with details than with the big
picture, so they can sometimes get bogged down in the day-to-
day stuff and lose any sense of direction or progression. You'll
both be great at getting things done: house projects, hobbies,
work, will all be approached in an efficient way, but every now
and again you might realise how bored you've become. It's just
because you haven't built any forward motion into your life. In
a sense, your relationship needs to be a project, too. Working
out where you both want to be in a few years' time, and then
setting goals to achieve that, will help keep you moving – and
making sure you revisit these goals regularly will prevent you
from getting your head so stuck into any one particular step of
the journey that you forget you're on it.

Finally, don't mistake your rules for anything serious. I know
they make you feel more comfortable, and I know they make
sense to you, but I've known many ground-birds who arrive late
for something important because they simply can't leave the
house without the washing-up done, or who'd love to go out for
a meal with their friends but Thursday is the night they wash
the hamster. Make it a personal development issue that you
identify these rules of yours that run your life just beneath the
surface of it, and massage some flexibility into them. Nobody on
their death-bed ever said, 'I wish I'd done just a little more dusting.'
(Unless they died from dust inhalation.)

Peacock and Peacock

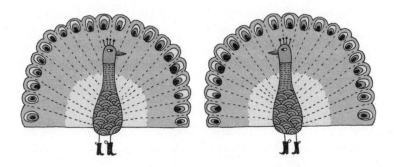

Peacock 1: 'Sometimes it feels like we're in a competition. If I get something that looks newer than his, he has to replace it. If he thinks I look better than him going out he'll spend another half an hour changing. It's exhausting.'

Peacock 2: 'It's like she has the Bible on taste. If I like something she doesn't, then I'm a Philistine, and I can't buy anything for the house without her approval or there's hell to pay.'

There is a lot going for you two because you'll tend to see the world in very similar ways. Peacocks are visual birds who put great emphasis on the appearance of things. They're also ground-birds who like to know the details of everything, make decisions based on facts and what is known, and tend to have rules they follow. All of this can contribute to a harmonious and well-run relationship – as I've said with other types who are similar, I see fewer coming for help in relationship therapy, so seeing eye to eye clearly helps. What I'm going to write about here is the challenges that being similar can sometimes throw up which can, for those experiencing them, be as damaging as difference.

Cuckoos in the nest

What you two see is what you pay most attention to – far more than what you hear or feel. In terms of relationships, how you and your partner look is likely to count a great deal. In Peacock houses I've visited, there are often loads of photos of the couple, usually dressed up for special occasions, and I've sometimes felt that they're almost as much a warning as a pleasant remembrance: 'You see how good you look, well, keep it up!' If you do slip from how good you looked when you started dating, you're likely to get wistful comments from your partner, which may become more barbed over time. You're both going to feel that your partner is somehow a statement about you, so if the world sees either of you looking ropey . . .

This can lead to a bit of appearance tyranny where neither of you feels able to relax and just let it all hang out. Like I said before, this might suit you – I often see immaculately turned out couples shopping in the supermarket, choosing not to queue behind the slob in the slippers – but if it's not that much of a drive for you, then a day off in your jammies in front of the telly should feel like a naughty treat, not an act of infidelity.

Ranging from home décor to personal fashion, you're both likely to have strong opinions and, for some of you, a strong interest in one or the other. In either case, outfits and rooms are never going to be just thrown together and unless your tastes are twinned there are likely to be . . . well, let's call them creative differences. Hopefully such differences can be negotiated, but if one's love of Queen Anne furniture jars with the other's desire for post-modern concrete chairs, then I predict a long cold winter of discontent. I've known Peacock couples live in near-empty houses for ages because they couldn't agree on how to style them.

Time together is something that tends to be a standard need for both of you. You won't deal well with being apart for long periods, and you'll both get upset if you feel your partner is choosing to do something in preference to spending time with you. Because you'll both be aware of this, it's something that usually doesn't arise as an issue. What can happen instead is that you become a bit set in your ways. Measuring how strong your relationship is by the amount of time you choose to spend together is great, but it can lead to a bit of a hermit-like existence, or one where neither of you has much chance to breathe as an individual or pursue individual interests. I'm aware as I write this that many of you will be shouting at me, 'But we like it that way!' and I'm really pleased for you – it might just not be true for both of you, all the time, always. And if either one of you wants to stretch their wings away from the nest, it's vital that it's not used as a barometer for the state of the relationship. Time away doesn't have to equal bad – quite the reverse: it could breathe some extra life into things.

When it comes to making decisions, you're both more comfortable with having all the facts to hand. The unknown is uncomfortable and ideas without evidence can seem just too pie in the sky to be trusted. This can keep you safe from dodgy salespeople or quick decisions you regret later, but it can also lead to your life becoming stuck in a bit of a rut where everything you do is measured and considered and achieved carefully step by step. Sometimes you both need to take a leap of faith, sometimes you need help to see the big picture, sometimes you need to dream a little larger. It'll be scary doing something by the seat of your pants instead of as a consequence of serious research and the deforestation of a continent in reading material, but it's another thing that can just let a little new light in. You won't regret it – actually, sometimes you probably will, but it's usually the things you don't do that you regret more.

Rules make your world run smoothly. I bet you've got a routine of who does what around the house, a plan for when the bills get paid, and an agreed way to stack the dishwasher. If you listen carefully in your home, you can hear the cogs whirring as the well-oiled machine that is a Peacock house glides along . . . unless you don't agree on the rules – then there's trouble. Big trouble. If one of you thinks the oil goes in first when making French dressing, and the other thinks it should be the vinegar, then you'll probably reach a point where you only dress the salad for your-self because you won't lower yourself to the stupidity of doing something 'wrong'. I've known Peacocks who will literally re-hang someone else's washing because it isn't hung 'right', and yet it dries perfectly well both ways. Rules can become a battleground for you both because you tend to treat them as real when oh, no, they're not. You have reasons for following yours and, here's the revelation, *your partner has reasons that are good for them for doing it their way* – and if both ways work, then neither one can be 'wrong'. Both of you need to sit down and work out what rules are causing discord and decide what you're going to do about them. I expect caring less is out of the question?

Feathers for the nest

What Peacocks living with Peacocks need to know
Do:
There are three basic ways Peacocks will know that they are loved – and because you two are the same, I realise I'm probably telling you something you're already aware of, but pointing out the obvious may still be helpful.

Firstly, the way your partner looks at you sometimes is likely to give you that rush of feeling that lets you *know*. Remember that the way you look at them will give them a feeling in turn – so make sure you know what look you're giving them, and use it when the occasion warrants it. Better still, *make* the occasion warrant it. It's one of the reasons why Peacocks prefer speaking face to face rather than on the phone: they get a lot from reading faces – so both of you be careful. Research shows that the biggest predictor of relationships not working out is the appearance of contempt or dismissal on the face of one partner about the other. So be careful not to have any expression that could be mistaken for either one – looks can cut like knives in particular for you two, and never be forgotten. The second thing that lets you know you're loved can be the giving and receiving of gifts. As an expression of affection and caring they can't be beaten for you two, and I'd expect you both to be great at picking up presents that the other loves. The way it seems to work is that you take the present as an indicator of how well the giver knows you, so a present that isn't your style or taste equals: 'They just don't get me'. It's why sight birds Peacocks and Swifts often fly off the handle on birthdays if they don't get what they hoped for. What this means is the present needs to be about the receiver, not about the sender; it needs to be something that fits their life, not something that reminds them of yours (although if you're a couple, there is obviously a crossover that will work, too).

The third thing is what I mentioned earlier – time. For both of you, absence makes the heart grow colder – at least that's what you feel and fear, so you'll always need to keep an eye on the balance between life and work, or life and hobbies, or life and anything else that keeps you from the embrace of your partner. Happily, we're all now members of the Skype generation (should we choose to be), so whenever you have to be apart for a period of time, use it to video-conference each other. You know that phone calls on their own don't cut much ice.

Don't:
There is a danger that small things can drag you two into conflict. There are certain things that you invest a lot of importance in, often without the rest of the world seeming to agree. It's why ground-birds such as yourselves generally find it harder to live with people the longer they're single: their life becomes so set in the way they like things done that they end up no longer being able to fit someone else in it. Do your best not to make your rules a prison for your partner; something to beat them up about, or to nag them over. Similarly, don't use their attachment to their rules as something to ridicule them for: in their world, they make as much sense as yours do. As a sky-bird, I don't really get this attachment to rules, which makes it easy for me to say there are only a few that will actually matter or make a difference to your life. Find out what they

are for both of you, honour each other's, and work on not letting the others become an issue.

How you look is important to you both, and can be something that bonds you – hours of shopping for clothes has to bring you together, right? This is another thing that can become a power play between you. When you go out together, don't make it a competition for who gets the most attention. I went to a birthday bash for a Peacock who looked incredibly stylish in an understated way. His partner arrived late in a garish lemon dress that grabbed attention, but gained her no fans. Shine equally, or agree who should dazzle most.

Peacocks are sometimes accused of being superficial because they place so much importance on the way things look, and there is a grain of truth in that. The world feels to you as if it values you through looking at everything connected to you; so, house, car and partner are all part of the package. Just be careful that you don't lose what you truly value in the pursuit of shiny things. Peacock couples can sometimes end up in big houses that look posh, but they allow no visitors inside because only one room is furnished. 'Lace curtains, no knickers,' was my mum's description. Don't egg each other on in making everything look picture-perfect, because you may over-extend yourselves.

Dove and Swift

Swift: 'I worked so hard the other day to finish work so we could spend some time together, seeing as we've been apart for a couple of days. I rang at 8 p.m. and he'd said it was getting a bit late and he'd see me tomorrow. I was so upset!'

Dove: 'She's cool and I love hanging out with her, but it's no big deal if stuff gets in the way. The truth is, once I get to a certain point in the evening I just don't have the energy to cope with hers.'

This is a couple who can work together if they can just understand a couple of things. Swifts tend to work at high speed and that will often be exhausting for Doves to keep up with. Doves are very much in the moment, so they can be happy in what they're doing and not miss what they're not. Swifts don't cope with absence well, and can mistake a Dove's calmness about it for a lack of care. The good thing is that they share a preference for the big picture of Life, so while your relationship may be a bit disorganised and full of plans that never quite reach fruition, you'll probably have fun playing with the ideas – and wasting a lot of money on things you should have spent more time thinking through.

Cuckoos in the nest

Think hare and tortoise. Swifts come out of the blocks fast – they open their eyes and launch themselves into the day. Doves are more likely to open their eyes only to find the duvet so they can snuggle down for another ten minutes. Swifts are visual, so pay most attention to stuff arriving in their brains at the speed of light; Doves pay most attention to their feelings, whether that means what their skin touches, or what their heart does. These things tend to move a lot slower than light, so one of the hardest things for this couple is to adjust to their difference in pace. Swifts could exhaust their partners, just from the difficulty of keeping up with their speed of thought and, after a while, they might actually hibernate during conversations rather than struggle to keep up. Doves can be mistaken by their partners for being a bit slow. They're not, it's just a different kind of intelligence, and one every bit as valuable. Their instincts are usually good, and they pick up things they're shown amazingly quickly, from a dance step to how to strip down a car engine. They just don't learn well in a conventional learning environment, and they don't process words that quickly. So pace them.

Swifts put a high value on appearance. They will pick a sofa for how it looks, which is madness to a Dove. For them, a sofa could look like a bag of spanners so long as it nestles you as gently as a mother's womb. Swifts will stagger around in ten-inch heels if they looked good in them in the shop; Doves won't make it out of the door in them. Whatever works for you, right? Not to a Swift. How you look is a reflection on how the world sees them, so they will expect their partner to dress the part of their partner – and you don't see them in a velour jumpsuit, do you? The Dove's love of comfort and cosiness can sometimes lead to interesting dress choices, just as it draws them towards their jimjams and dressing gown of an evening. If this is done too early in a relationship you're going to get a raised eyebrow from your Swift. For them, not 'putting effort' into your appearance is the same as not caring for them.

Doves pursue comfort; Swifts pursue style. This can mean the Dove never seems content with what they have. A feeling bird I know changed her sofa three times in a year because the comfort she was after eluded her (I'm expecting number four to arrive any day). Things are often too hot, too cold, too tight, too baggy – and that's just their partner. This can be a bit of a tiring mystery to the Swift, who is happy as long as it looks right. A restaurant meal that looks delicious will taste delicious to them, whereas for the Dove the look is irrelevant – why didn't they warm the plate?

Both partners avoid the details of life; frankly, these bore them. This can mean that you live in a state of perpetual near-chaos, being chased for late bill payments, depending on lastminute. com for . . . everything. You'll have loads of fabulous ideas; you'll even start some of them. Bouncing from one idea to another isn't a problem as such, not if you both enjoy where it takes you and what you get from it – it is just a shame you have to live with so many things half-completed. You'll have tons of fun investigating different hobbies and interests, but you probably won't stick with many of them. All this is fine. Well, the late credit card bills waste a lot of your money in penalties so it's an idea to work out responsibilities and check on each other; automate everything you can; and, if at all possible, recruit a friend or family member who is a ground-bird to set up a system that you can follow – and they can check on. I know one couple whose fourteen-year-old runs the family finances because she's more dependable. (Mysteriously, she gets the highest pocket money in the neighbourhood.)

Doves are very much 'in the moment' people. They can absorb themselves fully in what they're doing and enjoy it without thinking beyond it. It means that they deal pretty well with the general absence of their partner. They'll love them when they get home; until then, well, there's cake. This is very different for a Swift. Loving equals spending time together, and if being apart is your fault, they will often feel you're making a choice between them and what you're doing. Your yoga or hockey session is a love rival? In a way, yes. This different attitude to time is probably going to be a niggle unless you sort it out by acknowledging it and talking it through.

Feathers for the nest

What Swifts need to know about Doves
Do:

Doves feel your love, literally. Every touch is likely to have some degree of significance – even if they're not always consciously aware of it. Over time, a lack of physical contact will bubble into their awareness as a feeling of distance between you, so don't underestimate the power of a hug, a kiss or a squeeze.

Also, be aware of the importance of mood to your partner, as nothing can happen unless their mood supports it. This means that if you want them to decide something they need to feel right before you ask them, or their mood will say 'no' for them. Logic is not their bag, feelings are; and these can be difficult to separate from those feelings that accompany the kind of day they're having. Wanting to make love as they come through the door straight from a two-hour traffic jam is probably not going to be on the cards. So, remember, set the mood before you ask anything of them.

Doves will also know that you love them by the things you do for them. This doesn't mean becoming their slave, just that they probably put a lot of thought into making your life nicer. Watch what they do for you (whether it matters to you or not), and do those things back for them. Anything that improves the quality of any sensory experience is probably going to work wonders for your status.

Don't:

Don't overwhelm Doves with the future. As a Swift, you are probably very good at seeing where you're going, and where you want the pair of you to be heading. It's possible that your partner can too – but some Doves do it poorly, and few as well as a Swift. Their emphasis is going to be much more on the present, so pace them – for Doves, something that's going to be great next year won't feel anywhere near as exciting as what's going to happen this week. I remember a Dove friend who took up home brewing. He loved the mixing and air locks and methods, but he realized – when he starting drinking straight from the demi-john rather than waiting for it to mature – that it probably wasn't the hobby for him. Delayed gratification is just not their thing.

Don't hassle Doves about their clothes choices. Doves often have quirky taste and I hope it's one of the things you like about them, because you're not going to change them. They will never elect to wear something that looks good but feels horrible. Don't see their appearance as a reflection on you, or any kind of indicator about how much they care for you. The fact they can be comfortable around you in a knackered old tracksuit is as much a sign of their happiness in the relationship as it is an issue for you.

Finally, slow down. You're probably a bit of a jack-in-the-box, mentally as well as physically. Doves don't find words for things as quickly as you do, and often need to dwell for a while before their opinion emerges. Let them take the time, and don't mistake this slower pacing for them being less able than you; they're often wonderfully intuitive.

What Doves need to know about Swifts
Do:
Your partner lives through their eyes. Give them a naughty look and their legs will buckle; dress up in what they like you in and they'll come over all unnecessary. To Swifts, how you look at them is a sign of how you feel about them – which is why they'll often check up with you with a 'What's up?' If you're worried about something and it shows on your face, when they look at

you they might make the look about how you feel about them. Look them in the eye when you tell them your feelings, to reassure them.

Swifts will let you know they love you by looking good for you, and they'll expect the same. Compliment them on how they look and, of course, their bum doesn't look big in that, just sexy. I know that for you comfort ranks higher than keeping up with fashion, but for your partner you're an extension of them, so going to a party in your comfy gardening shorts is a fashion crime of capital proportions. Think of it as them liking to show you off.

Time is weirdly important to Swifts. How much of yours you spend with them will be taken as a sign of how important the relationship is to you. If you start spending too much time on something else, they'll often see that as you expressing a preference. Separation from you for anything – especially something out of the ordinary – can make them anxious. Their fear is that out of your sight is out of your mind. Skype might help.

Don't:
Don't rain on their parade. By that, I mean that Swifts will often map out a great future for the two of you that to you will seem a bit vague and woolly. Not that you like detail, but things too far ahead are probably a bit too misty to excite you. Accept that, not only is it clearer to them, it excites them. Indulge them as best you can – often you'll love it when you get there.

Don't think just because they go off at 100 miles an hour that they know better than you. Trust your instincts and gut feelings, and realise that it's normal for you to take longer to work things out in your head than it does in theirs. Just because they get an answer more quickly than you doesn't mean they're always going to be right.

Don't expect them to care about making life as nice as you'd like. Instead, they'll decorate your living room so beautifully that it could be a magazine cover, even though an evening on the sofa they chose means a trip to the osteopath. (They probably didn't even try it – if it was okay for Brangelina in their *Hello!* feature, it's good enough for you two.)

Peacock and Robin

Peacock: 'I'm sorry; she can tell me she loves me all she likes over the phone, but she could be pulling faces while she does it. Seeing is believing in my book.'

Robin: 'He's like the fashion police. I can't buy anything without him having an opinion on how I could improve it. He treats me like a Barbie doll.'

Robins are song birds, so sounds are paramount, whereas Peacocks are sight birds, so it's what they see that matters most. This can lead to some pressures within the relationship where both partners are working to show their love and appreciation to each other, but in such different ways that neither sees it.

Something that binds you together is that you're both ground-birds, so your house is likely to be one that is run with more precision than a Japanese railway, and with more rules than a pedants' paradise – just how you like it.

Cuckoos in the nest

The fundamental need of a Robin is to be heard. Most of them seem to think more clearly when they speak their thoughts aloud,

Lovebirds

so to be with them is often to be buffeted by an apparent stream of consciousness without end – which can be quite exhausting. If you try to shut them down, or end their sentences, it usually only sends them back to the beginning. If the Peacock is trying to enjoy the visual pleasure of watching a sunset or a good film, appreciating a picture in a gallery or cheering on their favourite team, it can be a challenge to have their partner giving a running commentary of their experience of it (so much so that if you're sharing a view near a cliff edge, it's understandable if only one of you makes the journey home).

Some people simply can't keep up with the flow of Robin chatter, but Peacocks are better equipped than most. They tend to process thoughts quite quickly and their pace of speech mirrors this. The difference is that they speak to communicate, unlike their partner who also speaks to think. This difference can confuse: when the Robin has a problem, for example, the Peacock will often be busy offering solutions and alternatives and get confused that these are being ignored while the Robin continues to spout their thoughts. It's actually because the Robin isn't ready for solutions as they haven't got clarity on their own thoughts yet. Peacocks need to be quiet and wait for the Robin to finish. (It'll probably be a while.)

This makes it sound like the problems are one-way, but I bet the Robin would argue that this isn't so. Peacocks can have a funny attitude towards time, in that they feel their partner should spend it with them to demonstrate that they care; spending time that their partner could be with them anywhere else can be perceived as their partner expressing a preference – i.e. they'd rather be out with their mates than going out with their partner. This can make life a little claustrophobic, as the Robin can feel as if they have to negotiate for every moment out of the relationship.

While we're on the subject of Peacocks being high maintenance, they can also be a bit of a fascist with fashion – they'll want things to look right. This will include their home, their car, and you. If the house needs doing up, expect to be breathing the smell of fresh paint until it is. Nor are Peacocks 'live in a pig-sty with potential' kind of people; they'll want to live somewhere while the house is being renovated. The car will probably be very clean, and you? Well, you need to remember that, as their partner, you're a showcase for their taste to the outside world. If you haven't heard them actually say, 'Are you really going out in that?', you've seen the equivalent eyebrow. Dress-down Friday probably won't happen in your house, and if it did, your partner would take as long to look like they'd just got out of bed as if they'd got dressed for a wedding. And you know those sloppy joes you used to love wearing around the house that mysteriously disappeared? Yep, it was them. For your Peacock partner, it's a matter of if you loved them, you'd look good for them – that's the message the eyebrow is conveying. And what looks good is what they say looks good.

Similarities between types usually means fewer problems, so as much as your separate preferences for what you see and what you hear will cause challenges, at least what you share is a liking for knowing the detail for things, basing decisions on logic and facts, and working out rules. The only shadow on this similarities horizon is if your rules conflict. If one of you thinks that the world will end if your DVD collection isn't filed in genre order, while the other insists the right way is to order it by leading man, you're going to have a war (and a constantly shuffled collection). I've used a glib example (because I'm a sky-bird who looks in wonder at my ground-bird wife's assembly of rules), but there is a point to be made here. Rules can become not only a cause of bad feeling; they can also be restrictive. Over time, if both partners stick to them, you can lose the benefits of innovation, difference and novelty. You're not listening, are you? Seriously, you two could get a bit, well, fuddy-duddy. Sometimes bracing yourself and trying a different way to do something might just bring a bit of freshness to the house. (And you can always be counselled afterwards for the trauma.)

Feathers for the nest

What Peacocks need to know about Robins
Do:

Your partner needs time to sort through their thoughts and, unfortunately for you, they'll often need someone as a sounding board to accomplish this. Give them as much time to do this as they need, and don't feel you have to contribute overly until the flow from them has subsided. If they're still at the point of talking over you or not responding to what you say, then you're wasting your efforts – keep quiet and let them go on. Helping them with different perspectives is a matter of timing – Robins need to know what their starting point is before they can work with any options.

Share everything with them. They will know you care about them by your voice tone and the words you use. Just hearing your voice can give them a boost, especially if you're focused on them and using the appropriate tone. Hearing you being appreciative is going to pay you dividends.

Music is likely to be an important part of a Robin's life, and often they'll have particular songs linked to particular memories of your relationship. It would do you no harm to keep a note of what they are – or are likely to be when they happen (because there will come a day when responding wrongly to, 'Do you remember what we were doing when we last listened to this? Shall we do it again now?' is going to get you some funny looks at your mother-in-law's Sunday dinner table).

For your partner, your words are a balm that can soothe the worst of days, or knives that can cut them deeper than anything else. Be sparing of your criticism and do your best to not make it about them personally. Being ground-birds, you're both going to be guilty of feeling that your way is the best way. I'm not saying surrender to your Robin partner, but if you're going to fight, don't personalise it, because what you say in a heated second can take years to heal. And most things just aren't that important. No, they're not.

Don't:

Never try to beat your Robin partner at Who Said What: they'll win. Even if you *are* right, they'll have such a belief that their verbal memory is perfect that they'll wear you down.

Don't think that empty vessels make most noise. Robins often get a bad press because of how talkative they are: 'A good act, but they're on too long' is a commonly held thought. That might be true, but it's a mistake to underestimate them; they're as sharp as anybody else, it's just that their route to knowing something happens outside their head, not in the privacy of it. After all, if people heard all your thinking process as you were coming to a decision, how would they view you?

Don't get so hung up on the way you think the world should work that you don't let your Robin help to keep it spinning, too. The clever trick our beliefs have is that they make themselves feel true; they have to, for you to feel you should act on them. In the main, they're actually not true, they're just useful. It's why two people can be at loggerheads over something, even though both ways work. Try to bear that in mind, or you'll live a life quibbling with each other over what could just be petty niggles.

What Robins need to know about Peacocks
Do:

Your partner looks at things the way you listen, so how things look, for them, is paramount. That's why it doesn't matter how many times you ring to say you love them over the phone – it won't count anywhere near as much as you looking them in the eye when you say it. 'Seeing is believing' is the Peacock's mantra, which might be why they place so much importance on the time you spend together as a barometer for the health of the relationship. Make sure you keep an eye on how much time you allocate to spending meaningfully with your partner, and how much is abstracted by your friends, family, hobbies and work. Measure it in their favour, or you'll soon hear about it.

Appearance matters to your Peacock, so a lot of that can be left to them. Home furnishings and garden design are things that will fall naturally within their talent and remit – they'd probably dress you, if you let them. Do honour their gift. Obviously you'll want to put in your tuppence-worth (who are we kidding, you'll want to put in a quid), but your Peacock partner is likely to have a touch you can trust.

On the subject of looks, keep in mind about taking care of yours. There can be a bit of pressure applied to you to keep in shape and well turned out. I remember one particularly insensitive Peacock showing his partner their wedding photo and threatening to sue her for breach of contract because she'd gained a stone. Hoho . . . not. Although said in apparent jest, there is a message – if you don't look good, in their eyes you look like you don't care enough about them to be bothered.

Don't:

Don't overwhelm your Peacock with your need to speak. As I write this, I recognise the impossibility of what I'm asking. So what I ask instead is to pay attention to your partner when you're talking to them. Don't wait until they slump comatose in their chair before you recognise that you've drained the will to live from them. Take a breath and let them contribute.

You are both people who like rules but, as I've already said to your partner: don't mistake rules for anything real, or you'll butt heads over things that really should be negotiable. If you both have different ways of doing the same thing, sit down and talk them through. If both work, then they don't matter. If one is better than the other, then adopt that one.

Don't accuse your partner of being precious or pedantic – they just happen to have strong opinions about taste and will often be very passionate about it. Just as you might rant about the Madonna cover of 'American Pie' being a crime against music, so they might go off the deep-end about mixing spots and stripes, or velour and corduroy. Fake outrage and it'll score you points, that's all I'm saying.

Owl and Kingfisher

Owl: '*I tell you, she's so, "This is the way you do things." What drives me mad the most is that she doesn't just ask me to do something, she then tells me how to do it, as well!*'

Kingfisher: '*He's got the attention span of a gnat. And the funniest thing is that he cocks something up by not paying attention, and then doesn't listen when I try to help him.*'

This is an interesting combination. With the pair of you both being thinking birds, the question of how you know you are loved is going to be best answered by reading what is here, and then reading the section that describes the bird that was your second type in the Lovebird quiz at the start of the book. So, for example, if the Owl's second strongest type was Swift and the Kingfisher's was Swan, then reading about Swifts and Swans in Part Two, and how they combine here in Part Three, will give you a richer idea of what you two might experience together.

The similarity between you is that you both spend a lot of time in your heads thinking, have a need to make sense of things and dislike being controlled by your emotions, or someone else's.

The difference is that Owls prefer the big picture to detail, and enjoy pursuing ideas, while Kingfishers are most comfortable when they have all the facts, rather than going with their intuition, and are happy with details. They also pay far more attention to rules than Owls. This relationship can be a bit of a duel.

Cuckoos in the nest

Owls love pursuing what Kingfishers would describe as flights of fancy. They're great at seeing things in new ways, finding creative solutions to problems and flying by the seat of their pants. Kingfishers are brilliant at methodically working through a problem, grinding out a solution and making a sensible decision based on a careful analysis of every scrap of information they can get their mitts on. The challenge this might bring is that Owls can feel undermined by their partner; every time they share an idea it can feel as if they're assaulted by a tide of 'realism', while Kingfishers can feel as if their common sense is wilfully ignored and they're constantly holding back their partner from disastrous undertakings.

Kingfishers have rules about how the world should be, and they cling to them particularly strongly. From how to fold clothes, to whether milk goes in before or after the tea, to when you should put up your Christmas decorations, there are certain ways of doing things – their way. Unfortunately, Owls don't live in that world; in fact, they don't live in a universe where rules matter much at all.

This is likely to be one of the central pressures between you. With the need Kingfishers have for the solidity of facts, and the preference Owls have for possibilities, it can be wearing for you both. If you embark on a joint project, like a new kitchen, the Owl will love briefly exploring the options and will probably settle on a preference quite quickly. The Kingfisher, on the other hand, will want to wade through all the catalogues, visit all the showrooms, and invite dozens of sales people to come and camp in your living room. This epic will not be even halfway completed before the Owl has given up in boredom. They'll accuse their partner of being anal, and be accused in turn of not caring enough about getting it right. And the kitchen will probably stay the same for another few years.

Both of you spend a lot of time in your head thinking, so in that respect you're very compatible; silence between you will be a comfortable necessity rather than a sign of disunity. A thing to beware of, though, is your habit of having conversations in your head and mistaking them for real ones. It's the easiest thing for you both to think you've said something to your partner, when in reality it's not left the confines of your head. Count how often the pair of you say to each other, 'I told you that!' and realise how many important things remain unsaid between you. It means that things can be going on in the life of your partner that you have no idea about. Beyond all others, Owls and Kingfishers are the ones who – no matter who they are in a relationship with – say to me the most: 'I didn't realise they were unhappy.' It's often because they're not listening enough to what's going on on the outside, or sharing enough of what's going on on the inside.

Neither of you are likely to be comfortable with feelings (unless Dove or Swan was your second type in the Lovebird quiz, in which case you'll probably be better than most of your type); you'll either bottle them up (and the bottle will be big enough to put a real ship inside) or avoid them. If you're not careful, you can become so good at keeping away from emotions that you end up more like siblings than lovers. I've said before that I believe thinking birds do this because of uncomfortable experiences when they were children that caused them to distance themselves from their feelings, or a lack of exposure to experiences that helped them connect to them. As a result, the danger is that, rather than use the relationship as a means by which the pair of you can explore intimacy in the safety of the love you have for each other, you'll strive to out-perform your partner in the 'I don't do emotion' stakes. In my opinion, this is a mistake of gargantuan proportions.

Reconnecting to the world through your senses will enrich

your life and increase the chance of the pair of you no longer feeling that you're on the outside of Life looking in at people who seem to 'belong' (in a way that you feel you never do). What you choose to achieve that is down to you; any artistic activity, or sport, yoga or Tai Chi. Anything that utilises your body and causes you to pay attention to what is happening to you, and around you, in the moment will strengthen your connection to your senses. Do it together. Make your relationship the first example of how you'd like to feel about the rest of the world and see where it takes you.

Feathers for the nest

What Owls and Kingfishers living together need to know
Do:
Sit down and start talking. I would recommend that you have a regular pow-wow, where each of you has to talk uninterrupted for a set period of time about anything and everything that's happening: in your life, in your head, in your work, and in the relationship. If you're honest, it will clear up any mind-reading that might be going on and ensure that you're not living with assumptions about your partner that could prove problematical if left to themselves.

Connect physically. I don't just mean sex, I mean as a form of intimacy. Hold hands, hug and give each other massages. I know some of you won't like it much to start with (feeling birds who were having a nose at your advice just ran shrieking from the room), but stick with it: your feeling muscles just aren't used to flexing. If the only time you touch is when you're getting naughty, you might have great sex, but you'll never know what making love feels like.

To the Owl: learn your partner's rules, or at least the really important ones (they'll be the ones you get nagged about most for not following). When you've learned them, do your best to follow them, without comment, ridicule or bad grace (as an Owl, I've done all three and none worked). Surrender is the best form of attack. (The good thing is that you're likely to fail consistently because your attention will always flick from thing to thing and you'll miss the 'rule' moment, so you'll never quite live up to your partner's hopes of you.) As I mentioned earlier in the book, I have a theory that this is a good thing. If you surrender and become who they think you should be they might start looking around for a new project. I mean partner.

Now that I've got the Kingfisher shouting at me, I might as well keep going. Cut your Owl partner some slack. You've seen the advice I've just given them; you see that I'm on your side? Well, your side of the bargain is to not keep trying to improve them. If you want them to do something, ask them, then leave them to it. Don't go on to give them detailed instructions about how it should be done; it's annoying and they won't do it anyway, which only gives you more opportunity to give them 'feedback' to try to 'help' them, which just sets off another row. Chill.

The two of you can be a brilliantly powerful and effective couple, and it largely comes down to how well you can use this difference between you. The Owl is the one who is most likely to be the ideas-engine of the partnership, and the Kingfisher will be the actual engine – they'll be the ones to turn the bright ideas into action. That will probably suit both of you: the trick is how to pick the best ideas of the Owl – bearing in mind that the Owl's butterfly interests can drive their ground-bird lover to distraction – and commit your efforts to them, rather than the Kingfisher's need for certainty before committing, which can suck the enthusiasm out of their partner.

Don't:

Don't support or encourage each other in avoiding feelings or emotions. It's easily done, and with the two of you likely to be quite competitive, it can almost become a shared virtue. It's really not – it will just cocoon you from a lot of the best things life can bring you, even though it opens you to some of the worst. I speak to you as an Owl who has learnt this from living for many years with a Swan. Feeling stuff is better, even if it's not always as easy (and it's really not like the on/off switch you might fear, as you can feel in degrees). Help each other.

To the Kingfisher: don't overwhelm your partner with detail. They are big-picture people – you know how you ask a question and you get a one-sentence reply? That's a full and complete answer to an Owl: it's not them being evasive. I know if you were asked the same question, you would give the Wikipedia version of the answer rather than the *Reader's Digest* version, and that's my point. Owls have no capacity to stay interested for that long; they just don't feel the need to know beyond what they consider useful. And that's a huge amount less than you would. So, to avoid them shutting down, or diving into a cupboard when you come home from work brimming with things to tell them, be gentle, and cut the detail down.

To the Owl: share a little more, for heaven's sake! Your partner needs to tell you what is going on in their life in minute detail – so learn to look interested or buy a mask of that expression. Look to expand your vocal contributions too – it's part of the evidence your partner needs to know you care. The most common refrain from ground-birds is, 'They never tell me anything, they just don't want me involved in their life.' It's only a short distance for them to wondering what you're hiding.

To both of you: you have a mutual need for things to make sense to you, and you probably don't endure trivia particularly well. There may have been occasions when you've gone to a dinner party, quickly been bored by the company, and clung together all evening like drowning passengers from the *Titanic*. Do your best not to make it too obvious. You can actually seem quite an intimidating couple to many people, so don't make it easier for people to avoid you (unless that's your intention) by appearing bored or disinterested in them.

Peacock and Nightingale

Peacock: 'I don't think he cares any more, he so rarely makes an effort to look good like he used to.'

Nightingale: 'I tell her she looks good all the time, and you'd think that'd be enough, but she's always moaning if I want to go out with my mates.'

There are two distinct challenges with you two. The first is that Nightingales filter the world through their ears more than anything else, while for Peacocks the eyes have it. The second is that Peacocks are grounded in facts and rules and reality, while Nightingales like to sing of what might be and hate to be dragged down into the details of life. There is nothing here that can't be used to turn you into a brilliant combination; you just have to understand where these differences can lead.

Cuckoos in the nest

Nightingales don't like to sing alone – an audience is required not only to appreciate the song, but also to help form it. Often this type doesn't seem to know what they think without hearing it first on the outside, and people are often used as the sounding board. Silence can be a real challenge for Nightingales – it's something to fill, not something to contemplate. (It would be fun to make them a librarian for a day and see how long they last.) Also, the difference between inside and outside can be a bit blurry, which can lead to them finishing a sentence with '. . . did I just say that out loud?' as they view the embarrassment that surrounds them.

Peacocks take in information pretty quickly, and tend to provide it at the same speed, so it's not a challenge to keep up with Nightingales in the words-per-minute stakes; it's just that they aren't driven to do it as much. Peacocks speak when they have something to say, Nightingales talk as a way of making sure their lungs are working. This can test the patience of the Peacock. In any situation where the Peacock's role is to listen and provide help, I suggest you wait until the end or risk your words being drowned under your Nightingale's. They need to get their thoughts straight before they can start listening to yours.

Nightingales are attracted to big ideas, while Peacocks are loath to trust anything that doesn't feel concrete. This can lead to the Nightingale feeling that their partner always crushes their dreams, while Peacocks can write off their partner as a dreamer who needs protecting from the reality of life, or needs to awaken to it. A saving factor in this is that Peacocks are more able to visualise than most other types, so are capable of joining the Nightingale's vision, goal or dream: they'll just want a lot more information before they trust it. Nevertheless, this can become a strength. The key to ground-birds and sky-birds becoming a successful partnership is in utilising the sky-bird's (in this case the Nightingale's) ability to think big-picture, with the ground-bird's (Peacock's) ability to organise the details that make it happen. A recipe for disaster is the Nightingale being responsible for the organisation of the couple. Leave appointments, credit card payments and holiday bookings to the ground-bird, as they'll get a kick from making things work, whereas Nightingales will get kicked for not making things work.

Peacocks will know that they are loved by the way you look at them, the care you take in your appearance for them, and by the time you choose to spend with them. Think of time as money, so spending it on one thing indicates you value it more than its alternative: a night out with your friends can mean you prefer them to your partner, while overtime at work can mean you enjoy work more than your partner. This can be perplexing to Nightingales, because as long as they get a phone call telling them they're missed at some point in the evening – and you sound sincere – they're likely to be happy. With the busy lives people have these days, this particular difference raises its head often, making sight birds seem the most jealous of the types. It's not necessarily so, but this connection between time and preference, coupled with Peacocks' ability to create vivid pictures out of their sense of rejection, can get them in all sorts of unnecessary rows.

Like all ground-birds, Peacocks feel secure with rules. Things need to be done in a certain way, and the way it's always been done is often a reason in itself for continuing in that vein. In any relationship, what emerges is a 'way things work': who does what, when you do it, and how you do it. We are all creatures of habit, so as this 'way' emerges it becomes largely invisible; it's just the way the two of you roll. However, for the Nightingale, it's just a loose alliance. If things aren't followed quite the way they should be, it's no big deal. But for the Peacock it's a case of, 'Are you crazy?' To them, it's the whole deal. Having a 'way' the relationship runs is a big source of their security, so it's not unusual for them to overreact in the face of a rule being broken or a role not fulfilled. If it's your job to clean the bedroom, make sure it's done when it should be, and make sure you learn the rules that constitute *clean* for your Peacock partner, because for them, if it's 5 per cent worse than they would have done it, it's like you haven't done it at all. Cue them cleaning it themselves with much muttering, while you feel unappreciated, probably with even more muttering.

Feathers for the nest

What Nightingales need to know about Peacocks

Do:

Peacocks will feel that they're loved by the way you make them look – both in terms of the place you two live in, and your appearance. In their eyes, when people look at you, they're making a judgement about them. Making an effort with your appearance sends the message that you care. Helping them make the house 'nice' is equally important. They will probably have an interest in art and style, and often tidiness will be a value for them. Indulge it.

The amount of time you spend with them will also be a key factor in their happiness. 'Out of sight is out of heart' is what they fear, so make sure there is plenty of contact time with them – and I mean face-to-face, not by text or phone. If you're putting in the hours at work you're going to get tired, because you're going to have to balance it with time with your Peacock. They will love sharing a visual experience, so the cinema or theatre is likely to be appreciated.

Gifts can also be something they prize as a sign of your love, but be careful. Because taste is important to them, make sure the gift you buy matches theirs, or you'll find it in a cupboard. A client of mine recounted how surprised he had been when he and his Peacock partner took a present for his mother's birthday to her party. His mother was delighted by the package – a Peacock's present will always be beautifully wrapped – and thrilled at the expense they'd clearly gone to for the gift. She should have been: it was a special present he'd bought his Peacock for their anniversary. To the Peacock it's not rudeness, it's just recycling – it was never going to go with anything she'd wear.

Don't:

For Peacocks, the world needs to look a certain way. Generally, that means their way. Don't fight it. I know you can take the mickey out of their need for order, for everything having its place, for cushions being plumped at the end of an evening – you can even occasionally indulge in some passive-aggressive mixing up of the knives and forks in their little compartments in the cutlery draw – but, overall, give in. I know it doesn't mean a thing to you, and most of what they stress about you won't even notice, but it matters to them, so learn the way they like things done and do your best to follow the house rules. You're going to forget – probably a lot – which is why I'm asking you to *focus* so that you do anything that's more than nothing.

Don't compliment the way someone else looks without careful thought. If they could even remotely be thought of as a love rival, you're in for a world of hurt, because how they look and how you feel about that are very closely related in your partner's eyes. If you realise your partner has caught you looking at some eye candy, quickly say something like, 'How could they think they could get away with wearing that?' With a bit of luck, you might get away with it, but don't push it.

Don't forget to tell your Peacock how good they look. Keep a close eye on what they wear for any additions to their wardrobe – they'll test you to see if you notice. Remember: not noticing equals not caring.

When you shop, as a Nightingale you need to talk through your options; your Peacock partner probably doesn't. Peacocks will know the right thing to buy the moment they see it, so give them the space to look. Point out choices, but don't overwhelm them with opinions until they ask for any – usually, it's just safer to confirm they're right, that they have impeccable taste. (In their eyes, I mean.)

What Peacocks need to know about Nightingales
Do:
Your partner will sometimes drive you crazy with their need to talk. Do be patient; they achieve all of the things you do in your head by turning them into words outside their head. On a regular basis, they're going to have ideas – for holidays, home alterations, business opportunities, a new kind of corkscrew; you name it,

they're going to come up with it. These ideas are likely to seem pie in the sky to you, and it would be easy for you to crush them. Instead, listen. Let them share them with you. Most will simply fizzle out once the words hit the air. But every now and again, your Nightingale will have an idea that could improve or even change your life. It would be a shame if the fear of your scorn drove them into silence, because there's no happiness in that place for them.

Nightingales will know that you love them simply by the fact that you tell them. 'I love you' needs to be a regular part of your conversation, but said meaningfully, not as a throwaway bit of punctuation at the end of a call. Take a moment, focus your attention on the fact that you mean what you're about to say, and deliver it. And any time you see something about them that you love or appreciate, tell them – it's all money in the love bank.

Don't:
Don't be harsh. Nightingales can be cut to the quick by your words, so any criticism can hurt out of proportion to your intention. This is going to be a challenge because you can have a propensity to . . . erm . . . nag. I know there are ways you like things to be done, and I know they will regularly fail to meet your standard . . . but you need to get used to it. This will be a continuing part of your relationship, and the most important thing I have to tell you is: give Nightingales feedback about their behaviour if you must, but avoid personalising it. Words wound them more than they do you, and in the end you might end up with a spotless kitchen, but nobody to cook for.

Don't expect them to care about the way things look as much as you do. Style and fashion should be your end of the relationship; Nightingales should fill the house with music – their taste in which will probably be as important to them as your talent for putting colours together is to you. Often music is a central part of their life, so pay attention to the music they choose for particular occasions, because it's probably for a reason. What mood is it evoking? What memories does it stir? They will love you saying, 'Didn't we dance to this when we were in the Maldives?'(just as long as it was with them you were dancing . . . or, indeed, went to the Maldives with). If you get it wrong, you can depend on a pout every time you hear that song for the rest of your life together.

Finally, don't argue about who said what. Nightingales are likely to have a brilliant recall for conversations, and will no doubt drag into any argument they have with you every insensitive, stupid or ill-advised comment you've ever made.

Swan and Swan

Swan 1: 'I love him to pieces, but sometimes we just get into these stupid rows over how things should be done. He's so stubborn, and then the bad feeling ruins the day.'

Swan 2: 'I love her to bits, but she doesn't always see that my way works best and she gets stupidly angry when I point it out. Then she sulks.'

As I write this, I imagine you two reading this scrunched on your comfy sofa all cuddled up. I'm probably wrong, but I hope you recognise the principle. The pair of you communicate a lot with your hands – your whole bodies, really – so the amount of tactile contact between you might be of almost conjoined-twin proportions. You know the sweet old couples you sometimes see hugging on a park bench, or sharing a tandem Zimmer frame? That could be you two.

A further level of similarity is that you both feel more comfortable with detail than you do with 'fluffy' ideas, and find rules a comfort. It sounds like a recipe for convivial bliss, but while I find it's the differences between couples that bring them to my practice more than their similarities, there *are* potential pitfalls that I'll do my best to outline below.

Cuckoos in the nest

Feeling birds like you tend to be very caring – and like being cared for, too. If you imagine a line where 'caring for' is at one end and 'being cared for' is at the other, most Swans will clump in the middle and like a bit of both, while some will be stronger one way than the other. If there's any kind of balance – both of you liking both, or one strongly one way and your partner the other – then there's likely to be a mutually enjoyable connection between you. If, however, you're both strongly the same, it can lead to a weird situation where neither of you feels able to either express their love, or feel loved, despite your best efforts. Two Swans who are 'care for others' types will be constantly trying to make the other person feel good, and it can almost seem like a competition for who cares the most. It's a bottomless task that can be exhausting, and without the feeling of reward. And if you're both 'care for self' types, you're going to feel loved by the care your partner shows – and sometimes this leads to a situation like you see when birds fledge – two people flapping their wings loudly asking to be fed by the other. To the outside world, this can seem a strange relationship; one that is quite whingy and demanding. To be honest, I don't see these couples making it very often, so it's lucky that few people are entirely down one end of the line.

Apart from the caring factor, the other way Swans communicate their love is through touch – you'll even find it difficult not to touch someone who's only stopped you to ask directions. Touch is as natural a part of communication as speech, but that's not how the rest of the world might view you and you've probably experienced being misunderstood. That can extend to your partner. If they see you touching someone who they consider has love-rival potential, they can fly into a fit of jealousy. Because they know how they feel when you touch them, and how you feel when you touch them in that way, it's easy for them to project that onto the rival, and onto you. So be careful. The rows between you can be quite incandescent, but it's usually better if they are, because they tend to blow over quickly and then you get to the fun part of making up. If you let things fester, then everything feels sour for ages.

Comfort is likely to be high on the agenda for both of you, so your house is likely to be very comfy. Both of you will be engaged in a search for the ultimate sensory experience in everything that forms part of your life; from the best coffee shop in the area and the comfiest car seat, to the nicest headphones for your iPod, the list will be endless. And expensive, if you're not careful. The thing is that both of you are great at detail – working with it as well as noticing it – so the degree of perfection you tend to demand can make you quite picky: together, that can add up to a lot of picking. What it can mean is that you're so involved in searching for – but never quite reaching – perfection, you don't enjoy what you have, as it's just a stepping stone to what you really want, which is a bit more, even if you're not quite sure what *of*. This is a shame because enjoying the moment is one of your skills, so it's a pity to focus on what isn't quite right, compared to what is.

While I'm talking about being in the moment, with both of you being ground-birds too, this feeling bird/ground-bird combination can have the effect of you getting particularly stuck in a negative moment longer than you need to, because you don't look up and see your way forward. Be careful that you don't drag each other down into a pit of despondency by your shared inability to see the big picture. All things pass: find a sky-bird friend to talk you out of it.

Another ground-bird propensity is your love of rules. Your house probably hums with contented order (if only you ruled the world) . . . unless your rules contradict your partner's, then it gets all kinds of nasty. You see, ground-birds each believe that *their* way is the right way. So if you have two under the same roof, there are two 'right ways' that are going to arm-wrestle unless you find a compromise, or one of you surrenders. It probably won't be a true surrender, though, more the beginning of the guerrilla phase of the war.

Feathers for the nest

What Swans living with Swans need to know
Do:
Look at the balance between the care you give and the care you demand. Are you both happy with the flow between you? If you understand that this is a river you both need to cross, you'll appreciate the effort you put in, and the effort your partner invests – plus the difference between what you need and what they need.

You're both quite deliberate, one-step-at-a-time kind of people, more comfortable with proven facts than speculative ideas or theories. This can make you too cautious, both in terms of opportunities you miss, and also novelties you decide not to pursue. Over time, your life can become quite set and uneventful – and doing the same events year after year isn't the same as eventful. Experiment a bit more, take some chances and trust your gut.

Do your best to make do, and enjoy what you have. If you invest too much time on trying to make things better – like an even better mattress topper than the three you've tried over the last year – then you don't sink into the enjoyment that's possible in the moment. As a couple, there will be occasions when others see you as high maintenance and difficult to please. It's for you to decide if what you get from your behaviour is truly worth it.

With both of you being happiest when immersed in the detail of things, your decision-making process could be a lengthy one, with you always wanting just a little more information before you make a decision . . . and there goes the opportunity. It can work to give yourselves a time limit for a decision, even if it means tossing a coin at the eleventh hour. Again, trust your instincts and take a leap of faith sometimes.

Often I find Swans build such a cosy life together that it can be hard for others to find a place within it, and often they feel no need for anyone else if they're particularly introverted. As with everything that I'm writing about similar types, this is only a problem if you both think it is. If you really feel your partner completes you and is your everything, that's truly lovely but if, sometimes, just sometimes, you would like to connect – in a non-jealousy-inducing kind of way – with a bigger social group than just your partner, then say so. A bit more connection to the world could energise you both.

Your intelligence tends to lean towards the practical, and it's often the activities that involve your hands that you get the most joy from. If you can find a shared hobby that is physically creative then it can be a thing that defines your whole relationship, because you'll both love diving into the detail of learning something new. And if it gives you a chance to talk to . . . what are they called? . . . oh, yes, other people, then so much the better.

Don't:
Don't start a war over a rule. I know your rules make sense, which means that any other rule on the subject clearly doesn't – which means your partner is wrong (you see, I just proved it for you) – but, the thing is, they feel the same way, and both ways probably work, so it's not a rule as such, just a strong preference. Work out a rota. Not really, but loosen up a bit about things you think matter, because mainly they don't as much as you think. It can become exhausting when rules become a battlefield for ground-birds. Sit down together with a list of them, from whether a scone should be jam first and then cream to whether socks should be paired before or after the wash: you know, the big stuff. Decide between you which ones you can change, and which ones could contribute to the end of Life As We Know It. Hopefully, the ones you dig in about won't be ones that oppose each other. If they do, really do work out a rota.

Don't lose yourself in the details of every day and miss living. I've known Swans get so bogged down in 'the things that need to be done' that they feel they can't get away for holidays, visit friends or take time to smell the roses (which they 'really should be pruning back by now – it's on the wall planner'!). An occasional missed payment or delay in getting to the dental hygienist is worth you taking a chance to get your head up and see the world you're in danger of letting pass you by.

This final point is probably unnecessary, but the way you (both) know you're loved is by the things you have done for you, and by the way you're touched and hugged. All of those things require you being together. If life does drag you apart, if work requires you to be there more than at home for a while, then make sure you set some time to refuel your touching tanks. Swans tend to have a tolerance for separation because they live in the moment, so as long as they're happy pottering or doing whatever they're doing, they can cope with your absence. But missing you can creep up on them without them realising that's what they're feeling, and a gulf will slowly creep between you that will take longer and longer to breach every time it happens. I remember when I was an instructor at Hendon Police College there was a number of Swans on the eighteen-week residential course who experienced marital difficulties because they'd 'grown apart' from their partner – and often found someone else to lean on. It's the downside of your physical intimacy: it's such a given in your life that you'll suffer from stroke deprivation more than most, and might drift towards something or someone to ease the loss.

Swift and Peacock

Swift: 'He's really picky about what I wear. He'll say something like, "Red and green must never be seen" like it's a law. I know what suits me, so I wish he'd butt out.'

Peacock: 'We see eye to eye on so many things, but she's always going off on these wild flights of fancy, planning things we can't afford, things that are way off in the future. I wish she'd take some reality medication.'

You two have a lot going for you, in the sense that, as sight birds, you share a strong preference for paying attention most to what you see. In the main, such similarities tend to help things, although I'm going to highlight the challenges they might also sometimes throw at you.

Trouble will tend to arise from the fact that one of you likes to keep things grounded in facts and evidence, and to organise your life around rules that make sense to you, where the other much prefers the realm of ideas and possibilities and gets strangled by any kind of detail or system. This can be something that potentially makes you a very powerful couple, but it can also drive you both bonkers.

Cuckoos in the nest

You're both visually oriented people, so what you see matters to you: in relationships that can mean both what you see in the mirror, and what you see beside you in bed. In many respects, you're going to view the world through the same eyes, with one significant difference: Swifts are sky-birds and Peacocks are ground-birds. As with every combination of this type, one of you is more comfortable with facts and the other with ideas; one with rules and the other with . . . well, treating rules as guidelines. I describe below some of the major challenges I've found you experiencing.

The way things look is likely to be of importance to both of you, so the style of your house will be an important part of your happiness. That's great if you share a similar taste in decor – if you're both into, say, Art Deco, then it could become a major source of intimacy and interest between you. If, however, one of you likes that style, but the other is into, say, post-modernism, then that's going to be a problem, ranging from a mild but on-going grumble to the Berlin Wall running through the living room. Compromise is the answer, but that's hard, isn't it, when your partner has no taste? (Of course, you could try to educate them – that'd be fun to watch . . .)

I've heard it said by women I know that you should never live with a man who takes longer in the bathroom than you. Whoever thinks that's true should strike both your types off their wish-list. Swifts and Peacocks of both genders are going to take an interest in their appearance. Now that could come in two flavours – you might pursue fashion, and dress to the hilt in all situations, or you might strike an anti-fashion attitude and put a lot of effort into looking beautifully dishevelled. Wherever you stand in the fashion war, you can bet the look isn't accidental. And this can lead to competition. It's not just the expense; it's the underlying, and probably unspoken, drive to look the best on a night out. A Swift and Peacock couple will set off for a dinner party (probably after about five hours of primping), both as taut as bowstrings as they will be waiting to see who gets the first, and then the most, comments on how they look. They'll leave the party, one quietly (or not) glowing; the other sulking. Just a little.

Don't let this competition lead to passive-aggressive under-mining – like the arched eyebrow and a comment like, 'Are you going to the party like *that*?' accompanied by feigned innocence in the face of the hurt such a comment would cause. Make no mistake: if you go down this route it will knock your partner's self-esteem, and probably cause the end of the rela-tionship when he or she meets someone who says, 'I love the way you're dressed!'

This next point is a sky- and ground-bird difference. Peacocks are most comfortable when they know where they stand, and their best place is knee-deep in details. If you ask them, 'How was your day?' have sandwiches handy because it could be a long answer. Similarly, they're likely to probe you for the ins and outs of your day, too. For the Swift, this is a chore. Your day will have been good, bad, or average, with maybe one little anecdote to relate. Such parsimony can be interpreted by the Peacock as 'not letting them in', and can be the start of a suspi-cion that you're hiding something. It's why Swifts, even when they know what's coming, have to gird their loins and ask, 'And did your meeting go well?' or similar, and look interested throughout the three-act reply.

Being visual creatures, you're both likely to be able to talk about the future in a meaningful way, but the Swift will prob-ably spend more time there. Often they will be the one who points the relationship in long-term directions, but it will be the Peacock who takes charge of how they get there. Peacocks are systematic, building one step at a time towards a goal. Swifts are more intuitive, happy to leap from one step to four ahead once they've discerned a pattern: they become bored quickly if made to proceed in a Peacock manner. This can be infuriating for both parties: Swifts can find their partners maddeningly cautious, paint-by-numbers unimaginative bores.

Peacocks can look at their partner and see a flighty, ADHD, head-in-the-clouds dreamer who would lead them to disaster but for their attention to the small stuff – which should be sweated over. It's just a difference, but it needs to be understood to avoid the negative labelling.

It'll come as no surprise that Peacocks are the rules people. They will have a set of them – neatly arranged, obviously. On a scale of personal importance to them, they rank alongside a Bible to a priest, so if you're in a relationship with a Peacock any contravention of their rules by you may be taken as a personal attack. Be ready for one of those, 'If you cared about me you'd . . .' conversations. What often happens with sky-ground-bird combinations is that the ground-bird gradually takes over running the relationship, from paying the bills to deciding what thing belongs in which drawer. This can lead to the Swift standing in the kitchen one day and not having a clue where the spoons are. It usually arises in the following way (but bear in mind I'm a sky-bird, so I'm viewing this with prejudiced eyes): you, in this case, the Swift, undertake to clean the bathroom. You can't tell much difference between how it was and how it is afterwards, but it seems clean to you. A little later, you find your partner cleaning it again. He or she will have a standard, and if you fall even a little below that bench-mark it's like you haven't done it at all. After a while it can feel quite hopeless even trying to reach this mythical bathroom cleaner nirvana. For your partner, it can feel easier to just do it themselves rather than endlessly instruct on what to them seems the obvious way to do things. Only yesterday my wife (who is a ground-bird, while I'm a sky-bird) asked me to help her fold a just-out-of-the-washing-machine duvet cover. I was happy to oblige. I took one end. She moved towards me. I was confused, as I thought we needed to stretch it so we could sort out the edges. I moved back. She moved forward. I said, 'What are we doing here?' Bex replied, as to an idiot, 'We need to give it a shake to get rid of some of the wrinkles. I'm trying to get you to back into the kitchen where we have room to do it.'

Obvious, really. A couple of hours later, she asked for my help again with folding. I took the edges of the duvet cover and started backing towards the kitchen. 'What are you doing?' she said, to the same idiot who had clearly taken an extra numpty tablet. 'I'm getting some room to give it a shake,' I said, a little nervous, clearly wrong in a big way but not knowing why. How withering can a simple phrase like, 'It's dry now!' be? Plenty, let me tell you.

I tell that story clearly hoping to get you to agree that my wife is a rule-obsessed Nazi. But, look at it from her point of view. She believes shaking helps, so how can I, after fifty years on the planet, not have noticed that, too? I've lived with her for twelve years and counting (boy, am I . . .) and this isn't the first time she's educated me into the rule. How can I not remember? And, finally, how could I not notice that it's the same duvet cover AND that it's now dry, so shaking it out is completely unnecessary? (What can I tell you? It's a talent.) Rules and a lack of attention to detail under the same roof are going to be a regular thorn for the two of you.

I mentioned in your profiles that Swifts and Peacocks often know that you're loved by the amount of time you spend together. With you both sharing this value, it's likely that you'll both work hard to spend quality time together, and miss each other equally when you're forced apart; while the knowledge of it mattering is likely to prevent it from being an issue when it occurs. The only drawback I come across is that it can lead to you becoming a bit exclusive, spending so much time together that you tend to neglect friendships and outside interests. You give up Sunday football to spend time at home, or make excuses to get out of the hen or stag weekend. A year into each other and you're a happy little island, which is fine unless things go sour and you're left sobbing, with nobody to call. It can be a good thing to pry yourselves apart occasionally. (It'll make the coming-home sex that much more spectacular. Especially if you don't wait until the front door is shut.)

Feathers for the nest

What Peacocks need to know about Swifts
Do:

Look at what similarities you have in terms of tastes. Focus on them and build your joint house-style around them. Agree areas in the house where you can both express your artistic differences: you get the bedroom, say, while they get the broom cupboard – that kind of thing.

Be aware of your rules. Maybe make a list of them so you get a grip on how pervasive they are in the way you order your world. Now, this is a hard thing to take on, but do your best: they're not THE rules. The world doesn't have to work this way, but I accept it feels that way to you. So, do your best to be flexible with them in the face of a breach by your partner. Why not go crazy by some days even breaking one yourself, just to prove that the world does keep spinning?

If you do work by rules, try tailoring the length of your explanations about things concerning them with the look on your partner's face. Them glazing over isn't a sign they're not interested or don't care, it's a sign they've heard enough to understand, and they care enough to have listened that long. Listen to their equivalent description of what they say. If that's enough words for them to communicate something, it's enough words for your meaning to be communicated to them. At least meet them halfway.

Your Swift partner always looks at the big picture. Sometimes they'll get very excited at the potential of something, from buying a holiday home to emigrating. Don't burst their bubble instantly; they're having fun. I know you can see the 101 reasons why it won't work – but 99 of those are probably just immediate issues that might not always be true, so try joining in the big idea and see what you can add to it constructively, rather than raining on their parade. Often their future vision will take you to a good place that your immediate objections shielded from your gaze.

Don't:

Don't treat a breach of a rule as a personal attack on you. Swifts
don't see rules. They can trip over the same shoebox on the floor
for days and not think of putting it away. It's not laziness, it's
just that their attention isn't on the minutiae of life; they usually
have their head in one cloud or another.

Don't grill them about everything that happened to them since
they left you that morning. Accept what they give you first time
of asking, and return to it in small chunks as the evening
progresses. Tease what you like to know out of them; don't beat
it from them with your tongue.

You probably do most things around the house, or most things
full stop. If you and your partner are happy with that, perfect.
If you're not, say something – don't blow up twice a year when
your simmering dissatisfaction at the inequality of the relationship
comes to the boil. Give them tasks that are their responsibility.
Which leads me to my next point . . .

Don't give Swifts something to do and then tell them how to
do it. They won't do it your way (anyway) but it will still work
out, more or less. Work at accepting the more or less bit. I know
you're only trying to be helpful by suggesting the very best way
to peel a potato, but please, step away from the utensil.

What Swifts need to know about Peacocks
Do:

This is the same piece of advice I gave your partner. How things
look is important to both of you, so if you have differing tastes
in how you like the house to look, or about art, then find the
similarities and build around that. Agree a corner of the house
that's yours to do with as you wish, and allow them to do
the same.

Learn the rules your partner feels are important, and follow
them whenever you can. They matter to them in a way you can't
imagine, and you'll get a lot of points for sticking to them.

Listen, also, to how your partner answers a request for
information. They will go into much more depth than you

require. Sometimes listening can reach a point where your will to live begins to slip a little. This is a need they have; so try to be patient. Give them about twice as much information as you feel they need when they ask you something, and I've asked them to give you about half of what they think you need. Generally, it's about finding a middle ground.

Pace your ideas. Your Peacock partner likes to deal in concrete facts and figures, so their enthusiasm for your great but vague plan will be proportionate to how clearly they can see how to achieve it. I know this is something you'll be happy to work out as the need arises, but that will make them uncomfortable, so meet them at their level of detail as best you can. They're not being anal; they just build an idea out of smaller bricks than you.

Don't:
Don't call their rules their 'little madnesses'. (I've tried it; it doesn't help.) And don't surrender all of the things that need to be done. I know it can be annoying when your Peacock insists you do something a certain way, and that it's so much easier to leave it to them, knowing that they won't be able to resist improving on your pathetic effort. Instead, put some effort into making some things around the house – or fulfilling some of the relationship duties like bills – your job. And work at it until your partner leaves you alone. The simplest thing to do is, within these specific tasks, learn how to do it their way and follow it religiously. (It took me a year to learn how to clean the bathroom properly.)

Kingfisher and Kingfisher

Kingfisher 1: 'I think we sometimes bring out the worst in each other – sometimes he is just so perfectionist about the oddest things.'

Kingfisher 2: 'She's even worse than me at getting hooked on something and disappearing on me – in front of the computer or just in her head.'

I've made the point every time I talk about thinking birds: that you are a particular challenge to describe. I'm reconciled to being stopped by readers of this book for years to come and told, 'It wasn't like me at all!' and knowing that most will be Owls or Kingfishers. The reason is that you're a bit of a special case. All the other types are based on the idea that we have a preference for which sense we pay most attention to: seeing, hearing or feeling. You, however, tend to *think* about what you see, hear or feel, as if these senses are one step removed. As a therapist, my opinion is that this is because when you were younger there were things you didn't enjoy experiencing and you found that thinking about things, instead of instantly feeling them, was easier. Or, your childhood didn't give you many opportunities to experience your feelings, especially in relation to others. It's why you spend a lot of time inside your own heads and often feel a bit of an observer of life – someone on the outside looking in. A consequence of this is that, when we're talking about relationships, how you know yourself to be loved won't be quite as straightforward as it is for others, as it will depend a lot on which type came second when you took the Lovebirds quiz at the start of the book. My advice is, read what follows, as I describe what tends to be generally true about Kingfishers, but then read the combinations of the second type of both of you, and them in relation to Kingfishers. By that, I mean that if Swan was your second type then, as well as reading this section, read about Swans, and how they combine with Kingfishers, and whatever was the second choice of your partner, too. A lot of reading, but out of it should emerge enough nodding-head moments for it to be useful.

Cuckoos in the nest

One of the most common things about thinking birds is that you tend to avoid emotions, wherever they're to be found. Chick-flicks are out; programmes about sick animals a definite no-no. A belief that emotions are all or nothing – and 'nothing' is safer – leads to a strong need to be in control, so you're often hard to read. (Poker could be a career option.)

A danger is that the two of you could inadvertently strengthen this position for each other so, over time, you become a couple who lead a very level life, devoid of emotional peaks and troughs. This might feel like a good idea to you, but I'd encourage you against it. Your relationship provides an opportunity to learn to engage with your emotions safely and actually explore what they could bring to your life: this will make it much richer.

Both of you like to spend time in your heads, exploring your thoughts and working things out. You have little time for trivia, and things need to make sense – you probably have a reputation for not suffering people you consider to be fools. This can mean that you're not ones for social gatherings, unless they're for a purpose that interests you: even just meeting for coffee for friends might feel a bit pointless unless they . . . well, have a point. This can compress your social network, i.e. leave you with only a few close friends. Now, many Kingfishers might not care about this, particularly if you're in a relationship, as your partner can feel like they are all you need. If both of you feel that way equally, then great, nail the door closed; but if one feels that way more than the other it can lead to a situation where one person's splendid isolation becomes another's loneliness.

You're going to be one of those couples who can spend a long time in each other's company without needing to say much – you define the expression 'companionable silence'. This will probably suit both of you because you'll be busy talking to yourself. And I would expect you to have moments of near-telepathy where you say the same thing at the same time, or one voices the thought of their partner. This is a great feeling to have; that you under-stand each other so well. The downside is that you think you know the other's thoughts all the time, and this can lead to one actually not feeling understood at all, because something is going on with them that their partner doesn't seem to notice. Kingfishers should regularly have pow-wows, where each person gets to talk without interruption about what's on their mind. You might surprise each other.

As ground-birds, you're most comfortable making decisions when you have all the facts; you're not ones for speculative leaps. With Kingfishers, the need for detail tends to be greater than most other ground-birds, to a point where sometimes you'll miss opportunities or just fail to take action because you feel that you need to know just one more thing before you can be sure enough to commit to something – and by the time you do, the moment is long gone. Also, you can be great nit-pickers. Have you ever seen restaurants put up a 'Closed' sign just as you get to the door? (No, of course not, they have a look out for you permanently and turn their sign to 'Closed' as soon as they see you come round the corner at the top of the high street.) A great many of you will mock perfectionists for not being particular enough, which means you might not get as much enjoyment out of things because they could always be just that little bit better.

Let's talk about rules. You both have them, and Kingfishers tend to be particularly wedded to them. In fairness, most of them are going to be sensible and well thought out, but that doesn't mean they deserve to be committed to stone. That's how you can be: there's a way of doing something, and it's the only way. If it's a rule you both agree with, you'll go to war with the world over it. If it's a rule only one of you adheres to or, even worse, a situation where your rules conflict or contradict, then there's going to be trouble between you. Being intransigent, or stubborn, or bloody-minded (depending on who is describing you), is something to be careful of in your relationship, because often Kingfishers will simmer for years and, as a couple, this could ruin what you have. Give a little.

Feathers for the nest

What Kingfishers living with Kingfishers need to know
Do:
I'm going to repeat the last thing I said. Give a little. You could make a stand about something you think is important to such an extent that you drive a wedge between you. Many a Kingfisher has sat in front of me shaking their head with regret: when the door slams as their partner leaves them, suddenly the rule doesn't appear quite so important. Sit down with each other, work out what the rules you think important are, get each other to understand them, and *be prepared to bend*. The world was spinning happily before you made these rules, after all.

Both of you should engage in some kind of physical skill. Kingfishers are often quite disconnected from their bodies, so the discipline of learning an instrument or a sport, or taking up painting or sculpture, for example, can really begin to knock down some internal walls. And that's just a start. Taking the time to massage each other might knock down some more. Using your love of each other to strengthen your connection to your body really is a very smart thing to do; it leads to a greater sense of intimacy and a stronger sense of yourself as a connected whole. It can also turn you from someone who is probably good at sex to someone who is good at making love.

As I mentioned earlier, how you know you're loved will largely depend on the second strongest Lovebird preference from the Lovebird quiz you took, and I've advised you to read up on that type too. So, in addition to what that might tell you, I've only one extra piece of advice: say what's in your mind. It's so easy for you Kingfishers to lavish your partner with praise they never hear because it doesn't actually make it past your lips. Verbalise every good thought that comes to your mind about your partner. I've already said to sit down and open your head to them; give them a chance to hear what you're happy about, what worries you, what you'd like to stay the same, what could do with changing. It's a necessary reality check because you two are so good at creating your own world inside your head and mistaking it for the one outside.

Take more chances. You love to be certain, and to be able to work things out before you take the plunge – how long did it take you to go on a date? But your caution could really lead to you missing out on life. Sometimes you should just roll a dice or flip a coin: things will work out okay. (You're hyperventilating, aren't you? Breathe . . .) Sometimes taking a walk on the wild side, before examining its health and safety policy, will really help you connect to life.

Don't:
You can have a strong sense of the way the world should work, and you're probably critical of a lot of it, but don't get cynical – it's easy for this to descend into 'everything's going down the pan and nothing works'. You both are very good at thinking clearly, and on many occasions you really do see things that others miss, but to make the leap to thinking you know best all

the time won't win you many friends, and can take the joy out of life.

Don't wear your 'I don't do emotion' as a badge, or encourage your partner to, either. It's a defence mechanism, not a quality. It can be useful and it does have some advantages – I'm a thinking bird myself and value the ability to be dispassionate about things, but not all things all the time, which was what I used to strive for. To learn that it's okay to feel emotion, and to express it, has improved my life and enhanced the quality of my relationships. Feeling some emotion doesn't mean that it's inevitable that a tsunami of feeling is hurtling towards you. I'm making the point strongly simply because I've seen so many clients whose need to stay in control of themselves has led to them squeezing the life out of their relationship. If that doesn't sound much like you, it's likely that Swan was your second preference in the quiz at the start of the book – it tends to make most Kingfishers who are like this more comfortable with their feelings.

If you are the kind of Kingfisher whose attention to detail has made you hard to please, have a word with yourself. I mean that kindly. If you focus too strongly on what's wrong with things, your brain becomes tuned to noticing more and more of what's wrong and, soon, you're living in a world that's going to hell in a handcart. Muslims have a saying: 'Perfection is for God.' Even though I'm an atheist, I use it a lot because it's spot on. Perfection doesn't exist, so why work so hard? The degree of increase to the quality of your experience through the pursuit of everything being perfect won't be matched to any degree by what you lose through not noticing what everyone else around you is finding pretty damn good. Chill.

Your life, and your household, is probably a very well-run affair, with an unwavering rhythm and regularity – and I would expect many of you to get comfort from that: certainty is safety for you. Now, this won't be true of some of you, but there will be Kingfishers who end up so set in their ways that nothing novel or out of the ordinary has a chance to wiggle its way into your life. I knew a Kingfisher who turned down a holiday to New York because the dates clashed with the British Grand Prix. He didn't have tickets for it; he just liked to watch it with his mates. It was a tradition. There's a danger with Kingfishers that you doing anything more than twice becomes a tradition. Live a little; don't feel you have to plan your spontaneity.

Owl and Nightingale

Owl: 'He drives me up the bloody wall! He just constantly jabbers in my ear all the time. I can't hear myself think!'

Nightingale: 'She is so moody. I try to talk to her but she just sulks and goes quiet on me. Sometimes I know she is deliberately keeping away from where I am.'

This couple have one main challenge to overcome, and it's a big one. When it comes to listening we have two choices: we can listen to what's happening on the outside of our head, or the inside. We can't do both. Owls spend a great deal of time talking to themselves on the inside, while Nightingales like to spend their day talking to anyone on the outside. I'll describe in a moment the problems this can lead to. You also share a similarity, so at least the problems this can cause, you tend to be equally guilty of.

Cuckoos in the nest

This can be a difficult pairing. I worked in an office with a Nightingale once. A nicer man you couldn't wish to meet, and he drove me to distraction. I cannot count the number of times he interrupted my thinking by coming in and chattering; he took my sitting quietly writing or working at the computer as a sign that I was available to listen to him. The trouble arose because people have only one audio channel: you can only listen effectively to one thing at once. As an Owl this drove me crazy because he was constantly jamming my thinking – until we evolved a sophisticated signal that would let him know he was doing it. (I would turn to him as he began to speak, smile, and say 'Shut the f*** up!' It worked, but don't try it at home – I'm sure you can come up with something more elegant.)

The Nightingale needs to be aware of the Owl's need to be quiet sometimes and the importance to them of a lull between conversations so that they can process their thinking. Don't think of quiet as something that necessarily has to be filled immediately. Wait until your Owl has come back to you. On the other hand, Owls need to be sensitive to their partner's need to have a sounding board and to process out loud what the Owl does in their head.

Owls are looking to make sense of things, so if presented with a problem they will cut to the chase and not want to go all around the houses discussing different options. This can lead them to interrupt the Nightingale, which in turn impedes the Nightingale's ability to think things through. Let them finish. One is not better than the other; they are just different.

Nightingales will usually know they are loved by being told that, and by the warmth and tone of the person saying it. They will often say 'I love you' to their partners several times a day, and when they ask 'Do you love me?' they're really telling you that you're not saying it often enough. To know how an Owl expresses or recognises love will largely depend on the Lovebird type that was their second strongest in the Lovebird quiz you took. If that happens to be Nightingale then there's a chance they will say it often enough to satisfy their partner – but the odds are in favour of them only saying it to their partner within their head, which is no use whatsoever. Also, as well as reading about Owls, you need to look at the section that describes their second strongest Lovebird type, and how it relates to yours.

In most circumstances, when it comes to actually communicating their love, Owls can be quite non-verbal. They may be doing a number of things that mean to *them* they love you, but that doesn't necessarily help you. If they look puzzled when you ask them, or say, 'Of course I do' in that slightly exasperated way they can have, then you know they think they are expressing it in a way that should be obvious to you. Ask how you should know and you will probably get a list of what they do for you.

Owls don't give much away. They can be quite guarded and difficult to get close to. If that sounds like a defence mechanism, that is probably because, in most cases, it is. This guardedness can extend to their voice tone, too. At first, people can find it quite hard to understand what their Owl partner really means because all they are left to rely on are the words spoken, not the inflection or tone. For a Nightingale, this absence of texture in an Owl's voice can leave them feeling insecure because they have nothing to judge their partner's sincerity with. For example:

Nightingale: 'I don't know where I stand.'

Owl: 'But I just told you.'

Nightingale: 'I know, but what do you really *mean*?'

The Owl is not deliberately being obstructive – for them the words are all there is, and they just used them to say how they felt. What more do you want? What the Nightingale wants is what *they* need in order to be convinced – what they recognise as sincerity, understanding and love in your voice, not in your words.

One similarity that might help you is that you are both sky-birds, so you value ideas above certain knowledge and trust your instincts more than seeking out hard evidence. It means you'll avoid detail like a biblical plague and live in a kind of rolling semi-chaos of missed bills and half-finished projects – and yet be quite happy with that state of affairs. The downside to this as a couple is that you might find yourself under-achieving, as individuals as well as a couple, because you have lots of ideas and grand schemes, but lack the attention to detail and systematic action that brings them to fruition. You probably need to make friends with a ground-bird.

My advice, which in this regard is rarely taken, is for you both to work out roles and responsibilities and then meet at least once every fortnight to check you've each done what you're supposed to. It'll save you money, and the disappointment of watching a plane leave without you in it.

Feathers for the nest

What Owls need to know about Nightingales
Do:

When you think 'I love you', remember to say it out loud. It matters. Don't believe people who say it's the thought that counts: with a Nightingale it's most definitely the words – and those must be said in the right way.

Give your partner some room to talk, even if it means singing a song in your head while they do it. Many Nightingales don't have much of a voice in their head, so they need to speak to order their thoughts. Their need to talk (and talk) isn't just verbal diarrhoea; it's an essential part of their thinking, so honour it as best you can. If you keep in mind that you only have one sound channel, so outside noises interfere with your ability to think, you can see why you can get so irritated at their need to speak about everything. It's a key area for both of you to work on.

For a great many Owls, emotions are things to be avoided. They can appear very controlled and reserved, but it's often more that everything appears calm on the surface, but they're working like mad underneath. A lot of energy can be expended in that, and all to avoid the fear that experiencing any level of emotion can lead to an uncontainable loss of control (unless you're a Dove for your second Lovebird type, in which case you're likely to be more open to your feelings and your partner's). This fear is, on the whole, completely ungrounded, and a loving relationship is a great place to work on getting more in touch with your feelings – which, in turn, makes it more likely that your relationship will work long-term.

While both of you have an aversion to detail, out of the two of you it's the Owl who is likely to be best at working things out and creating systems. If that sounds true (to both of you), then I'd advise that you drive the organisation of things like holidays and bill paying. This isn't giving your partner an absolution from helping, it's just you making sure that what needs doing gets done, because you know what you can both be like.

Owls like to know things. They hate secrets or the thought of something going on that they're not a party to. This can make you a bit inquisitorial, and Nightingales, with their ears finely tuned for nuance, can interpret your questions about where they've been, what they've done and why they've done it, to be a sign of a lack of trust in them (at the very least, turn the spotlight off before you start questioning your partner). Seriously, leave them with a few secrets; you don't need to know everything.

Don't:
Sometimes you'll feel an irresistible urge to shut your partner up, whether it's by finishing their sentences or interrupting them. It won't work; they'll only go back to the beginning of their story and start again. It will also make them feel unloved, because for a Nightingale, if you loved them you'd listen. So, I'm afraid, you're just going to have to bear it, even if you can't bring yourself to grin.

Don't assume your partner knows what's going on in your head. They need to hear from you as a means of connecting to you and feeling a part of your life. Silence between you has a meaning for them; make sure it's a good meaning.

What Nightingales need to know about Owls
Do:
Leave your Owl the space to think. If they go quiet, let them. One of the things that irritates your Owl more than anything is to be brought out of their head when they're in the middle of something. Timing is everything. I know you need to talk to think, but your partner is the exact opposite; they're as busy when they're quiet as you are when you're talking – and you know how distracting it is when someone interrupts *your* flow.

Owls aren't great at showing their emotions, and they'll often avoid situations where feelings are present, whether that's in a soppy film or where someone is upset. It's not that they're unfeeling, it's that they're nervous of what those feelings could lead to – like a loss of control. Encourage them, slowly, to engage in things of this kind that make them nervous. When they get more comfortable with expressing their emotions you might actually get them to a point where they voluntarily listen to Sinead O'Connor singing 'Nothing Compares 2U'.

A problem can be that Nightingales make sense of things by talking them out, whereas your Owl partner works them out before speaking. This can make listening to you a bit of a trial for an Owl because they have a low tolerance for things or people who don't make sense, and listening to anyone for an extended period of time can feel like really hard work. You're aware, I'm sure, of their dislike of trivia and small talk? What I'm trying to say is work (really hard) on cutting back on the number of words you need to convey something, and allow more spaces for silence.

Don't:
There will be many occasions when it becomes clear to you that your partner hasn't listened to you. Don't mistake this for them not caring. You already know about their internal dialogue, so if they're listening to it, they can't be listening to you. Balance that with the moments when what you say causes them to have a thought about it and you can see that you've lost them again, but this time because they were interested in what you said. Overall, the thing not to do is make them not hearing you personal – it's just about their bird type. What needs to happen is for you to learn to watch for when you have their attention, and when you lose it.

You'll tend to share everything with them: what happens in your day, your adventure on the way home, what you saw on the internet when you were bored at work – they'll get chapter and verse (and at least that will satisfy their need to know everything about you). Owls tend to keep important things to themselves, especially their worries, until they've resolved them. This comes under the heading of 'They need to open up more.' Encourage them to do so, but don't rush or push it. They're big-picture people anyway, so detail is never going to be their bag (it isn't yours either, but song bird usually trumps sky-bird, so you'll talk more than the other sky-birds), but with their aversion to trivia, detail and emotion, there is a lot less on their minds to converse about. Let's hope you like the strong, silent type – and that they're strong.

Conclusion to Part Four

Before you move on, I'd like you to take the time to think about the answers that come from the following questions. It's perfectly okay to read this book just for what you find out about yourself, but you will get so much more benefit from it if you learn how to use it to improve relationships you have with others, whoever they are.

1. When you look back at previous relationships, how does what you've learned here explain some of the problems you experienced?

2. When you think about your present relationship, how does what you've learned explain some of the problems you're experiencing?

3. Looking at what you've written or thought, are there any patterns in what you do, or what your partners did, that run through your relationship history?

4. What needs to change for these patterns to no longer cause you a problem?

5. What three actions could you take that, by taking them, would lead to this change? Write these down.

Share what you've written with each other.

PART FIVE

Staying together

This is the part of the book I've been especially looking forward to writing. (I'm doing it on New Year's Day, so you can see how keen I am about what I want to tell you.) I hope that what you've read so far is helping you to understand yourself and your partner better. I often say that relationship therapy is largely a process of education, but information without action is useless, so in this next part I'm going to take you through some of the coaching processes I use to engage my couples that really help them to focus and make the differences between them into things that make them stronger.

In effect, I ask them to turn their relationship into a project.

I can just see some of the romantics among you throwing your hands in the air at this (which probably means my book is hitting a wall at this moment somewhere). A *project*? Where are the warm fuzzies in that? My reply is, if what you've been doing so far hasn't worked, why not try a different approach and see what happens? Just because your relationship becomes something you think about, study and practise doesn't mean it can't be magical.

The Relationship Rut

I think it's natural for relationships to be a challenge. Quite apart from the differences I've described, there are still other ways our brains organise things that create problems. I mentioned at the beginning about the way we are first attracted to a partner and how the release of oxytocin, the 'love chemical', creates in us a state akin to a mental disorder (that's a double whammy for the romantics!). In those early days, we fall in love with the feeling of love as much as we do with the person themselves, which means that when we start to come down from the high, the person we wake up beside may suddenly be someone riddled with irritating features your addiction had masked.

Attraction breeds appreciation

During the initial period of intense attraction, most of us are on our best behaviour; keen, if not desperate, to be seen by our love in the best light. We do things for them, and we go out of our way to be considerate and thoughtful. Our new love does the same thing, and we both appreciate these acts of caring – with oxytocin flowing, they're not just nice things, they can take on an almost mystical significance that has us exclaiming to our friends, 'They're just so unbelievably considerate!' in response to quite average kindnesses. This period of attraction and appreciation characterises the first (and most irritating to your friends) phase of a relationship.

Being a couple becomes a habit

After a while, things begin to settle down a little. We are creatures of habit and, if you've been in more than one relationship, you'll know that they settle into a pattern. There are things you do, and times when you do them. Each partner will tend to assume responsibility for certain functions of the relationship, and a kind of rhythm begins to emerge, to your day, your week, your month, your year. This rhythm can be so gentle that it lulls you both to sleep, and time passes in a cosy kind of relationship hibernation. Our brains like this. Nothing makes it happier than the certainty of knowing what is going to happen next – and the further out into the future your certainty extends, the better. Therefore, habituation is a natural, and pretty much unavoidable, feature of a relationship, and many people live a life of gentle contentment within the comforting rhythm it brings.

You're expected . . .

What can disturb that contentment is the fact that, after a while, what the brain takes to be a constant begins to become invisible – it's why a knick-knack that's been in your living room for years could disappear and you probably wouldn't notice it's gone for ages. In relationship terms, what it means is that what you used to appreciate your partner for doing now becomes part of the fabric of your life, about as noticeable and predictable as the presence of your wallpaper. This can be the things they do for you, as well as the qualities you value. When I first began living with Bex, for example, I'd get up every morning and take her tea in bed, and it was a thing she appreciated. After a period of time, it just became part of her day. Until I didn't do it.

'I'm so disappointed . . .'

Here can be the problem: when appreciation slips into habituation, it can breed expectation, and the trouble with that is if your expectations aren't realised, you're usually disappointed. So, you no longer get appreciation from your partner for what you do, but you get criticised by your partner for what you don't do – or they at least suffer in silent disappointment. Over time, the steady drip of disappointments can build into a giant stalactite of dissatisfaction – especially if you stop doing something your partner takes to be a symbol of you loving them (which can be something as simple as bringing them a cup of tea in the morning). I remember a client whose partner had gone to police training college. My client was a song bird, so his partner's evening phone call was a lifeline for him. Two years after she had graduated, he could trace the decline of her love for him (in his mind) from just one night when she'd forgotten to call.

Expectation can be the start of a slippery slope, and the intention of the exercises that follow is to regularly get you to revisit your appreciation of each other so that your habituated relationship remains a positive one, with the minimum of accidental disappointments.

For this part of the book to work, you have to engage with me and actually do the exercises. Some of you – the sky-birds and the thinking birds especially – will be tempted to read through them and 'get the idea' and think they've served their purpose. They won't have done. You need to sit down and give them your best shot; if you do, I'm pretty sure you'll be surprised at the benefit they bring.

The reason I frame this chapter as a project is because a successful project has certain characteristics, like goals, a need to make the project a focus of attention, and regular reviews of the current situation.

So many relationships drift into a rut of expectation and habit where the essence of what brought two people together just evaporates, almost without its loss being noticed, until something wakes one or other of them up to its absence. Relationships need a regular dose of appreciation of each other to prevent this slumber from becoming terminal. The following exercises will help you achieve that.

Project You2

One of the key purposes of these tasks is to utilise a principle from psychology called priming. You know when you're thinking of having a baby and suddenly everyone around you seems pregnant? Or you have your heart set on a new car and the model you're think of appears on every corner? That's priming: what's on your mind is brought to mind.

What these exercises are geared towards is priming your brain to notice more and more positive things about your relationship, tuning it to make your life as a couple one that you appreciate more because there's more to appreciate.

Week One: Making a start
Over the next week, both of you do three things for your partner that you think they will recognise as you loving them from what

you've learned about their bird type. Don't tell them when you're doing these things, and don't make them so extravagantly different that you make it obvious you're doing something. Keep a note, too, of what you think your partner has done for you.

One week later, answer these questions:

- What are the three things you did for your partner? What was their response?

- What do you think they did for you to suit *your* type?

- Over the last week, what have you noticed your partner doing as a sign they love you that fits *their* bird type as you understand it? Include things you like and things you don't.

Now, sit with your partner and compare with them what you've both written. Did you spot what they did for you? What else did they do that you thought was them loving you (especially those things where you did feel loved by them doing it)?

- How has this helped your relationship over the last week?

Week Two and onwards: The Project Generator
A key to getting the most out of these projects is attention – don't cheat by counting things that happened or were going to happen anyway. Project You2 is about you making a deliberate impact on your life together, so pay attention and look for situations where you can fulfil a project, or put effort into creating situations where you feed your relationship with something positive. For this, you can use the Project Generator.

Decide how often each week you're going to use the Project Generator (see below) – I suggest twice a week as a minimum.

Have a dice each. Here are six things you could do, but if you can think of other things that suit you better but achieve the same goal, feel free to change them.

On the days you decide to do this, just roll the dice and do what it tells you.

1. Do something today that is purely for your partner's pleasure

Clearly it's a nice thing to receive something pleasurable, but research has shown that actually the act of giving someone pleasure is at least equal in benefit. We're back here in oxytocin-land, creating surges of it from the attention we give and receive.

2. Do something today that is usually 'their job'

Not only will this be nice for them (if you're a bad cook, take them out or get a takeaway), but it might make you appreciate the things that otherwise go unnoticed.

3. Do something today that will make your partner laugh

This brings benefit from the attention you need to pay to create or utilise a situation that your partner will laugh at (note of caution: a friend of mine surprised her husband by opening the door naked, other than a pair of those novelty spectacles which has eyeballs on springs. It turned out to be her neighbour, and I think his eyeballs probably looked about the same as hers). As the saying goes, laughter is the best medicine, and I think that's especially true of an ailing relationship.

4. Notice something you appreciate in your partner. Let them know

You already know why I suggest this as a specific task: appreciation is an inoculation against expectation and disappointment, and the ground from which the seeds of love can be re-sewn and refreshed. The more you put your attention on what you appreciate about your partner, the more your brain becomes primed to notice those things above anything else. Typically, clients whose relationships are in trouble who've come to see me have become primed over a period of months to notice everything they find wrong in their partner, and you get more of what you pay attention to. This exercise begins to reverse the trend, and by letting your partner know about what you're appreciating, they feel better about you too. One of the most common complaints from someone in a crumbling relationship is the cry, 'I'm not valued.' Our psychology is such that we value people most who value us.

5. Surprise your partner

Again, not necessarily with novelty specs; just something that will create a good feeling that wouldn't otherwise have been a part of their day. You'll definitely need to choose based on your partner's Lovebird type here; thinking birds tend to hate spontaneous surprises, and ground-birds can be a bit reluctant to embrace new experiences, so don't make it too big a surprise.

6. Spend time remembering a good time you've had with your partner. Share the memory with them

Your past is a great resource, and many of your memories contain good feelings that a bad patch in your relationship has probably blocked from your present. Having a nostalgia-fest can give you a chance to remember how you came to be together, and to bring some of the old good stuff back into the present.

It would be a good idea to keep a note of what you did and how it was received etc. Something along these lines would suffice:

Date:

What task were you given by the Project Generator?

What did you do?

How did it go?

Is it worth doing again?

Is there anything you'd do differently?

Goals

All relationships can become just a habit – how many friends do we have who we lost any real connection to years ago, but we still keep seeing them? If we're not careful, we end up being with people because of what we used to have with them, not what we have now, so it's important to keep creating new, positive memories that strengthen the bond between you as they happen.

Research has shown that people who make goals are more successful at what they set out to do. Writing them down makes the chances of success even more likely, so I'm going to encourage you to write some goals for your relationship – and keep revisiting them.

Make sure any goal you set fulfils the following 'S-M-A-R-T' critera:

Specific – be very clear about the goal. Not 'We'll have had a holiday,' but 'We'll have had two weeks in the Caribbean, full-board.'

Measurable – be able to answer questions like how much, how many, how often, how will we know when we have it?

Achievable – is this goal within your abilities as a couple to reach?

Realistic – are you able to work towards this goal? Do you have the resources and the will?

Time – set a specific timeframe for the achievement of the goal e.g. 'By [day] of [month] we will have . . .'

With these SMART criteria in mind, begin to build some goals for the pair of you as a couple. I suggest you think of one big goal, and as many small ones as you want, and divide them into short-term (in the next 1–2 months); mid-term (in the next 3–6 months); and long-term (7–12 months).

First, brainstorm ideas for things you'd like to accomplish **as a couple** over the next 12 months. Think of small achievements, like a weekly treat (if you have a young family, just managing a pizza and a DVD might rank as a treat) as well as big projects, like a holiday. Sort them into short-, mid- and long-term. Post them somewhere visible, like on your fridge. Mark them off as you achieve them. For example:

Weekly goals sheet:

This week, as a couple, the goal we are going to achieve is:

This week, what we're going to do to achieve our mid-term goal is:

This week, what we're going to do towards our long-term goal is:

Monthly Review
Put a date in the calendar every month to have an evening together where you talk. If that's over a drink, that's great; but don't drink too much (a clear head makes for a clearer conversation). Use the following questions to guide the conversation:

1. What things has your partner done this month that you've really appreciated? Is your partner aware of them?

2. When were the moments when you had the thought that you love your partner? Where were you, what were you doing, etc.? Is your partner aware of them?

3. What were your favourite things you did in response to the Project Generator? Why?

4. What were the favourite things that were done for you from the Project Generator? Why?

5. What wouldn't you want to lose from your relationship from the last month?

6. What would you like to change from your relationship from the last month (i.e. anything that annoyed you)?

7. Review your goals:

Are they progressing?

Do they need adjusting?

Are there any new ones you could add?

Conclusion

The message of this book is that a relationship is a verb, not a noun: it's a thing we do, not a thing we have. It's about relating, and to be able to do that well you need to know who you're relating to, and what language they speak. Knowledge is power, so I really hope this has given you the desire to make the effort to learn to spot differences from you in your partner, learn to speak their language, and use their differences to improve the quality of your relating and the power of you as a couple. At the beginning of the book I made the point that 'do unto others as you would have done to you' is wrong when it comes to relationships, and I hope now you can see why I think that. 'Do unto your partner as he or she would like done to them' is the motto I'd like you to leave here with.

If you're lucky, you could have a lifetime with the privilege of learning deeply about someone else, and they you. You can help your luck by keeping your relationship like your garden: something you attend to. Nurture it, prune it, feed it and, above all, enjoy it.

Rubin Battino, a friend who has huge experience with helping people in coming to terms with terminal illness, says that at the end of life all that remains of importance is two things: nature and people. I agree. Love those close to you with all your heart for as long as the love is there. If it leaves, leave with it; you're getting in the way of who could love them next, and keeping yourself from who is out there who will love you better. And know that if you follow the principles in this book, the only relationship you'll lose is one that you should.

I began the book by saying that I believe relationships don't usually fail from a lack of love, but from a lack of understanding and a failure to nourish. I hope this book has provided you with the means to both understand, and nourish, the person you love. And I hope they've read it with you.

Good luck.